S0-ASF-711

CREATIVE SELF-HYPNOSIS

*New, Wide-Awake,
Nontrance Techniques
to Empower Your Life,
Work, and Relationships*

ROGER A. STRAUS, Ph.D.

PRENTICE HALL PRESS

NEW YORK   LONDON   TORONTO   SYDNEY   TOKYO

Prentice Hall Press
Gulf + Western Building
One Gulf + Western Plaza
New York, New York 10023

Copyright © 1989 by Roger A. Straus

All rights reserved,
including the right of reproduction
in whole or in part in any form.

PRENTICE HALL PRESS and colophon are registered
trademarks of Simon & Schuster Inc.

Library of Congress Cataloging in Publication Data

Straus, Roger A. (Roger Austin), 1948–
   Creative self-hypnosis : new, wide-awake, nontrance techniques to
empower your life, work, and relationships/Roger A. Straus.
      p.   cm.
   Bibliography: p.
   Includes index.
   ISBN 0-13-191198-8 : $9.95
   1. Hypnotism.   2. Conduct of life.   I. Title.
BF1141.S85   1989   88-39351
154.7—dc19   CIP

Manufactured in the United States of America

10   9   8   7   6   5   4   3   2   1

First Edition

To Diane
for all the logical reasons,
and the rest as well

ACKNOWLEDGMENTS

I would like to express my appreciation to all my friends and colleagues whose work and ideas have influenced my own and, however greatly transmuted, appear in these pages, as well as those whose unstinting support has kept me going and growing over the past several years. In addition to Ted Barber, Theodore Sarbin, Al and Betty Lee, John Glass, and Susan Hillier Parks whose names appear in these pages, many others come to mind: Ross Koppel, Robin and Fernando Roth-Barriero, Ellen Gurian, Sandra and Mike Connolly, Bill and Barb Castle, Jan Fritz, Pam Elizabeth, Al Goldman, Margaret Walker, and Erica and Amber Straus.

I would like to thank my editor, P. J. Dempsey, and senior production editor, Alice Fellows, both of Prentice Hall Press, for their enormous help and patience in midwifing this book.

CONTENTS

INTRODUCTION

In a word, this book is about *empowerment*.

It is more than another book about self-hypnosis (although it is that). In these pages you will find a complete training program that will show you how to start taking more active, inner-directed control over your life, work, and relationships.

While the core technique you will be learning is called *creative self-hypnosis*, it is probably very different from what you're accustomed to thinking of as hypnosis. In fact, it may be close to the direct opposite! You will find that there is no need to put yourself into a trance. You don't have to surrender control; you don't have to go through any yoga contortions of the mind or spirit in order to liberate your potentials for creative and effective living.

Rather, you will learn how to use your entire mind—reason, intuition, will, and imagination—to become an agent of change in your own life, to create new internal and external realities for yourself, and to take control of the processes by which the world influences you and you influence it.

This book will not tell you what to do with your life or how to live your life. It is a book about process—about the process of transforming your everyday life into whatever it is you want it to be. This book will show you how to get to where you want to be.

That is not to say that this book is value-free. The value I am talking about is simply genuine consideration for others—the conviction that you have the right to be treated with the same dignity and respect you would like from others. That we are in this life together and we might as well make the best of it; that it is better to share than to take, to nurture than to break. That "dead serious" is all too apt a metaphor (and that it is better to live than to be unalive).

Now, let's focus on how to gain new power over your thoughts, feelings, and actions so that you can create some desired changes in your everyday world. How, in actual practice, to become more fully alive.

This is not a how-to-do-it "cookbook." Rather, it teaches you how to discover your own best way to deal with every new problem or situation in your life. It does not prescribe. Instead, it teaches you the skills you need to clarify what it is you want for yourself and then to break out of whatever self-limiting and self-destructive habits and patterns lie between you and your chosen goals. It will show you how to become more awake, more fully conscious, and to achieve new freedom and power with respect to everyday living, working, learning, and relationships.

This book contains a great deal of information about perspectives, about ways of understanding the experiences, events, and relationships in our lives. But it also breaks the flow of my talking to you through the medium of print and has you explore concepts and discover things for yourself. Then, rather than provide the type of highly structured techniques found in my earlier book, *Strategic Self-Hypnosis*, this book teaches you some simple, almost effortless methods for releasing and channeling your creativity, intelligence, and imagination so as to make your entire life the vehicle by which you move toward attaining your goals. The only way to get there, I am convinced, is to do it your own way.

Some of the material this book contains might seem pretty radical, but everything you find here is grounded in contemporary social and behavioral science. The concepts and methods represent the fruit of more than a dozen years of research, teaching, and practice as a clinical sociologist. In fact, a secondary objective of this book is to introduce some of the perspectives and methods developed by social science practitioners who have devoted their lives to facilitating personal, family, organizational, and community growth.

In summary, I have intended this book to be unlike anything you have ever read. To inform you, but even more important, to change you—or, rather, to set you up with the tools, know-how, and motivation to creatively transform your life, work, and relationships in a way that perfectly suits yourself. I hope and I trust that *Creative Self-Hypnosis* stretches your mind, tickles your fancy, and sends you on a journey toward your highest dreams and goals.

HOW TO USE THIS BOOK

Depending on your needs, *Creative Self-Hypnosis* can be used as a text, a handbook of techniques, or a self-contained training manual. You can use it on your own, with one or more friends, with a college or adult school class, or with the guidance of a professional counselor, therapist, or hypnosis practitioner. It's yours to do with as you wish.

If you want, you can simply dig in and mine the material for whatever you find to be of value. Feel free to do so. However, this book is explicitly organized to serve as a training program. I have written it to be the workbook I would assign you to use if you were my student and I were training you in creative self-hypnosis.

Form follows function, at least in this case. You will find that the following pages contain text for you to read, with forty-one *Key Principles* and twenty-five *Key Tactics* set off from the rest, several *exercises* for you to work with in every chapter, and seven *techniques* for you to practice (one at the end of each chapter). The chapters are carefully organized to provide a programmed learning experience, and I suggest that you work through them in sequence. I'd advise you go through one chapter per week over a seven-week period, although this program can be learned in half that time if you devote considerably more time each day to the readings and the exercises.

But in order to get the most from this book, take it slowly. The reason for this is twofold. First, you need some time practicing each new exercise before you can profitably move on to the next. Second, there is a great deal of experiential material to cover. Much of what you will learn from this book you will learn by doing. So don't go through it too quickly.

I also suggest that you don't drink anything alcoholic for at least a couple of hours before you do the exercises and techniques. Because the effects of the so-called recreational drugs linger longer than a few hours, it is best to avoid them completely during the seven weeks you are working through the program.

I anticipate that most readers will be going through this book on their own and I have designed the exercises accordingly. However, there is a great deal to be gained from working with a partner or a group (be it several friends or a class). In this way you can tap the power of group dynamics, more fully explore some of the issues and concepts we will be considering, and take advantage of the social support others can offer as you work to change your own life and relationships.

Special instructions are provided in the exercises for those who choose the team alternative. As an overall principle, I recommend that you read through the material on your own and meet together at least once a week to discuss one chapter at a time and to go through the group exercises as suggested. It would be best if you agreed not to practice the technique for that chapter until after you have met to discuss the material and do the exercises.

Whichever way you choose to work through this program, keep a written journal documenting what you do and what you experience. Those of my students and clients who have faithfully kept journals have invariably reported getting a lot more out of the program than those who have not. The key seems to be keeping an *intensive* journal—not just listing times and writing out answers to questions but recording thoughts, feelings, observations, worries, fears, problems, insights, and inspirations. This technique is so powerful that it has been adopted by counselors and therapists of virtually every discipline and school of thought.

Trust me. While nothing is more important than actually doing the activities and practicing the exercises, your journal is the single best way to guarantee that you will get the most out of the program.

KEEPING A JOURNAL

- Use a blank spiral-bound or other notebook.
- This is to be your private journal, for your eyes alone. You can share it with anybody you'd like, of course, but don't let that influence how you keep the journal. Don't worry about spelling, grammar, or what others would think. It's for you and for you alone.
- Be creative in keeping your journal. It doesn't have to please or make sense to anybody else but yourself. Use any way that strikes your fancy of representing what you want to record: doodles, sketches, diagrams, words, music, whatever.
- Every time you do one of the exercises in this book, write down which one it was, what you did, when you did it, what you felt, what you noticed, and what you learned.
- Between exercises or practice sessions, or even as you read this book, feel free to jot down any changes you notice and anything else you think appropriate: thoughts, reactions, odd or special experiences, flashes, insights, annoyances, hassles, gains, losses, pleasures, problems, and possible solutions that come to mind. If you want to, record your dreams, your daydreams, your fantasies, your hopes, and your fears. Be sure to date (and preferably time) each entry.
- It is particularly important to make a record of what works for you and what doesn't work for you, both with respect to creative self-hypnosis and to what is going on in the rest of your life.

ONE

Self-Management

Have you ever imagined what it would be like to be free, to be like a child again, to recapture the richness and the brilliance and the wonder and the infinite possibilities of every new moment? Have you ever said to yourself that this has gone on long enough, that life is too precious to waste? That starting right now, or tomorrow morning, or on New Year's Day it's going to be different; you're going to take control of your life; you're going to really start to live?

And what happened? Chances are, you never got around to doing anything about it.

That's what this chapter is all about—doing something about it.

Exercise 1-A: Awakening

DIRECTIONS
1. Close your eyes.
2. Imagine waking up.
3. Record what you did and what you experienced in your journal.

You see, we are all hypnotized, so to speak. We are all walking around in something like a trance, sleepwalking

1

through our lives, following what amounts to a set of "post-natal suggestions" to be a certain kind of person and to think and behave in a certain way. We perform the same tired old scripts over and over, making the same old choices, the same old mistakes, again and again and again. Most of the time we just go along with it, doing what we can, trying to make the best of things.

But then, if we somehow mobilize the energy or spite or whatever it is to do something different, we feel odd. Out of character. We hear those internal voices telling us, "This isn't me. I'm not being myself."

What gives?

If you're looking for answers from me, I can't give them to you. But by applying what you learn from this book, you will be able to get all the answers you need from yourself.

Exercise 1-B: A Snapshot of Yourself

DIRECTIONS

1. Close your eyes. Ask yourself, "*Who* am I? *What* am I really like?"

   Hint: The only trick here is to let your thoughts, images, and feelings flow.

2. Think about it for a minute or two. When you are ready, open your eyes again and write down as many answers as you can. Not only those you thought about but whatever others come to mind. Write until you run down, so to speak. Until nothing more seems to come.

   Note: This method of generating answers or ideas is known as *brainstorming*. We'll be using it a lot.

3. Now, with your eyes open, write down your answer(s) to this second question: "How do I know these things to be so?"

SUGGESTIONS FOR TEAMS

If you are working with a partner or group, share whatever you are willing to reveal about what you learned from this activity and discuss your answers to step 3. Can you arrive at a consensus about how we "know" things about ourselves?

There are no right or wrong answers to a thought experiment like this. Rather, the purpose is to sensitize you to the fact that you are carrying around an image, an understanding, a definition of what it means to be "you." You have come to accept this as who and what you are.

In a word, as your *self*.

But can you explain precisely what this *self* of yours is?

THE SELF

You can't see it; you can't touch it; you can take your brain and body apart cell by cell and you'll never find out where it lives. Why? Because it is not you or any part of you.

It exists at an entirely different order of reality than, say, your hand or this book. Those are things. Your *self* is not a thing or even a spiritual entity (a term this book leaves you to define). The *self* we are talking about is an abstraction—an idea, a symbol, a concept. It represents the total of all your answers to the question "Who am I?"

At least, that is how clinical sociologists like myself have come to understand it. We trace our approach to this question back to just before 1900 when Charles Horton Cooley, a pioneering American sociologist, decided to investigate how we come to "be ourselves."

One of the first low-budget researchers, Cooley observed his two daughters growing up. He concluded that, while your self seems to reflect some inner essence of your being, it really reflects your image of how others see you. That is, you build up your ideas about what you are really like from the way the people in your life respond to your behavior and your appearance. To capture this process, Cooley termed his concept the "looking-glass self."

Around the same time, the great psychologist William James pointed out that we are actually as many *selves* as there are people or relationships in our lives. Aren't you a "different" person with your parents, your friends, your lovers, with strangers on the street, or with your fiercest rivals? Why, then, aren't we all multiple personalities? How is it that we see ourselves as the "same person" despite the fact that we are such different characters in various situations and relationships and look and act so very differently at different periods in our lives?

George Herbert Mead, a University of Chicago social philosopher who died in 1931, took the concept of the looking-glass self a few steps further in order to answer these questions. It was clear to him that it is not just anybody's opinion of us that counts. There are *significant others*. As infants and children, we are most deeply attached to and influenced by our family members. It is their positive responses we crave and seek to obtain by imitating them and trying to please them.

At this point, then, our emerging self-image is tied to the actual responses of a small set of significant others. They smile at us and we feel great; they frown at us and we ache. But then we make a developmental leap.

Kittens and puppies play-fight and play-hunt and so build up the skills they need to be cats and dogs. The *function* of their play is to prepare them for grown-up life. Similarly, Mead argued, human children play games, the function of which is to prepare themselves to live in society.

The function of little kids' fantasy games is to give them a feel for the different scenes and characters in life. They play at being mommy and they play at being Masters of the Universe (being little kids, they haven't learned the difference between fantasy and reality). One thing is clear to them— none of these roles are "themselves," although they ignore the difference while they are playing. It is as if they are dressing up in different selves, trying them on, so to speak, just as they may dress up in mommy's and daddy's old clothes or simply make believe they are in costume.

Older kids play in a different league (like Mead, we'll use the analogy of baseball to illustrate his concepts). Notice the difference in the nature of the games they play. Young children play make-believe games in which they make up the rules as they go along. Older kids learn to play organized games that have complicated *rules* that they must follow, *roles* they must learn to master, and a system of *relationships* among those roles within which they must learn to function.

Such games reflect the social world and prepare us for life in society. In the process, they teach us to go beyond the looking glass, so to speak (all references to Lewis Carroll intended), and see ourselves in a larger context. That is their function.

Think about baseball (or, if you prefer, softball). Like other organized games, it involves a set of rules, roles, and relationships that the players must learn to master and that they cannot change.

For example, the rules of baseball designate certain preset *roles* or *positions*. While any player can be assigned to any of these roles at different times, whoever occupies a position is expected to carry out the role assigned to it. Whether you're currently shortstop, pitcher, or center left field, you have a specific job to do. Everyone learns what each position entails, so that all the players know what to expect, regardless of who currently occupies each role. What is more, each player alternates between two sets of roles in any single game, depending on whether one's team is at bat or in the field.

As a kid, you learn at least two things from playing baseball (or any other team sport). You learn the concept of a *social system*, a network of roles and rules and relationships external to yourself. You learn to work within that network of relationships, meeting your mutual obligations to your teammates. At the same time, perhaps, you are learning how to compete for personal advantage within that group context. In any case, you are learning how to cooperate in society.

You are also learning to conceptualize *yourself*. As you shift between the different roles expected of you, from the ways in which the others in the system respond to your actions, personality, and appearance, you build an "objective" concept of yourself as it seems that you are viewed from the outside. You make it up, but you don't make it up on your own. That is Mead's central point.

But there's an easily overlooked implication here: *The looking glass is inside your head.* Actually, it has by this point become more like a video monitor on which you watch yourself acting from a back row seat in the imaginary audience. Perhaps, even more significantly, you begin to perform for that imaginary audience among whom you sit.

You literally create yourself, your character in life's drama (or is it comedy?), by an act of imagination. And then, by creative imagination, you keep yourself "you." That's pretty amazing, but it is also a trap.

THE OTHER SIDE OF THE SELF

You've been coached, wheedled, bribed, coerced, conned, and bullied into seeing things in a certain way. Yet you imagine that this is how the world actually is—that there is only the one way to see it. Social scientists call this *socialization.* Let's be blunt (and a little outrageous)—what we are talking about is virtually identical to "being hypnotized."

As I've said, it's all a matter of postnatal suggestion. Used in this sense, "suggestion" has a double meaning, since nothing is spelled out or engraved in stone. On your side, it is all a matter of guesswork and imagination, but your ideas about the world are not entirely your own. You were born into an ongoing world and brought up to accept its rules—the ones they teach you in church and synagogue and school, the ones that are beaten into you by those with more power or strength or authority than yourself, and the ones you pick up on by hints and by innuendo.

There is something very peculiar about this kind of learning. Look at your answers to the second question in Exercise 1-B. I'll bet you find nothing there that is concrete or tangible.

You can describe your hands or the cover of this book in terms of what you directly perceive, but you can only describe your *self* in terms of what you *infer* from others and from experience.

Let's look a bit further, shall we?

Exercise 1-C: Defining Ourselves

DIRECTIONS
1. Look at your responses to the first question you asked yourself in Exercise 1-B. If you think of anything else as you do this, write it down in your journal as well. Now, complete the following exercise.
2. Think of your answers to this question as adding up to 100 percent.
   a. What percentage of your answers referred to positives—something you are, something you can do, something you have accomplished?   _____%
   b. What percentage of your answers referred to negatives—to what you are not, to what you cannot do, to what you have not accomplished?   _____%

   Total   100%

SUGGESTIONS FOR TEAMS
Share your findings from this activity with one another. What conclusions are suggested about how we define ourselves?

It seems that we are far more aware of what we are not than of what we are. We look out at the world, not in at ourselves. When we look out at the world, we never see ourselves in the picture. We can see the world around us. We can see what we are not; but we can only use our imagination to "see" ourselves.

Consequently, we have little alternative but to identify ourselves by a process of elimination and inference. This identification is what we tapped into when you answered the question, "Who am I?" in Exercise 1-A.

Moreover, there is a kind of security in identifying safe limits for ourselves. It is as if we secrete a mental fence around ourselves, so that we don't even accidentally put ourselves at risk of harm. We've "learned" that it does not pay to press any further, that we'll only falter, fail or fall flat on our faces and embarrass ourselves. Or worse.

So we accept our limits and we don't press our luck. Yet we have no direct means of ascertaining what those limits really are.

Think about it. You can't know what is possible for you; you can only know what you have tried and what you seem to have accomplished to date. You can't know your limits, your boundaries—you can only infer them. Yes, once again it's all a matter of inference with lots and lots of room for error.

SELF-ESTEEM

Okay. You have an image of yourself. How do you feel about that person you see on the video monitor of your mind?

Exercise 1-D: Rating Yourself

DIRECTIONS

Using a 5-point scale, where A = outstanding, B = pretty good, C = okay, D = poor, and F = failure, grade yourself on the following:

		Grade
1.	Overall value as a human being	_____
2.	Accomplishments in life	_____
3.	Realization of your potential	_____
4.	Success as a student or success in your job or profession	_____
5.	Quality of your relationships	_____
6.	Desirability as a friend	_____
7.	Physical attractiveness	_____
8.	Being somebody others can depend on	_____
9.	Being somebody others can look up to	_____
10.	Living a life you can be proud of	_____

_____   Total

Now, let's calculate your self-regard score. Let A = 4, B = 3, C = 2, D = 1, and F = 0. Add up the numbers corresponding to your grades and divide the sum by 10.

If your self-regard score is above 3.75, you are probably not being honest with yourself; if it's below 2.0, you are probably being too harsh on yourself. There is no "ideal" score, but somewhere around 3.0 represents a healthy but realistic self-regard.

What do you think? How do you feel about your score?

SUGGESTIONS FOR TEAMS

If you feel that you are willing to do so, share your ratings with one another and discuss your responses to what you learned in this activity. You may be surprised to discover how much you share with one another.

What we're exploring in this exercise is the concept of positive self-regard or *self-esteem*. You not only have an image of yourself but you have feelings about that image. Like the way in which you define yourself, those feelings tend to be framed by negatives.

There is at least one major difference between self-regard and self-image, however. It's not only the outlines but also what lies within the outlines that tends to be dominated by negatives. Who can honestly say that deep inside he or she is okay? That anyone is really happy with him- or herself?

Yet the way in which you regard yourself is perhaps the key factor governing the quality of your life. While it is important to understand that self-esteem is a relative matter, again and again we find that people with low self-esteem tend to have more problems than others—school problems, job problems, emotional problems, financial problems, family problems, medical problems, mental problems, coping problems, drug problems.

Those with positive self-esteem, in contrast, are more likely to live happy and fruitful lives. They're the ones who succeed where others fail, who enjoy life, who find joy in life. Obviously, we're going to be doing a lot of work on your self-esteem.

Don't get me wrong, however. The cure for low self-esteem is not self-worship. By positive self-esteem, I don't mean that you're your own fan club. That's not self-esteem, that's disgusting. What I do mean is that you can accept yourself and feel that it's good to be alive, that maybe you're not perfect, but you are okay. And if you're not pretty good yet, you're well on your way to getting there. But let's backtrack a bit and take a look at where you started from. How do we acquire self-esteem? What is the natural history of self-regard?

These questions lead us right back to Cooley:

> A self-idea of this sort seems to have three principal elements: the imagination of our appearance to the other person; the imagination of his judgment of that appearance, and some sort of self-feeling, such as pride or mortification. The comparison with a looking glass hardly suggests the second element, the imagined judgment, which is quite essential. The thing that moves us to pride or shame is not the mere mechanical reflection of ourselves, but an imputed sentiment, the imagined effect of this reflection upon another's mind.

Taking Cooley a bit further, we base our self-regard on how we imagine others judge us. In childhood, our significant others are all important; while those others might change over the course of our lives, we never cease to direct our actions toward the imagined judgment of those who are most important to us.

Have you ever considered how much you concern yourself with how you will appear in the eyes of significant others? How often have you done and said things, or not done and not said things, in order to convey a desired impression of yourself, in order to get the other person to see you in a certain way? And how often have you learned at a later time that you predicted wrongly what that other person would think, how that person would respond?

Going a bit deeper, to your core sense of self, your overarching self-image, you also carry a basic self-judgment. When we make that leap to imagining ourselves in the eyes of a generalized other, we also imagine how the world-as-a-whole regards us. Once again, however, it seems that we place more emphasis on negatives than on positives.

In part, perhaps, that is because each of us in our hearts knows all the reasons why others would despise us or reject us if they only knew. . . . You are always the world's best authority on your own failings.

Sure, we can attribute this preoccupation to some inner psychological process, but have you ever wondered whether there might be an external reason why so many of us feel so lousy about ourselves? Could this be a way to control us, to keep us in line, to keep us down?

Exercise 1-E: Secrets

DIRECTIONS
Note: In these exercises, you can always open your eyes to look at the directions and then close your eyes again and continue.

1. Close your eyes and take a couple of deep breaths to relax and let yourself loosen up a bit.
2. Think about what you consider to be your failings and the secrets about yourself that you feel (however irrationally) would cause others you care about to reject, laugh at, or despise you if they found out.
3. What words or judgments are you associating with these things? What feelings do you attach to those words or judgments—guilt, shame, embarrassment, feeling bad, unworthy?
4. Open your eyes. Make three columns across the top of your journal page labeled "Nonissues," "Change Issues," and "Coping Issues."
    *   *Nonissues* are the things that, on reflection, aren't really worth bothering about because they are somebody else's hang-ups, or you only imagined them to be problems at the time and they really aren't any longer.
    *   *Change issues* are those things you have thought of

that *you realistically can do something about,* for example, by changing your behavior.

- *Coping issues* are those things that you cannot realistically change but that *you must learn to cope with so that they no longer represent a problem (or as much of a problem) for you.*

5. Now sort each of the things you thought about when your eyes were closed into one of these categories by simply listing them by name under the appropriate column heading. Feel free to use code names or abbreviations if you feel nervous about somebody else reading your list of secrets, just as long as you know what each refers to.

6. When you are done, read through each list, doing the following:

   - As you come to each new "nonissue," tell yourself that you now realize it's no longer worth troubling yourself over it.

   - As you come to each new "change issue," if it is something you are willing to change, tell yourself that you choose to change this behavior (or whatever it is) so that it will no longer be a problem for you. If it is not something you are willing to change, cross it out and list it under the "coping issues" column. You have a right to decide what you are and are not willing to change about yourself and your life!

   - As you come to each new "coping issue," tell yourself that you accept it as an aspect of yourself and that you choose to find new, creative ways of coping with it so that it is no longer a source of trouble for you.

7. Now close your eyes again and take a couple of deep breaths again. Then imagine you are feeling more and more able to accept yourself exactly as you are now and *make believe you are feeling this way.* Let whatever words, images, fantasies seem appropriate pass through your mind, perhaps imagining that you are literally embracing yourself in a hug of forgiveness

and acceptance or whatever strikes your fancy. When you are ready to do so, open your eyes and continue.

SUGGESTIONS FOR TEAMS
Revealing as much as you feel comfortable about your own personal "secrets," discuss what you have learned from doing the exercise and, perhaps, talk about how we come to feel guilty, ashamed, sinful, and bad about ourselves, what the consequences are of attaching these *labels* to ourselves, and what we can do about them.

Negative self-feelings are, indeed, a control mechanism. They are part of the hypnotizing routine by which the world controls us. We are taught to feel embarrassed about ourselves, to feel guilty, rotten, shameful, inferior.

To the degree that we accept these feelings, we accept whatever the world hands us—and we do so gratefully. In any case, we don't come up with these feelings or others about ourselves entirely on our own. We get lots and lots of "help."

SOCIAL GROUPS

So far, we have concentrated on the other individuals in your life and the consequences that your relationships with them have had for you. Let's change focus a bit now and think about the *social groups* to which you belong.

Exercise 1-F: Your Groups

DIRECTIONS
1. In your journal, make a heading called "My Groups" and list all the social groups to which you presently belong or have belonged to in the past. Include, for example, your country, community, the family into which you were born, your own family or household, groups of friends, schools, companies, work groups

or workplace, religious organizations, professional organizations, political organizations, clubs, teams, volunteer associations, and so forth.

2. Go through the the list and circle the three groups that you feel are the most important to you at the *present* time.

3. Now, for each of these three groups:
   a. Describe your *role* in that group (what part do you play, what is your position officially/unofficially).
   b. Describe what you feel is your *standing* in that group (that is, your *status*—how important is your role, where do you stand in the group's "pecking order").
   c. Describe how you think other group members perceive you (what kind of person do they see you as, how do they feel about you, how do they evaluate you).

SUGGESTIONS FOR TEAMS

Compare your lists (or at least as much as each of you is willing to share about your lists), which groups each of you selected in step 2 and how you answered the questions in step 3. Again, you may find that sharing your responses to step 3 is a revelation.

We human beings are social creatures; not only do we make our lives within groups of other human beings but our very selves reflect and are shaped by group belonging. As an early sociology textbook, *Introduction to the Science of Sociology* by Park and Burgess (1926), put it:

> The person is an individual who has status. We come into the world as individuals. We acquire status and become persons. Status means position in society. The individual inevitably has some status in every social group of which he is a member. In a given group the status of every member is determined by his relation to every other member of that group.

The fact that we are not merely isolated individuals but persons affects us in two very important ways.

First, what we do and how we go about doing it invariably reflects our status in all the social groups of which we are a member. We *internalize* our social relationships as part of our very selves, possibly because other people tend to relate to us according to what they perceive to be our social status. In any case, we commonly identify ourselves in terms of status. No doubt, when you answered the "Who am I" question in Exercise 1-A, you listed some statuses, such as your place in your family or your position at work.

Second, we tend to adopt the perspectives of our *reference groups.* A reference group is a social group that is psychologically important to us; for example, one in which we actually participate or one to which we see ourselves as belonging. We tend to absorb the values, beliefs, understandings, and ways of speaking, seeing, and doing things of our reference groups. This is not very surprising, since we normally find our significant others within our reference groups. After all, these are the people with whom we identify and with whom we tend to associate.

Not only our "in-groups" influence us but also our "out" groups—those groups that we see ourselves as not being part of, to which we do not want to belong. They serve as negative reference groups, giving us a sense of who are not "our kind" of people. A lot of groups, in fact, seem to define themselves negatively, in terms of what they are *not* more than in terms of what they share among themselves. This seems to be particularly true of groups that perceive themselves as minorities. Our group participation has a critical impact on every facet of our lives (for example, our self-esteem).

Our first group experience is almost invariably our family. For this reason, Cooley labeled the family our *primary group.* Both clinicians and researchers agree that one of the most important influences on our self-regard is the family in which we were raised.

Some families seem to facilitate the development of positive self-esteem in their children. They are supportive, nurturing, accepting of all family members. They hold up nonjudgmental mirrors to one another, defining each member's status as worthy of trust and respect. They provide opportunities for children to take on responsibility and to develop a sense of competency and control.

Even the best of families can, however, squash their children, stunt their emotional and intellectual growth, do violence to their self-esteem. For example, there's our neighbor Paul. His parents are both college professors, pillars of their community. Everyone gets dressed up and goes to church on Sunday. The family is like something out of a 1950s sitcom.

Everything about this household is neat and tidy and, above all else, orderly. For example, when the three kids come home from school there is always a snack waiting. They are expected to eat that snack, and then, of course, they are expected to eat their dinner, do their chores, do their lessons, relax for a while, and go to bed.

These people are so "straight" that Paul's dad expressed shock when my wife drove by with some of the neighborhood kids in the car and rock music on the stereo.

"But . . . you're a *mother*," he stammered.

Now, it turns out that there is a bit more to the story than first appears. Paul's sister can do no wrong in her status as the darling little girl of the family. His little brother, the family's "genius" child, can do no wrong, and plays the part he is assigned to the hilt. Paul, however, can't do anything right.

A bright, personable child, year after year he keeps on trying. It is he who does the dishes, mows the lawns, does anything and everything to please his dad. It never gets him very far. He's criticized for everything.

Paul keeps on trying, but he can never be good enough. If anything, his situation keeps getting worse and worse. He finds himself responding to his low status by going through the motions and keeping his inner self aloof. In school, he is considered an underachiever. At home, his family considers him a loser. He can't get any respect.

When I last ran into him, Paul was on the verge of being thrown out of his house permanently. His Dad was just disgusted with him. He'd gotten into what most people would consider the "wrong" crowd at school.

I am not suggesting that Paul has been "ruined" by his family or that he has turned out rotten. Sure, you might conclude from this story that poor self-esteem "caused" Paul to become involved with the "party crowd," but I think you'd be missing the real point.

Some children would have retreated into passivity. Not Paul. He has not allowed his low status in his family to rob him of self-respect.

Granted, in terms of his family's social world, Paul has pretty much become what his parents were most afraid of, what they'd always accused him of being. He's stopped trying to change their image of him, their reactions to him as a person. Now, it may well have cost him his opportunity to create a conventional life for himself, but he's accepted the judgment of his family that he'll never make it as one of "their kind" of people.

So Paul took the implied hint and changed reference groups. His parents might consider his group to be the "wrong crowd," but for him it represents an opportunity for achieving what he could never get from his own family—an esteemed status and significant others who respond to him positively.

While there are many questions about the long-term consequences of this particular move, Paul has at least taken some first steps toward creating a better quality of life for himself. The "moral" of this story is that you can change your life without drastically changing yourself by changing your social relationships.

There are times when changing social relationships is perhaps your best alternative. There are, for example, marriages that have deteriorated to the point where divorce is the only way out, jobs for which you may be a total mismatch, friends who really *are* a bad crowd and that will only get you into trouble.

At other times, social relationships can be reconstructed so as to bring about desired change. This objective is a major one in the interventions conducted by many professional clinical sociologists and "systems change" consultants. We will discuss some of their tactics in subsequent chapters.

SELF-MANAGEMENT AND YOUR TRUE SELF

Let's go back to a point we skipped earlier. As William James pointed out, we do not act the same in every situation. Paul was not the "same person" around his parents as he was in church or around his peers. In fact, *I* was not the "same person" around the various crowds with which I was involved in Paul's community. We each play different roles in different social situations. Call them roles or masks or faces or aspects of ourselves; we act like different people.

John Lofland has described this concept as our *situated selves*. We are aware that we play different roles and exhibit different selves in the various concrete social situations in which we find ourselves. Yet we can only be or "do" one of these selves at a time. While I was being a neighbor, I was one person. While I was being a professor lecturing, I was another. While I was hanging around with my friends at a buddy's handmade, wood-fired sauna in the woods, I was being a third person entirely.

Which is the "real" me?

Unless we assume that there is an inner self revealed in our behavior—a hypothesis I dismissed above—then this is a major question.

The first part of the answer is to suggest that Mead was oversimplifying matters somewhat. Most of us manage to organize a consistent self-definition in childhood, and by *ongoing* self-management tactics, maintain an overarching sense of a "true" self throughout the ever-shifting situations of our lives.

This fact, in turn, suggests two ideas worth noting. The first is that we have to keep at it constantly. Our true self is a continual, never-ending project, an always unfinished work of art. Like a living collage, it keeps on growing, becoming more complex, incorporating more and more elements. Your own creative acts bring it together into an artistically consistent whole.

A second implication is that an integrated self is a kind of miracle we are expected to bring off without even thinking about it. It is understandable that some of us do a better job than others. Since we are really multiple selves, it is not surprising that some people never succeed in becoming un-*fragmented*. Most of us exhibit some degree of fragmentation, having different sides or faces or moods that come into play at different times and in different situations.

Most of the time, these different selves or facets of self communicate and hang together. A few of us exist as a sort of group of selves who may never talk to each other or even know of each other's existence. This, of course, is the phenomenon of multiple personality. Some counselors and psychologists feel that people who are severely abused as children quite commonly exhibit some degree of multiple personality, as if their ability to trust themselves is stifled by the pain and humiliation they have suffered at the hands of adults. I know of no research into the phenomenon from such a perspective, but it could be a useful line of inquiry to pursue.

We are led back to the question: Which is your true self? Since this is a kind of multiple choice question, my answer is, of course, "all of the above."

Okay, so I'm being facetious. You're in deep trouble if you can't take a joke—particularly about yourself. Actually, it appears to be true that we integrate an overarching self-concept out of the bits and pieces of our various social selves. In addition, as Cooley hints but most who have followed in his footsteps have ignored, the idea of a "true self" involves both your abstract conceptualization of your role in the world according to Mead and your image of yourself as a physical organism.

Apparently, by our teenage years we develop a physical or *somatic* self-image just as we develop our more abstract self-concept. Maintaining our somatic self-image is perhaps even trickier than keeping our social selves together, since we all mature physically. Doubtlessly, part of the troubles of even the most normal adolescence involves reconciling our new sexually and physically maturing bodies with our childhood images of self.

Our somatic selves may be highly unrealistic. First of all, until the advent of films and video equipment, we had no means of observing ourselves behaving. In any case, few of us spend much time as children or adults looking at our bodies. Rather, our somatic self-perception appears to be largely based on how we perceive others to respond to us, on how we imagine we appear, and on our own fantasies about how we ought to look.

Old images can, for example, haunt us for years. I was in my late twenties when I recognized that I was still carrying around a self-image of myself as a fat thirteen-year-old with braces and a big nose. Many of us tyrannize ourselves with unrealistically negative somatic images of this sort—and with these images, the imagined judgments that Cooley described as part of the looking-glass self.

You can run into other types of conflict between your somatic self-image and the physical self you actually present. We may have an idealized picture of ourselves that leads us to discredit ourselves in the eyes of others by inappropriate behavior. The image of the obese, middle-aged man or woman dressing and acting like a twenty-year-old comes to mind.

It is probably a good idea to monitor your somatic self-image and to revise it from time to time. By all means use positive thinking to the extent of visualizing yourself as you would choose to be, but keep it realistic. I am not and never will be a six-foot-tall California surfer with golden hair, darn it. And I would look awfully stupid strutting around in a skimpy bikini.

Exercise 1-G: Somatic Self-Image

DIRECTIONS

This exercise has two parts. Unlike most other exercises in the book, this one you'll want to do by yourself in complete privacy.

A. *Thinking about your physical self*
    1. Close your eyes and think about your body, how you look. Try to remember how you generally visualize your appearance from the outside. Don't

try to be accurate or scientific, but think about how you are accustomed to seeing yourself in your mind's eye.

2. How do you feel when you do this? How do you feel about the way you think you look? What do you like? What don't you like? What would you like to be different?

3. Record your answers to step 2 in your journal along with a brief summary of how you customarily visualize the way you look.

B. *Mirror exercise*

1. Stand in front of the biggest mirror available, in good lighting.

2. Look at what you see in the mirror. Pretend you are looking at somebody else in the mirror and pay close attention to everything you see. Turn around and see your image from all angles.

3. Take off all your clothes and repeat step 2. Perhaps do this first after peeling down to your underwear and then nude. For some, it may be very difficult or even embarrassing to do this. Just take a few deep breaths and do it anyway.

4. Now, as if you were a little child, fool around. I mean goof around. Move your limbs. Dance. Hop. Make funny faces. Stand on one leg. Twirl like a top. Strike various poses—heroic poses, serious poses, businesslike poses, sensual and sexy poses. And keep on observing what you see in the mirror.

5. As you watch, tell yourself, "This is me. This is what I look like at the moment. I'm okay, and I can make myself better if I so choose." Use your own words to say the same thing if you prefer. But keep on looking and keep on saying these words over and over.

6. Sit down, if you'd like (perhaps dress first, it's your option), and close your eyes. Remember how you looked in the mirror. Think about any alterations you might want to make in your current

physical appearance and how you might accomplish them.

Hint: It would be beneficial to do part B of this exercise more than once, perhaps several days in a row.

SUGGESTIONS FOR TEAMS

Since it is highly unlikely you would want to do this exercise as a group (joke), perhaps share what you learned about yourself from this exercise and how you felt while and after doing it. If you feel comfortable doing so, perhaps share some of the negative things you have felt about your somatic selves and how those negative images have affected you. You may find this to be a very powerful sharing experience.

DOING SOMETHING ABOUT IT

While, as I suggested earlier, a lot of the problems you may experience with your self have to do with the other people or the situations in your life, these are not generally easy to change. A lot of the time it is most appropriate to at least begin by changing yourself, which is the main thrust of this book.

What, then, is the solution to low self-esteem? How do you fix a bad self-image? How do you change yourself?

The general answer to these questions lies in our first key principle:

Key Principle One: The way to be changed is to act changed. Hold on there, you say. That sounds suspiciously like the sort of advice you've found in all those pop psychology books—you know, like "go with the flow" and "just take a deep breath and relax."

I agree. Of course, if you can just go ahead and do it, all power to you. However, I don't mean to suggest that transforming yourself is an easy task—anything but that.

Nevertheless, our discussion regarding the self suggests a basic line of approach. What Cooley and Mead tell us is that you internalize a self-image and then rely on that self-concept to organize your subsequent behavior. In effect, through the process of socialization, you have accepted those postnatal suggestions and let the world program you to be "yourself" as others define you to be.

What is more, you set up a bunch of backup programs to let yourself know if you're stepping out of character. Then you take your conscious attention off the whole thing and get on with the task of living and the whole process proceeds at a literally subconscious level. To act "like yourself," you merely have to glance at the monitor to see how you can be expected to behave in a given situation.

Going back to the beginning of this chapter, if you try to behave "out of character" your inner alarms go off. It feels wrong. You *know* how you "really" are, what you "naturally" do. You might struggle for a while, but in the end you generally find yourself acting out the suggestions you give yourself on that internal video screen.

You have worked for a lifetime to become the person you are. It would not only be unrealistic but downright stupid to expect that you or I or anyone could just wave some sort of magic wand and change. If this were true, there wouldn't be a multibillion-dollar therapy and life-changing industry, all the cults would be out of business, and I could leave the rest of this book blank.

If, for example, you know that you eat too much, that you are a compulsive overeater, it is, indeed, only natural for you to take that second helping, to gobble up that dessert. To do anything else requires you to literally fight "yourself."

That's *always* going to be a losing proposition. Which brings us to our second key principle:

Key Principle Two: Expect resistance and outflank it. As your own experience has proven, no doubt, it is shockingly hard to act contrary to your accustomed norm, even when you are alone, even in the privacy of your own imagination.

Exercise 1-H: Not Being Yourself

DIRECTIONS
1. Think about how you normally dress and act when you are with your closest friends (or, alternatively, your parents or children).
2. Now imagine going out in public with them but dressing and acting completely different. If you are normally neat and proper, imagine being sloppy and foul-mouthed. If you are normally quiet, imagine being loud.
3. As you imagine acting this way, picture the other people in the scene, how they would be acting and reacting. Also pay attention to what passes through your mind as you do this exercise; how it feels.
4. Now debrief yourself:
   a. What expressions could you see on the faces of the others? Surprise, concern, consternation?
   b. What were you imagining them saying and doing? Was anyone saying "What's wrong, you're not acting like yourself at all?"
   c. What did you feel like inside?
   d. What words passed through your mind? *In whose voice were those words—your own or whose?*

SUGGESTIONS FOR TEAMS
Why not share your answers to step 4? Then make a game of seeing who can imagine being *most* unlike their normal selves (that is, who can imagine being most outrageous) and put your heads together to imagine what responses such behavior could provoke. You'll get more benefit from this and all the other exercises, if you do them playfully.

There are three points to the exercise.
First, notice how your significant others depend on you to be the same person and will tend to talk you back into

character if you depart from the script they have in their minds for you. *Expect resistance from other people in your life.*

Second, notice how difficult it is to even imagine stepping so drastically out of character. Notice how severely you judge yourself. *The primary source of resistance to changing yourself is yourself.*

Third, notice how many of those voices inside your head are really not your own. Rather, you probably get the sense of parents' voices, children's voices (if you are a parent), friends' voices, lovers' voices, bosses' voices—all manner of voices.

A lot of the resistance within yourself is actually the resistance you imagine will come from others. It appears that we each carry around our own internalized reference group.

There was, in fact, a British psychiatrist, John Richmond, who in the 1940s wrote a book about this resistance titled *The Internal Society.* He and Ron Lippitt felt that these internal voices—in essence, our internalized images of significant others holding up their looking glasses to our thoughts and actions—were a major source of resistance to change:

> Everyone of us has an internal group holding conversations inside us all the time. It helps a lot if we can learn to listen to, and deal with, these internal voices.

One of Lippitt's greatest skills was the ability to turn resistance into positive energy for change. Resistance into resources, so to speak. For example, Lippitt might have asked you to listen quietly to those voices and notice both those counseling caution against starting new things or initiating changes and also those supporting your efforts. He might then have suggested that you listen to what the negative voices are telling you and try to learn from them.

This lesson is an example of outflanking resistance. However, working both with actual and imaginary others is probably not the best place to start a program of desired change. Rather, begin with your self and then act to recruit the resistance of significant others.

TAKING STOCK

We are now at a point where action is called for; the curtain is rising and you are about to go on stage.

First, let's pause for a moment. This is a good time to take stock of yourself.

Exercise 1-I: Your Personal Balance Sheet

DIRECTIONS

Go to the next blank page of your journal and divide it into quarters with two lines. Then enter titles for each part, so that it looks like this:

Exercise 1-I (today's date here)

Bads	Goods
Minuses	Pluses

This is your personal balance sheet. The part above the horizontal line represents your present; the part below it represents your past.

1. Begin with your past. In the "minuses" space on the bottom left, write down all things you have done or not done in your past that you feel were mistakes or failures—all the things you feel sorry about.

   In the "pluses" space on the bottom right, write down all the things you have done or not done in the past that you feel good about, including accomplishments and relationships.

   You can go back and forth between these two sides, but enter everything you can think of as honestly as you can until you run out of things to write or you have filled up all the available space.

2. Now let's move on to your present. On the "bads" side, write down all your current feelings of pain, all your worries, concerns, problems, and negative situations.

   On the "goods" side, write down all the things you feel good about right now, including the good things you have, the good things you are doing, your strengths and assets. Continue until you run out of things to write or you run out of room.

   You can always make an updated balance sheet for yourself. But right now continue with the other steps.

3. Read over your balance sheet. Really familiarize yourself with it.

4. As if you were somebody else entirely who had just read this material in a dossier, perhaps, write a *brief* paragraph describing this person as he or she is at the present time.

5. This step is the hardest part. If you wanted to capture the essence of this person, how he or she is right now, in a still photograph or in a thirty-second movie clip, what scene would you pick? What would be going on? Be creative; use your imagination and your intuition. *Do not, however, write this down. Instead, just imagine it in your mind.*

SUGGESTIONS FOR TEAMS

This activity is one you might or might not want to share. However, you would very likely benefit from sharing your responses and reactions to doing step 5 as well as sharing any problems you came across in doing the activity and how you solved those problems.

What you have done in steps 4 and 5 is to *scan your present*. The balance sheet was mainly to take stock of where you are. The paragraph is to help you identify what are, for you, the key features of your present self and situation.

***Key Principle Three: The best place to start anything is
here and now.*** There are a lot of people who will tell you
that the past is the key to the future. For example, Freud,
following Wordsworth, wrote that "the child is father to the
man."

It is true that those who are ignorant of history, including
their own personal history, are doomed to repeat it. And it is
also true that past experience has great influence on our
present selves, as our preceding discussion has suggested.

Let's not go overboard, however. We are not robots (although, to be sure, we often act as if we were).

***Key Principle Four: The power of the past flows from the
imagination.*** Our past does not control our future except,
that is, *to the degree that we act as if it did so.* You act in the
here and now and you connect your past and your future by
keeping your past selves alive in your thoughts, feelings, and
imaginations.

This means that to transform yourself and your life, you
don't have to resolve all the conflicts from your past or work
through your past in any way. To do so would, of course, be
nice and you could probably get a lot out of going through
the sort of therapy or program that would have such a result,
but it is not necessary.

While there is much to gain by taking inventory of your
past for lessons and resources, this can become a fixation and
you can lose track of the simple fact that the only value of the
past is to serve as a platform for creating your future. You can
simply stop agreeing to act as if the past controls your future
and start to focus on the future you want for your self. The
way to be changed is to act changed, remember? Not to
endlessly rehash the past.

TAKE NOTHING FOR GRANTED

There is one complication that I am obliged to tell you about:
It isn't generally what you are consciously aware of that most
influences your behavior.

As Louis Wirth (yes, another famous dead sociologist) pointed out, perhaps the most important information you can learn about anyone is what she or he takes for granted. That's where you find the "subconscious" rules that govern how a person thinks, feels, and imagines.

Key Principle Five: Don't take anything for granted. To put this rule another way, take a good look at what you presume to be "only natural"—that is, the way things are; whatever is so familiar and commonplace that you don't question it.

Hypnotized people are notorious for taking for granted whatever the hypnotist tells them. Posthypnotic suggestions depend on taking for granted the "fact" that the suggestions will be acted out without thinking. It is, perhaps, your ability to act this way that determines how you would score on the various tests of hypnotic suggestibility used to determine your aptitude as a hypnotic subject.

This goes for postnatal suggestions and the "hypnosis" of daily life, as well. *To break the pattern of automatic behavior, you need to stop taking things for granted and make your own decisions regarding what it is that you choose for yourself.*

CREATING YOUR FUTURE

The first step in taking control of your life is to take a good hard look at your present self and situation as we have been doing.

The second step is to explore and familiarize yourself with your options by *mocking up* preferred futures for yourself. I use that term in the sense of "creating a scenario" for use in "running" a computer simulation. You do not need to try to predict what the future is going to be. You do not have to detail the exact future you would like to bring about. You only need to sketch out futures that would meet your personal conditions for feeling good about yourself, for feeling that your life is worthwhile.

This procedure involves a radically different orientation toward future planning than that to which you are probably accustomed. We are trained to think in terms of a *logical future* that can be extrapolated from past and present conditions. However, what we will be concentrating on in this program is the *preferred future* that we bring about by our deliberate choices.

Exercise 1-J: Possible Futures

DIRECTIONS
    A. Look over these ten basic issues from Exercise 1-D:
        1. Overall value as a human being
        2. Accomplishments in life
        3. Realization of your potential
        4. Success as a student or success in your job or profession
        5. Quality of your relationships
        6. Desirability as a friend
        7. Physical attractiveness
        8. Being somebody others can depend on
        9. Being somebody others can look up to
      10. Living a life you can be proud of
    B. Now, go through these ten items doing the following with each in turn:
        1. Read the item.
        2. Close your eyes.
        3. Imagine that you are very, very old and, looking back, you are *really feeling good* about this aspect of your life.
        4. Think about what accomplishments, activities, relationships, and events could have made you feel this way.
        5. Open your eyes and jot down these thoughts in your journal.

SUGGESTIONS FOR TEAMS
    Consider your first time through (while reading this) as a trial run. Now do it for real. Work in teams of two. One partner will take the role of consultant and the other of

subject. The consultant reads the item and then coaches the subject through these steps while the subject (whose eyes are closed) calls out what comes to mind in step 4 and the consultant writes it down. After completing all ten items, switch roles.

When performing this exercise, you may have noticed that in order to feel we are really alive and that our lives have been well-lived, we need to feel that we have accomplished something. We need to feel that we have made a difference. Our objectives might be grand and glamorous, or they might be small and homely. In either case, what is important is to have caused an effect, to have created something, to have done something well.

Is there a secret method for bringing these things about? Are there rules for successfully creating a future?

Nope. Sorry. Anyone who sells you a foolproof plan for becoming a millionaire, becoming happy, getting what you want from life is asking you to prove that you are a fool. How do you get to the future you want?

It has been said time and again, but I'll repeat it:

Key Principle Six: *You create your future as you go along.*

SUMMARY

This chapter focused on your *self*. It suggested that you have been tricked into believing that what you seem to be is what you are and all that you can be. In exploring this idea, you have been introduced to some of the basic concepts of *clinical sociology* regarding the nature and development of the *self* and of *self-esteem*. On the way, you have explored your own self-concept. Then we turned to the question of how you can transform yourself. We have worked on two steps of the self-transformation process: *scanning your present* and *mocking up your future*. We have also developed the following Key Principles:

ONE: The way to be changed is to act changed.
TWO: Expect resistance and outflank it.
THREE: The best place to start anything is here and now.
FOUR: The power of the past flows from the imagination.
FIVE: Don't take anything for granted.
SIX: You create your future as you go along.

Technique One: Creative Hypnosis

PURPOSE
This technique is designed to reinforce what you have already learned, to give you an opportunity to do some further work on initial steps, and to mobilize your resources for change at the same time as you experience what is meant by "creative self-hypnosis."

METHOD (INCLUDING SUGGESTIONS FOR TEAMS)
This first exercise can be done in either (or both) of two ways. You can tape-record yourself reading through the script below and then listen to your tape recording. Or those who are working with a partner or group have the option of selecting one individual to take the role of consultant to read the script for the others. Either this reading should be taped for the consultant's use or someone else should then read the script for the consultant. It would be best, however, if each person working with this program made a tape for his or her own use.

The script provides cues regarding the best way to actually read it. Words to be emphasized are in italics and ellipses (. . .) are used to denote a brief pause. Instructions to the reader will be found in parentheses.

This session will take approximately 20 minutes for reading or listening.

When you are ready to begin listening to this session, make yourself comfortable. Dim lights, shut off stereos or televisions, unplug or turn down the phone. Loosen tight clothing, take off your glasses, take out your contacts. It is best to listen in a semireclining position (for example, in a recliner chair), although you can lie down or sit in a comfortable, well-upholstered chair. If it is comfortable for you, you might try sitting cross-legged on a nicely padded wall-to-wall carpet, or even in lotus position, listening to the session through stereo headphones.

When actually listening, some people like to imagine that they are saying the words to themselves. Others prefer to concentrate on what they are hearing. In either case, *lead with your imagination.* That is, allow yourself to feel and otherwise experience whatever the words are suggesting. For example, if the script is describing the feel and taste of a juicy, sweet orange, let yourself imagine that you are actually tasting the orange. And feel free to pretend that you are actually holding and biting into the orange—use your hand and mouth as if it were actually happening.

HINTS

1. When reading this script, speak in a calm, natural voice. Don't try to sound hypnotic or use a monotone. Feel free to be expressive, to convey the meaning of the words by your tone and volume and pacing.
2. If possible, record with a stereo microphone, so that the tape sounds better if played on a stereo or personal cassette player.
3. I find it helpful to add appropriate music at low volume to the background when I record tapes for my own use. The music should be somewhat mystical or meditative, to fit the mood of the session. If it contains any voices, it should be without words. Although I have sometimes used classical music (for example, excerpts from Debussy), I find that Celtic harp music works particularly well, although many "New Age" albums offer good choices. My personal favorites are Alan Stivell's *Renaissance of the Celtic Harp,* side one, and *New Age Symphony,* side three (both albums are on Rounder Records). Generally, I begin with very

low volume and slowly "fade" to a quiet, background level. In parts of the tape where my voice is silent, I may raise the level of the music and then lower it again when my voice comes back.

SCRIPT

Read aloud everything not in parentheses:

"Make yourself comfortable and prepare yourself for a wonderful experience. In a moment, I will ask you to take a deep breath and tense every muscle of your body. That means squeezing every muscle you can feel: your feet, your toes, your lower legs, and your thighs . . . tensing your butt and bottom . . . squeezing every muscle you can feel down there . . . squeezing your belly and your lower back . . . your chest . . . squeezing your shoulder blades together and tensing the long, strong muscles of your back . . . I mean making a fist and squeezing both your hands, your lower arms, and your upper arms . . . making a horrible face, squeezing your face, your eyes, your mouth, your neck . . . tensing your forehead . . . squeezing everything you can . . . and then, when you can't hold your breath any longer, I want you to breathe out . . . as slowly as you can . . . letting your body relax as you breathe out . . . letting go of every muscle of your body . . . and as you breathe out . . . as your muscles relax . . . just imagine you can feel yourself blowing out every last bit of tension and tightness and uptightness and nervousness and discomfort . . . ill health and tiredness and stress and strain and self-consciousness . . . just breathing yourself calm and clear. . . .

"Okay, here we go. Start to inhale . . . squeezing every muscle of your body . . . every muscle . . . holding your breath . . . squeeze . . . feeling every muscle . . . and, when you are ready, breathe out as slowly as you can . . . feeling your muscles let go and relax as you breathe out . . . just letting go of your muscles . . . letting them become limp and loose and calm and relaxed . . . letting yourself go now . . . exhaling from your mind and body and spirit every last bit of tightness and tension, stress and strain, and discomfort now . . . just letting go now . . . letting it all go now . . . let yourself begin to breathe in and breathe out naturally . . . at your own natural rate. . . .

"And with every breath you breathe in, feel yourself breathing in, sucking in, the wonderful, refreshing life-giving air . . . letting yourself feel yourself sucking this wonderful, life-giving air into your lungs and in through your lungs into your bloodstream . . . turning your blood bright, bright red with health and energy . . . and sending that health and fresh air and comfort to every part of your body . . . every cell, every nerve, every muscle, every organ . . . filling yourself with calm, wonderful, peaceful energy. . . ."

(Let your voice become slower, calmer, quieter, and more soothing for the next few paragraphs, drawing out the spaces between words more and more. Lengthen and emphasize the words themselves as appropriate.)

"And now, as you breathe in and breathe out . . . at your own natural rate . . . just imagine and dream along with my voice . . . feeling yourself beginning to awaken in a new way . . . beginning to open . . . in a new way . . . unfolding . . . like a marvellous flower . . . of life and joy and peace and energy . . . feeling your innermost self opening up . . . feeling yourself unfolding into level after level of new calmness and peace . . . and energy and strength . . . just letting yourself unfold . . . open up . . . all the way . . . into calmness, peace, energy . . . and strength . . . feeling these words . . . even as I say them, feeling what they can mean for you . . . calmness . . . peace . . . energy . . . strength . . . feeling your body flowing now . . . moving freely now . . . your breath moving freely . . . your breath, your mind, your consciousness moving freely now . . . opening up into calmness . . . peace . . . energy . . . strength . . . flowing freely now . . . awakening . . . opening up . . . feeling yourself becoming calmness . . . peace . . . energy . . . and strength . . . calmness . . . peace . . . energy . . . and strength . . .

flowing . . . flowing with life . . . flowing with everything around you . . . opening up . . . calmness . . . peace . . . energy . . . and strength. . . ."

(Pause 15 to 20 seconds. Music starts here, very quietly at first.)

"Flowing . . . into a magical place . . . deep inside yourself . . . your own personal center place . . . power here . . . calmness . . . peace and strength . . . feeling yourself in that center place . . . focusing now . . . able to focus your mind . . . your body . . . your complete concentration . . . finding yourself in a magical place . . . deep inside yourself . . . a place of calmness . . . peace . . . energy . . . and strength . . . of perfect safety . . . a healing place where you are in touch with every level of your being . . . and of life and love that goes beyond your own being . . . and as you feel yourself . . . settling in here . . . rediscovering the feelings of power and calmness, peace, energy, and strength . . . you find yourself awakening now . . . your deep power awakening . . . your abilities awakening . . . your true potential awakening . . . becoming your own . . . to focus and apply and use . . . calmly . . . moving freely now . . . flowing with life . . . feeling a new sense of power . . . energy . . . ability . . . peace and strength . . . and health . . . and wonder . . . as your mind and body awaken to new levels upon levels being alive . . . fully conscious . . . fully awake . . . fully alive . . . feeling your body letting go of all blockages and barriers to power and calmness . . . and energy . . . health and strength. . . .

"Feeling your body awakening now . . . as if you're starting to glow from the center . . . and this wonderful, wonderful feeling is filling you and your body with calmness, peace, healing . . . health, light, and strength . . . and you just begin to drift in this wonderful place . . . free of gravity . . . free of everything holding you down . . . a place of your own magic . . . the magic that's in you . . . that has always been in you . . . your birthright . . . your full potential . . . feeling yourself waking up into calmness, power . . . peace, health . . . energy and strength

. . . as you just drift and imagine these things you can *feel* them more and more . . . as real as reality itself . . . they *are* your reality. . . . And as you feel these things, you might notice thoughts surfacing in your mind . . . they tell you that you *can* do it now . . . just reaching into yourself when you choose to, when you need to, when you have to . . . and tap your true power, calmness, creativity, energy, and strength . . . you focus yourself . . . and act with full concentration . . . applying yourself fully . . . with calmness, peace, energy, and strength . . . allowing yourself to remember all you need to know . . . and doing whatever you need to do and should be doing to make it all go right. . . .

"Finding yourself flowing with life now . . . feeling an inner sense of reverence and joy and respect . . . reverence and respect for your body, for yourself, for others, for all life and all the miracles of life . . . feeling new respect for the gifts of the food we eat, the beverages we drink, the air we breathe, the world we share . . . finding the wonder of your own being . . . that sense of freshness you had as a child becomes your own again and you feel whole . . . you feel complete once again . . . you feel how good it can feel to be alive. . . .

"And an image begins to form in your mind . . . a symbol or a picture or a scene or a memory or a fantasy . . . and it tells you in more ways than words could ever express that it's okay now . . . you can do it . . . you're free . . . you're really okay now . . . it tells you that you can move and flow now . . . in mind and body and spirit . . . with peace and strength and concentration and power . . . that whatever it is . . . whatever the situation, you can deal with it calmly, with peace and confidence and energy and strength . . . and let memory and power flow and allow yourself to operate to your full potential . . . with energy and power and calmness and confidence and strength . . . you can feel this image now . . . it may be a brand new image you have never had before, it may be a familiar image, it may take you by surprise . . . it may be the most spiritual or beautiful thing you have ever imag-

ined . . . it may move and flow and change as you
experience it . . . but it always tells you that you are okay
. . . that you have the power and the creativity and the
energy and the freedom and all the strength you need . . .
to move and flow and learn and grow . . . and go beyond
whatever you once thought your limits were and discover
how much more you are and you can be and will be than
you ever dared or hoped to believe or be. . . .

"Every time your need is there an image will be
there, too . . . from deep inside . . . to tell you everything
you need to feel and hear and know . . . to awaken you to
full potential . . . and freedom, calmness, peace, creativity, energy, health, and strength . . . just let mind and
imagination flow . . . finding the image comes to mind
that is exactly right for you right now . . . that gives you
what you need . . . that helps and guides you to reach
into your deepest depths and realize and tap the calmness, power, energy, skill, and knowledge . . . creativity,
insight, and strength . . . concentration, confidence . . .
focus or ability you need . . . right now, just let yourself
flow . . . and float, and dream, and drift . . . finding you
can trust yourself now . . . you accept yourself now . . .
you can be yourself now . . . and this wonderful, magical
image, fantasy or memory . . . begins to crystalize for you,
so you can see and feel and sense it as real as life itself . . . becoming more and more real . . . until it becomes
more real than real. . . ."

(Pause 15 to 20 seconds. If playing music, make it a
bit louder.)

"Telling you in words, pictures, feelings everything
you really need to hear, everything you really need to
know . . . feeling so good . . . *so* good . . . so alive. . . ."

(Pause 1 minute. If you are using music, gradually
make it a bit louder still and then fade it before you start
speaking again.)

"So good . . . feeling so alive . . . let this imagery now
sort of fade . . . becoming part of you . . . sinking down
through your mind to your very core . . . it will always be

there for you . . . whenever you need it, it will be there for you . . . to remind you . . . to tell you whatever you need to be told . . . to give you the calmness, peace, focus, energy, and strength to let your ability flow . . . to make it all go right . . . calmly and naturally . . . you can bring it back intentionally at any time or it will come back automatically when you need it . . . you can even forget about it now . . . just let it go. . . ."

(If using music, lower, the volume even further now.)

"And, just for a moment, pretend you are somebody else looking at your life as it is right now . . . at the present time . . . and tell yourself what you see . . . what you like . . . and what you don't like, also . . . as if you were seeing your life from the outside . . . as somebody who cares would see you . . . somebody from whom there is not anything you can hide . . . see yourself as you are right now . . . not judging, not passing judgment but seeing it all . . . and if that person had to draw one single picture or tell it all in a very few words, what would that be, what story would that person show or tell?

"Now, as if you are turning to a new page of a book, a page that shows and tells about you as you would like yourself to be two years, five years, or ten years from now, what kind of story would there be to tell? . . . What could you be doing, what might you be like? What could you be seeing that tells you that you *are* okay, that you *have* done it, that you *have* made your life go right for you? What pictures or stories set in this future now make you feel alright? Make you feel positively good about yourself . . . proud of being yourself . . . glad to be alive . . . make you feel that you have proven to yourself that you *are* worthwhile and your life has been worthwhile? Be there now in your imagination . . . really feel it now . . . feel how good you can feel about yourself, how good it can feel to be alive. . . .

"And tell yourself that you *are* going to feel this way . . . that you *are* going to allow youself to be this way . . . that starting now you are on your way to doing it . . . that this is the kind of future you are now creating for yourself and that nothing and nobody, not even your old self, can stop you now. . . .

"Hear now in the depths of your mind whatever suggestions you need to hear right now . . . to really feel that it is good to be you, good to be alive . . . and imagine how you would like yourself to feel and be for the next few hours or days . . . whatever you feel appropriate. . . . Imagine how it would feel if you make it happen in just that way . . . imagine that you do. . . .

"And now, whenever you're ready, just take a deep breath, a moderately deep breath, and breathe out and, just for a moment, imagine being and feeling exactly how you'd like yourself to be and feel for the next few hours or days . . . and tell yourself you choose to do it this way now . . . and anything else you'd like to suggest to yourself . . . you're free . . . and just open your eyes and enjoy the feelings you've given yourself and go on and do whatever you've told yourself you want to do and choose to do for yourself now . . . feeling great, calm, peaceful, full of energy, health, confidence, certainty, and strength!"

(*End of script*. If you are using background music, make it swell louder now and then fade slowly in about 30 seconds.)

USING THIS SESSION

Like the chapter as a whole, this is a training session that introduces you to many of the themes and methods we will be developing throughout the book. Ideally, you should listen to this tape at least once daily until ready to start the next technique, at the end of Chapter Two, at which time you'll receive further instructions. You can, of course, use Technique One whenever you'd like, but you will be learning other techniques that will probably be even more helpful on a day-to-day basis.

TWO

Mind Control

You have been hypnotized by the world and the things of the world; your mind is not your own. That's the bad news.

However, you don't have to play along with it. That's the good news. You can use your mind to break the trance, to break out of this slavish hypnosis. By using your mind creatively, you can do things that would otherwise be exceedingly difficult, if not downright impossible. That's the best news of all.

And that is what creative self-hypnosis is all about: doing what you have really been doing all along, but doing it for yourself. Chapter One introduced you to this idea.

Chapter One also serves as the booster of a space rocket designed to give you the velocity you need to break free and venture onward and outward on your mission to explore the uncharted reaches of possibility. Now you've got to take over the controls, you've got to go from creative hypnosis to creative self-hypnosis. By the end of this chapter, you'll be on your way.

First we'd better familiarize you with your equipment, show you the propulsion system, get you used to working with the controls. The first thing you ought to know is:

Key Principle Seven: You can do it by mindwork. Defining mindwork is like trying to define what you do when you play

41

or when you create something; the best definition is doing the thing yourself. That's why I had you do Key Technique One. It's a good example of one form of mindwork, which I call creative hypnosis. If you want a more formal definition: *Mindwork means using your mind to do things that would otherwise be exceedingly difficult, if not downright impossible.*

"Hold on there," you say, "mindwork means using your mind? You can't define something by itself."

I agree. So we'll begin this chapter by taking a closer look at the "mind" that does the work and then go on to recommend some new ways to use it. To start, however, let's clarify our terms.

THE BRAIN

In the past few years, there has been an enormous expansion in our knowledge about the structure of the human brain and how its various parts operate.

Researchers have shed new light on how the brain interacts with the rest of the body at every level. Studies have explored the brain's chemical and anatomical structure and developed provocative evidence regarding how this organ functions to influence thoughts, feelings, behavior, and physical condition.

Probably the best-known finding from brain research is that the human brain is *lateralized* with respect to many cognitive functions. The left side or hemisphere is more specialized for speech, reading, writing, and analytical thought, while the right side specializes in a range of other less clearly elucidated cognitive functions having to do with pattern recognition and sensory thinking. Several recent books discuss these findings in depth (see the "Notes and References" section for titles).

These are things we can reasonably claim to know about the brain. However, evidence and logic have never slowed pop psychology. A lot of pundits don't stop at attributing different, complementary mental processes to the two hemispheres of the brain. They tell you that the left side of your brain is your rational, conscious mind and the right side is your nonrational, subconscious mind. Or they take sides, literally. Some claim, for example, that the right side is feminine and the left side is masculine and all the evils of our society are due to the male chauvinist suppression of right hemispherical thinking.

Without your brain, not only are you not "you" but you're not alive to worry about it. However, just because these statements are true they do not necessarily imply that your mind and brain are the same thing, that your mind exists somewhere within your brain, or that perfect understanding of the brain's structure and function yields the measure of your soul.

MINDING THE WORLD

A short time after birth, we become aware of things going on around us and we're aware of being aware of things happening.

But we do not and cannot apparently leave it at that. We find ourselves compulsively trying to make sense out of what we are experiencing. This process is, to all extents and purposes, what we mean when we refer to "the mind."

We don't have a mind; we *do* mind. Think of mind as a verb, not as an object or a thing, as a function of the human brain but also as a function of the entire human body.

Through mind we become conscious of a world that makes sense to us. This task is not an easy one. Things don't make sense; human beings do. We make things make sense to us by perceiving and understanding the world in terms of familiar *types* or *categories* of things, events, or situations rather than as one novel experience after another.

This way of using our minds enables us to proceed from what we are already familiar with and add on to it, to see the world as a system of things that have an understandable relationship, one to the other.

Beginning in earliest childhood, as we learn to master our native language we learn rules for dividing the world into meaningful categories and for communicating in terms of familiar categories to one another (but also to ourselves). Linguistic anthropologists have shown us that different types of languages have us organize experience differently.

The English language forces you to be very clear about whether something happened in the past, is happening in the present, or will happen in the future. Japanese forces you to be very clear about social standing vis à vis the person you are talking to—different words and different grammatical forms are used for speaking to a peer or to somebody of higher social status than oneself.

Vocabulary is also important. Words encode our collective understanding about the objects of those words. "Snake," for example, does not only denote a legless reptile but also connotes a range of associated feelings and understandings that are generally negative for most people in our culture. If you were to say, "You snake," to somebody, you would probably not be understood as complimenting that person or describing his or her sinuous elegance and grace.

Just as we are learning a language of words, we are learning a language of movements, feelings, tastes, sounds, images, and ways of organizing them. We are learning how to perceive the things in our world.

I mean that literally. We don't just learn a vocabulary of words; we also learn a vocabulary of the senses, even of rhythms. We learn how to see and feel and smell, what to look for, what to notice. I am *not* talking about right hemisphere/left hemisphere; I am talking about how you organize what leaks in through your senses.

There is, for example, some fascinating research suggesting that we learn the rhythm of our native language as well as the words. A study was done in which Chinese-speaking and English-speaking mothers and their infants were videotaped, and the sound and pictures were analyzed frame by frame. Whenever the mother's voice paused or inflected, the infant's body responded by making a motion of some type. Since the rhythms of English and Mandarin are very different, the children were learning to dance a different dance, to hear even inside of their heads a very different tune—literally.

What I'm trying to convey is that what you do "in your mind" is more like poetry than prose, more like Impressionist painting than journalistic photography. We don't live, think, or feel in a literal transcription of the world, but rather in a metaphor, a humanized reworking of the world.

Making sense out of new experience involves the construction of a metaphor, an imaginative image representing the new, the unfamiliar, in terms of the already known, the familiar.

If you do not believe me, try the next exercise. If you do believe me, try it anyway.

Exercise 2-A: Pine Street Experiment

This experiment is named in honor of the house in San Francisco in which I lived for a brief time in 1966. There was an empty lot next to my front stairs and a white, wood-shingled building on the other side of the lot. At night, you could sit on the stairs and watch the shifting patterns thrown onto the wall by the headlights of cars going down Pine Street. Best movie in town.

DIRECTIONS

Here are three alternatives. Try any or all of them.

- *Version 1.* Go outside on a day when there are distinct clouds. Lie down and look up. Watch the clouds for at least five minutes. What do you see?
- *Version 2.* Turn on the television set to an unused channel. Sit down and watch it for at least a couple of minutes. What do you see?
- *Version 3.* Close your eyes. Take your fingers and press in on your eyelids for at least a couple of minutes. What do you see?

Some of you will have noticed that when you are observing an essentially random event, for example, cloud patterns or an empty television channel, you compulsively "warp" it into a meaningful pattern. The randomness becomes order—shapes, lines, motions emerge. Then, very often, it goes beyond that. You begin to see stories—you begin, that is, to fit a story to the order you superimpose onto the random events. Sometimes it goes a step further. You begin to fill out the stories into virtual movies, seeing imaginary, semihallucinated events, entire dramas and comedies.

We compulsively make sense, even out of the senseless. And I am intentionally making a pun here—by sense I don't mean just making things rationally intelligible but also turning random noise into intelligible sensory experiences. We do this by making *perceptual* metaphors. This pattern is like a line, a sphere, the image of a dog's head.

The science fiction satirist Robert Sheckley, in his wonderful novel, *Mindswap*, took this idea to new dimensions. Sheckley points out that Don Quixote cannot help but see a windmill as a giant. But Sancho Panza cannot see a giant, even when one strides right up to him. Panza can see only a funny sort of windmill, because giants don't exist in his reality. They can't. So they don't.

Sheckley calls this idea "Panzaism" or *metaphoric deformation*. In his novel, he suggests that under an overload of novelty we warp oncoming sensory information into familiar perceptual categories that we then experience as cases of the familiar.

This same analysis can be applied to the very world we perceive to be the authentic, state-certified reality. Hindu and Buddhist meditative traditions, for example, teach that if you can just shut up inside your head and stop warping the inputs into familiar human terms, you just might catch a glimpse of what's really going on. According to the Buddhists, in fact, *everything* we experience is one big metaphoric deformation.

Coming down to everyday life on spaceship Earth, the concept that we not only think in metaphors but perceive in metaphors suggests that maybe part of the postnatal suggestion scam is to get you to experience things in a certain, self-limiting and perpetually self-defeating way.

As William James suggested in his *Essays on Radical*

Empiricism, another implication is that consciousness itself is not a thing or a state but rather a process. A process of selectively noticing and selectively perceiving the world. Of bringing an organized, intelligible world into our awareness.

While I have been speaking as if this act were of a creative sort, in which you add connections to what is out there to notice, it may very well be that consciousness involves a *subtractive* rather than an additive process. Aldous Huxley suggested, for example, that the brain and central nervous system function as *reducing valves*.

That is, there is a first-order reality out there that as human beings we cannot and do not directly or completely grasp. William James described this raw reality as a big, blooming, buzzing confusion. Huxley was suggesting that our brain functions to selectively present a mere trickle of information about this outside reality to our awareness. Our sense organs screen out more raw information than they let in and our brain further organizes these inputs to present us, at the conscious level, with only a tiny slice of "reality."

The other side of this theory is that what our senses do let in and our brain does convey to us is sharply focused, intelligible, and usable. Our eyes, for example, only respond to a tiny portion of the electromagnetic spectrum (not, for example, the wavelengths used to transmit radio or television). What is more, they are positioned so that we only see what is in front of our heads. So we miss most of what is going on around us. However, what we do see, we see with great acuity and stereo vision. In fact, our visual system is coordinated with our species' unique grasping hands, upright posture, and vocal apparatus, all of which, taken together, seem to have given us that special edge on survival that has enabled us to create civilizations and (over)populate the Earth.

A BRIEF DIGRESSION

Have you ever wondered what a worm perceives? Or even a dog, with its less acute vision but far, far more acute sense of smell? Certainly, to a very great extent, the quality of our experience is related to the organization of our brain and central nervous system.

So, even the raw stuff out of which we construct the objects of our conscious awareness is already structured, patterned, and tailored for human consumption.

Is there *any* escape? Can we ever perceive the world directly? Apparently not, or at least not easily, not completely. I'm enough of a mystic to believe that there are hints and perhaps even clues left scattered about here and there in a sort of cosmic treasure hunt. I've come into contact with many groups and individuals who claim to have found a trailhead and to have put up signposts saying, in the immortal words of P. T. Barnum, "This Way to the Egress."

It may all be nothing more than a story we humans make up in order to give ourselves hope, but the rumors are there: That to see the world truly is to wise up to the scam, completely—to shake loose every vestige of that postnatal trance and to awaken completely. The Buddhists say that if you awaken completely, you're gone—gone beyond. All the way beyond—but breaking *that* far out of the everyday world mindset is beyond the purpose of this book, which is to show you how to develop calm, easy control over your life, work, and relationships.

THINKING

Once you've got something to notice, what do you do with it? Sometimes you just react. You perceive that the fire is causing a sensation of pain in your hand and you pull the hand out of the fire. Or you notice a high-pitched humming sound, you feel a momentary sensation, you look down, and you swat the blasted mosquito.

But what do you do the *rest* of the time?

You stop and you think.

Which seems like a good idea to me; let's think about thinking.

Exercise 2-B: Thinking about Thinking

DIRECTIONS
1. When you finish reading these directions, stop and think about the last time you practiced Technique One.
2. When you've thought for a minute or two, write in your journal exactly what you did as you thought, what "passed through your mind," what you noticed, and what you experienced.
3. When you "think," what is it that you *do*?

Thinking is one of the uniquely human things we do. Our brains are specially equipped for it. There's that intricately folded, one-eighth inch of gray matter wrapped around the top of our brain, called the cerebral cortex. It is the part of the brain that we use to think, the part that gives our species its special edge.

But just what is it that we do when we "think?"

Before we get in over our heads, we need to be clear about the fact that we are dealing with a many-layered situation very much like the layered structure of an onion. There are levels upon levels of things going on, but you can't talk about them all at once. Trying to do so would be like listening to a radio that played all the stations at the same time. You couldn't make sense out of them. (As I told you, the brain is like a reducing valve. It allows us to focus on just one thing at a time.)

So we are not going to talk about the amazing architecture of the cerebral cortex. And we are not going to talk about the levels of data processing that go on "below" or "above" the threshold of conscious awareness, at least not yet. For now we're going to stick to the level of normal, everyday garden-variety consciousness.

STORYTELLING

The anthropologist and philosopher Gregory Bateson tells the story of the world's greatest scientist who, having some time on his hands, turns to his trusty super-ultra-high-tech-state-of-the-art-and-then-some megacomputer and programs in the question, "How do human beings know anything?"

Now, this is the world's fastest computer. So he's rather surprised to discover that a minute goes by and all he can get from the computer is the message, "Please wait."

So he waits. And waits. He finally goes home and goes to bed, comes back the next day, and it's still chunking away.

So he waits. And waits. And waits. And waits.

He's getting pretty nervous because *nothing* has ever taken this computer such a long time and he's used about a zillion dollars of computer time.

Finally, he sees the monitor screen blink. He rushes up to the screen and reads, "That reminds me of a story. . . ."

Let's see how this tale relates to the way you make sense out of your life and the world in which you live. Let's do an exercise!

Exercise 2-C: What's What?

DIRECTIONS

1. You can do this exercise in one of two ways. I would strongly recommend that you try the first way. Only try the second way if you are really pressed for time or are otherwise unable to use the first way.
    -   *The best way.* Go somewhere and, for a minute or two, actually observe people doing something—anything. Go to some public place where there are lots of unfamiliar people, for example, a shopping mall, a coffee shop, a hairdresser's, a store, a busy city street, or a beach, swimming pool, ice skating rink, or park.
    -   *The next best way.* Turn on a television to an unfamiliar program but turn the sound all the way down. Watch what is going on for a few minutes.

2. Feel free to take notes, in either case. Then write in your journal what you observed—what was happening, who was who, what was what.
3. Now, look at what you wrote and ask yourself these questions:
   a. How much of what you think was going on was based on objective *evidence*?
   b. How much of the story did *you* put there; how much was based on your *inferences* from what you noticed?
   c. To what degree did the *labels* and *names* you used influence your inferences about what was happening?
4. Write a brief account fitting a different interpretation or story line to the same observations.
5. Which account do you feel is more plausible—the first or the second—and why do you feel that way?

SUGGESTIONS FOR TEAMS

This exercise is perfect for doing with a partner or group. Perhaps hold off doing it until you have a partner. You can either go somewhere and watch the action together or turn on the television. Maybe watch people from a window. If nobody can hear you, you can call out what you think is going on, thereby creating a "round robin" story effect. Then share your interpretations and discuss them.

Your account of your observations is nothing more or less than a story you create around the things you notice. It's your map of the situation, which, like any map, tells you what is important to be aware of in that particular situation and how the pieces fit together. Social scientists who have made a study of people's accounts feel that such accounts shed invaluable light on how we *do* our everyday lives.

As we go about the business of living, we engage ourselves in a running conversation. Actually, it's more like an ongoing presentation of an all-senses movie we present to ourselves for approval, complete with voice-over soundtrack.

Some people are more verbal in their thinking than others. They tend to focus on the narrative—the internal dialogue or stream of consciousness that writers like James Joyce have tried to capture in their novels and stories. Others tend to be more attuned to mental imagery. They focus on the pictures more than the words.

But in either case, *"thinking" involves telling stories to ourselves,* fitting them to what we notice going on. The stories are a lot like the new choose-your-own-plot books or interactive computer games, where you can select the next move and see what transpires.

Of course, you can also think about what might be going on outside of your part of the story, or what might have gone on already or might go on in the future.

Key Principle Eight: We make sense of the world by telling ourselves stories about it. Cognitive psychologists suggest that in the final analysis all thinking involves filling in gaps in our evidence. As Robyn Dawes states, thinking is "the creation of mental representations of what *is not* in the environment."

If everything were there for you to see, you wouldn't need to think about it. But because you are filling in the gaps, you are going beyond the facts. Trying to work out the rest of the story, you toy with these facts. Examining the possibilities. Evaluating probabilities. Figuring out intentions. Feeling things out as you imagine how the story might be.

COMMON AND UNCOMMON SENSE

Whatever the universe out there may be, it ain't human. And we can't stand that thought.

So we transform it into a human reality. In effect, we domesticate it by the operation of brain, mind, and consciousness.

Our brains and nervous systems screen and shape what presents itself for our consciousness to process. The very act of perceiving involves fitting words and pictures to what we're about to notice in order for us to see the world as something that makes sense to us. We compulsively try to make sense out of what's out there by breaking everything into bits and pieces that we can deal with—words, images, categories, ideas.

We sure go to a lot of trouble to make the world tell a story we can understand!

Now, we all go around organizing these elements into some kind of picture or story to which we can relate. That is what a *theory* really is.

Most of the time we operate on the basis of common sense, which is a potpourri of theories about the world and the things in the world. These theories are based on what we infer from our own experiences, glean from others, or borrow from what others suppose to be the truth. The problem with common sense is that it lets us down all too often, because we're putting together the wrong story line.

Key Principle Nine: *Things are rarely what they seem to be.* The best alternative to common sense that humanity has yet come up with is *science*. Science is a method for generating theory that works.

The ultimate test of truth is not whether it is logical or fits our ideas about natural laws or how the whole game is rigged. For a truth to be worth calling by that name, it must satisfy the test of simple pragmatism: Does it work?

For a map to work, it must provide a route through the actual territory one seeks to traverse.

Science is *not* a series of beliefs about the world; belief has nothing to do with science. Science is a method for creating maps by working out story lines that best fit the evidence. It is a method for systematically building our arsenal of trustworthy theories about the world, theories that allow us to predict, manipulate, and control what's happening. To get us to this point, we establish stiff criteria for what is scientifically acceptable: A scientific theory must always be derived from, restricted to, and tested against the external reality we directly or indirectly observe or experience.

The fact remains that even science is a bunch of stories about the world. These stories are called fancy names like *theory* and *hypothesis*, but they are stories, nonetheless.

Theories and hypotheses are not true. They are *not truths*. They are stories. The truth is always bigger, wilder, simpler, infinitely more subtle, and more complex than our stories. Stories can only approximate the truth. They can be supported by the evidence. But, to quote Charles Horton Cooley, "The constructive part of science is, in truth, an art."

Art and science make uncommon sense. And that is the good stuff. Here's why.

CLEAR AND UNCLEAR THINKING

Let's go back to my original contention that we go about our lives in a kind of daze, acting out postnatal suggestions. Yet, in this chapter, I have also argued that we, ourselves, create those suggestions, implying that everyday life consciousness is a perverse sort of self-hypnosis to which this book offers a partial remedy, a way to turn the process around to put you back in charge. Like all hypnosis, it is done by sleight-of-mind. We make it up, but then we lose track of the fact that we have done so.

We construct our internal images of the world and of the things in it. We do this by making up stories about what is going on so that life makes sense to us. In doing so, we create imaginative linkages between things so that we can find a pattern that repeats in our experiences. This, in turn, requires us to fit new events into the ongoing story we are imagining for ourselves.

There is a very simple trick to this process, a kind of mental shorthand: We engage in *symbolic thinking*. We imbue words, images (involving any or all senses), or both with meanings that remind us of whole snippets of the stories we see around us. We construct figures of speech (or figures of thought), allowing us to be reminded of the sense or feeling of that larger story. The technical term for something that represents other things is a *symbol*.

We most often employ a specific type of symbol, known as a metaphor, in which one thing stands in our mind for another and invokes a whole range of ideas and associations, implying a larger pattern connecting them into a whole. We categorize things or events by likening them to something else: An annoyance is a headache, life is a game, and "it's a jungle out there."

And then we lose track of what we are doing. Or, perhaps, we are never fully aware that we are inventing stories about the things we experience in the world (and in our bodies and our selves). After all, like any poet, we construct most of our metaphors by feel or by association or we borrow them from sources we cannot remember.

We assume that we are seeing what we are only imagining to be the case. We forget that *as if* thinking is a kind of mental shorthand. We believe our stories; we equate them with the truth. This process transforms our metaphors into myths, as if the metaphor were a literal prose or photographic description of the thing we are trying to grasp.

And so we set into concrete all the subtle influences and biases that creep into any creative act. And we let ourselves be guided by our myths.

It's an old, old story. It's been said any number of times before: We are like children who have forgotten that we are only playing.

And our metaphor-to-myth transformations permeate our lives. While there may be practical benefits from transforming our metaphors into myths and getting on with the show, there are also liabilities. One is that we lose the richness, the wonder, and the openness of our experience. We lose the sense of creativity and play. We give ourselves, instead, a postnatal trance. We turn life gray and humdrum. We turn our "what ifs" into "so therefores," our symbols into things, and, in a sense, hypnotize ourselves into second-rate lives.

Count Alfred Korzybski felt that this difference was the difference between sane and "unsane," clear-headedness and hopeless confusion. The premise of his "science" of general semantics was recognition of this difference, suggesting that sane thinking requires us to recognize certain laws.

Key Principle Ten: The map is not the territory. This is Korzybski's first law of general semantics. He was trying to make the point that every time we say that this *is* that, we are making a myth. We confuse the symbol with what we created it to represent. The name, in other words, is not the thing named. It is merely a label we apply in order to communicate (or remember) what our experience of whatever we are symbolizing was *like*.

It might seem obvious, but we keep forgetting to remember. We confuse our ideas or opinions about the way things are with the reality we are trying to understand and we forget that a metaphor is not a statement of fact. We engage in metaphor-to-myth transformation and start to believe and do the oddest things.

I'm sure that an appreciable proportion of readers feel embarrassed about their bodies. Some, perhaps, feel that they're too skinny. A lot more probably feel that they're too fat. Our American middle-class culture puts a lot of emphasis on one's physical shape. This has been the case for a very long while, but it has gotten out of hand with our current fitness craze. Certainly it is healthier to be fit, but this craze goes beyond any rational considerations for healthiness or even aesthetics. It is not just a matter of taste, you see, but of how we evaluate ourselves and other people.

To be conspicuously overweight is like having a particularly disgusting blemish on your moral character. To be overweight is to be treated as if there is something wrong with you, as if you are an embarrassment to yourself and everyone around you. And, very often, you react that same way to yourself.

Most of the hundreds of clients who have come to me for help in losing weight and keeping it off have really come with a deeper agenda. They may claim lack of willpower or being a compulsive overeater, but what they are *really* asking for is to have their minds repaired. They are certain there is something wrong with them, something that needs fixing.

There are a lot of people out there who will sell them an expensive mind-repair job. But that is not what typical overweight Americans need. Ninety-nine percent of the time, there is nothing wrong with them. Rather, they have accustomed themselves to eating certain amounts and types of food. Very often they have been trained from childhood to eat as a way of managing stress. Eating is probably one of the major social activities they enjoy with friends, family, and co-workers. And, of course, entire industries are out there trying to coax them to consume high-calorie, processed foods.

A *workable* solution must address all these things. Effective problem solving demands practical understanding of the problem. The usefulness of any map depends on how closely it approximates the territory. There is, in summary, no substitute for a clear and careful evaluation of any situation that you are trying to change.

LEVELS OF REALITY

One of the most useful concepts I have run across in years is Gregory Bateson's theory of logical types. Actually, Bateson expanded on an idea he borrowed from his mentor, Bertrand Russell, whom he served as secretary for many years.

The concept comes down to this: any set (or class or category) of things exists at a different, higher level of logical type than the things that make up the set. For example, you can look at every single tree in a forest and never find a forest. Why? Because the forest is what we call all the trees *taken together*. A forest exists at a different level of reality or logical type than the trees that make up the forest.

Similarly, the map is not the territory, a name is not the thing named, and a family is not the people who individually make up the family. In each case, there is a difference in logical type between the two kinds of entities described.

The more abstract and inclusive, the "higher" the logical type in Bateson's scheme. A forest exists at a higher level of reality than the individual trees and a symbol is of a higher logical type than the concrete phenomenon it represents.

Notice that I generally use the term "reality" when speaking of things that I mentally assign to the objective, physical world and I use "logical type" when referring to concepts, categories, and processes of mind. I suppose Bateson would say that the difference is entirely arbitrary. However, it makes practical sense to me.

Bateson argues, and I have come to agree, that we are not only talking about abstract thinking here. He points out that the processes by which we make ourselves conscious cannot themselves be "conscious" processes. They are of a lower logical type than consciousness.

From the operation of the nerve endings in our sense organs, through the marvellous data processing of our brains, through the metaphoric processes of perception and conception, through the internal thinking process (at least most of the time), the activities that bear their fruit in our conscious awareness go on outside of our consciousness. They are some of the other layers of the onion.

So it is silly to deny that unconscious or subconscious processes exist. But it is important to recognize that they involve different levels or types of mental processes than conscious thought or self-awareness.

In these myriad stages of creating our conscious selves and actions, there is a potential for unconscious influences, biases, sources of knowledge, and sources of error. One way to deal with them is to treat them like the enemy and seek to overcome them, to operate entirely on the basis of rational consciousness. Another is to let our unconscious be our teacher and our guide, presuming "it" knows more and has more resources than "we" do. Yet a third way is to channel our unconscious or subconscious energies, to throw on a saddle and bridle and ride them off into the future.

However, we can also view all the levels of our mind and consciousness as potential resources to tap rather than forces to channel or deflect. We can deliberately enlist these processes in accomplishing our goals.

Now, we are automatically tapping into these levels upon levels of flowing mental process whenever we employ symbols and metaphors, but normally we treat the ripples of feeling, meaning, and imagery that they evoke as mental noise and give them little, if any, notice. Our internal voices are somewhere in there as well, murmuring their comments and speculations in the background. Where artists and creative scientists differ from most of us is that they tune into these levels of thinking, feeling, and imagining while we go about our business ignoring all but the tip of the infinite iceberg.

What would happen if you trained yourself to be open to these other levels of your mind? Well, if you stick with this program, you're going to find out because this is precisely what you *are* doing when you work with creative self-hypnosis. The reason you are being asked to fill in the details is to allow your creative imagination to flow.

VISUALIZING

One of the most important tools you have for working with your entire mind is visualization. All of us experience some degree of mental imagery; for some of us, as I have said, it is the primary mode of thought. So let's take a look.

Exercise 2-D: Images

DIRECTIONS
1. Recall the most recent time you listened to Technique One. Close your eyes and recall the image you were working with to remind yourself of calmness, peace, energy, and strength. Focus on that image for a few moments. If you are working by yourself, open your eyes and write down the ways in which you experienced or sensed that image—words, sounds, sights, colors, motions, smells, tactile feelings, whatever.
2. Conceptualize a range of possible ways of imagining things, from just getting words in your mind that describe what is going on to having an intense, almost physical, experience involving all your senses. Where did your experience seem to fit in to this? How does it compare to the way in which you normally daydream, fantasize, think, or imagine?

SUGGESTIONS FOR TEAMS

If you are working with a partner, do this exercise in turns so that one of you visualizes the image and, with your eyes still closed, calls out which imaginary senses are involved, while the other writes this information down. Then switch roles and compare your lists.

Most of us experience, with a limited range of senses, at a relatively vague level of realism. However, there are also what Ted Barber and Sheryl Wilson call "superimaginers" who have ultrarealistic imaginary experiences of almost psychedelic intensity. None of these ways are right or wrong. They are just mental styles.

Let me clarify a few points. By imagery, I strictly mean experiencing something almost indistinguishable from normal sensory experience but occurring in the absence of an external stimulus. As Robert Sommer has stressed in his excellent book on imagery, *The Mind's Eye*, we are not just referring to visual thinking but *sensory thinking* as well, involving any or all possible imaginary senses—audio, visual, olfactory, kinesthetic (feeling body position or motion), gustatory (taste), and tactile.

However, in this book, when I refer to "imagery" or "image," unless further qualified (for example, visual image), I mean either a verbal representation or a sensory image or both.

I will also use the term *visualize* generically, to mean conjure up an imaginary image with any or all available internal senses. Used in this sense, visualization can be considered a *skill* that can be improved through training and practice. However, like any other human potential, visualization skill (or, perhaps, skills—assuming that different sensory modes involve different talents) is not found in all individuals in equal measure. A few are gifted in this respect, such as the superimaginers I mentioned above, while others are without any talent. Most of us are going to find our visualization abilities somewhere in between these two extremes.

As you work with this program, you can expect that your

mental imagery will become more vivid, more realistic, encompassing an increasing number of imaginary senses. The reason it is worth working with imagery is that mental imagery operates like a kind of inner shorthand. Imagine something—for example, a warm, glowing sun. It's like dropping a pebble into still water, only the ripples are all the meanings and ideas and feelings you associate with that image. A mental image can echo through every layer of your mind; it is a kind of metaphor that cuts beneath and across words.

YOUR INNER REALITY

We carry about a map, a concept or representation of the world in our minds, and this internalized *reality* governs our thinking, our feeling, our imagining, and our behaving.

It is far from novel to suggest that we humans live simultaneously in two realities. One is the *objective universe* of raw experience, of matter, energy, space, and time. The other is a *symbolic world* we carve out of what William James termed "big blooming buzzing confusion." It is this latter reality that concerns us directly, for it is the ever-emergent reality we perceive, the evolving universe within which we live our lives. Which, in the last analysis, is our personal metaphor for the world of raw experience.

Our concern in this book is not with that which is but with the human reality in which we are each making our lives. We, ourselves, continually construct and reconstruct this symbolic reality in the images and narrations running at all times in the theater of the mind.

Human beings don't just react to external events. We don't follow preset programs. We are not robots. Between stimulus and response, input and action, linking the two, there is always *interpretation*. We respond to how we symbolize the world to ourselves, to the metaphors by which we make sense out of that world.

Or, as W. I. Thomas and Dorothy Swaine Thomas put it, "What a man defines to be real is real in its consequences." This quote is perhaps the only thing remembered from their book, *The Child in America: Behavior Problems and Programs*. It appears at the end of a story about how a prison warden refused to release a certain convicted felon. This prisoner was somewhat hard of hearing, very proud, and very paranoid. If anybody said something he didn't quite catch, he'd assume that it was an insult and stomp the person.

Key Principle Eleven: We respond to how we imagine things to be. Change what you imagine to be so, and you can change yourself.

Definitions of any situation exist at a level of logical type immediately below normal everyday consciousness. They serve as memory resident programs that pop out whenever your mental computer searches for the appropriate metaphor for understanding something. They tell you how that memory was experienced at the time it happened, what is important about it, and what your standardized response to it has been ever since. These programs allow you to string together a line of action from modular units and respond almost instantaneously to the situation confronting you, without having to stop and think about it. They act to stereotype your responses, make you mentally lazy, by making it too easy to get by without examining your assumptions.

Actually, your definition of any situation seems to form a whole stratum or level of mental process, the highest of which is your basic image or metaphor for how *everything* fits together, the big picture.

The key to change lies in breaking your addiction to reliance on these old mental maps. Training yourself to continually challenge and upgrade your assumptions about what is going on, what you imagine to be true regarding yourself, your self-worth, your life, your world. Again, it is as if you have been hypnotized and you have been sleepwalking through your life, seeing things as you have been led to imagine they are, responding to them as you have been led to imagine you must. Now is the time to shake off the trance. To rouse yourself and take control of your life and yourself from your past and from the world around you. You can do that by using your creative imagination, by changing how you symbolize the world in your mind, by learning to reconstruct your internal metaphors.

LETTING GO

What I am telling you is that you can choose your inner realities to get what you want out of yourself, your life, work, and relationships. First you have to choose intelligently and then make yourself support your choice by engraining these new realities in your mental process. That is a fairly tall order. This book and the techniques it contains will help you accomplish this goal. Choosing your reality and implementing that choice is what creative self-hypnosis is all about.

Let's now focus on how you can use your mind to create a new internal reality of your choice, by using creative self-hypnosis. As you experienced in Technique One, there are two basic parts of this process. The first is to let go of old realities. The following exercise will help you clear the screen so that you can input new realities.

Exercise 2-E: Letting Go

DIRECTIONS
1. By either reviewing your journal or by letting your mind wander, think of a goal for yourself that seems nearly impossible to attain.
2. Close your eyes and try to believe that you have already attained this goal. Do this for as long as you'd like; then open your eyes.
3. Using a 6-point scale in which 1 = completely unreal and 6 = as real as life, rate how vivid and realistic your imagined goal coming true feels for you.
4. Close your eyes and, just like you have been doing in Technique One, take a deep breath and tense all your muscles; then relax and breathe out. Tell yourself or imagine that you are letting go of all tightness and tension, just as you do in Technique One. Give it a little while. Then try to believe that your nearly im-

possible goal is already true. When you are ready, open your eyes.

5. Now, using the same scale as you did in step 3, rate the realism of your imagined goal.

6. What effect, if any, did the tense/relax routine seem to have on your ability to imagine an almost impossible goal?

7. How can you explain this effect (or lack of effect)?

I cannot tell a lie: I tricked you. Mindwork, recall, means using your mind to make new things possible. Bodywork means using your body (or manipulating your body) toward the same ends. This activity employed bodywork and was designed to show you that it is one of the quickest and easiest ways to break the ongoing flow of everyday reality. In order to do effective mindwork, it is helpful to employ a form of bodywork.

"New Age" theorists stress the holism of mind, body, and spirit. Bodywork has become very popular in New Age and humanistic psychology circles as an alternative to conventional talk therapies. The tense-and-relax method is based on one of the oldest forms of bodywork, Edmond Jacobsen's progressive relaxation, although I first learned it from Swami Satchidananda (of Integral Yoga® fame) as quick yoga relaxation. Call it what you wish—it works.

How can something as simple as closing your eyes, taking a deep breath, tensing and relaxing your muscles have such a liberating effect? The reason appears to be that this procedure interferes with some of the ongoing processes by which we make ourselves conscious. For example:

1. It releases the muscle tensions that remind us of what to worry about and how dangerous it all is.

2. It interferes with the movements of our voluntary and involuntary muscles (ideomotor responses) with which we are continually responding to our thoughts and images.

3. It blocks the visual and proprioceptive (body-feeling)

cues through which we anchor ourselves in the here-
and-now.

4. It creates some conspicuous, out-of-the ordinary physical sensations (such as light-headedness).

This combination serves to break the ongoing flow of our
thoughts, feelings, and responses and to make us feel different by disrupting our accustomed physical rhythms. In turn,
we are provided with a good jumping-off place for letting go
of our sense of everyday reality.

There are many other ways of accomplishing the same
objective. In my earlier book, for example, I asked readers to
roll their eyes up as far as they could. The idea in both cases
is the same.

***Key Principle Twelve: Physical sensation undercuts
thought.*** This principle literally goes right to the heart of the
matter. We give meaning to sensations by the thoughts and
images we attach to them, but we also give meaning to our
thoughts and images by the physical sensations we associate
with them. Any poet, writer, or artist knows this to be so.

This is not to say that you must use a bodywork technique to let go. You can accomplish the same thing through
mindwork alone. For example, conventional *hypnotic inductions* often rely exclusively on visualization or thinking along
with suggestions, "You are getting very sleepy," and the like.

If your goal is simply to let go of your everyday reality,
combining real physical sensations with thinking and imagining works well. However, most hypnotists have the additional objective of convincing you that they are placing you
into an altered state of consciousness in which you are "more
suggestible." By drawing out the process, they are able to
weave in the necessary suggestions to convince you that you
are not only letting go and shifting gears but *entering a trance.*

TRANCE?

The moment you say *hypnosis*, people think *trance*. I really
don't know what that word means, and I have done lots and

lots of hypnosis with myself and with other people. Personally, I consider *trance* a metaphor—when you are doing hypnosis, it's *as if* you were in an altered state of consciousness, feeling differently, processing reality differently—not being yourself.

It is fair to assert that doing hypnosis is qualitatively different from the way we normally operate in everyday life. This fact is not the same as claiming that in order to do hypnosis you must first enter a special "trance state" entirely separate from your normal consciousness. While saying that certainly makes hypnosis seem mysterious and powerful, it is nothing more than a classic metaphor-to-myth transformation. One to which I object because it suggests that you cannot access your own power without entering that hypnotic trance state.

There is a vast amount of scientific literature on hypnosis but there is an absence of evidence that a tangible psychological or physiological difference exists between the normal waking state and the hypnotic trance. I am *not* saying, however, that there is no value in hypnosis or that it cannot help you, but simply that hypnosis isn't a *thing*—it is a label for a process or a whole set of processes. Doing hypnosis is, indeed, different than doing virtually anything else. But, *you* are doing it. It's your own power that you are accessing in this fashion. And, as my colleagues Theodore R. Sarbin and T. X. Barber have been arguing for more than thirty years, there is no need to enter a special trance state in order to get the benefits of hypnosis.

Think of hypnosis as a remarkable way of using your mind. You don't have to give up anything to do it and you never have to surrender your consciousness or will. All you have to do is let go and let yourself think and feel along with your suggestions *as if you were actually experiencing what you are only imagining*. If you prefer to call this a trance, fine. Go ahead. Or use any other metaphor that makes you feel comfortable. Milton H. Erickson described hypnosis as "relying on your unconscious." That's a sort of double bind, since it asks you to consciously let go and rely on your unconscious.

What is important is that you want to break the flow of everyday life consciousness and do something different with your mind in order to liberate your imagination and create and experience new realities as if they were actually or already true.

BUILDING NEW REALITIES

There are two basic ways to go about imagining the world, your life, or yourself as you would prefer them to be. The first is to set up a detailed description or *script* and use it to guide your imagination.

The second approach is to start with a basic idea, sense, or feeling about what you want to imagine and then let your imagination play with it. You can do this by invoking a symbol or metaphor and letting your creative imagination fill in the rest of the picture or story. The beauty of allowing your creativity to flow in this way is that it allows you to rely on your entire mind (conscious and unconscious) and to give equal play to rational or "propositional" thought and intuition, feeling, or "appositional" thought. Think of it as a way to combine the powers of a scientist and an artist.

I will show you a number of variations on this second approach. All of them are premised on Key Principle Thirteen.

Key Principle Thirteen: Imagination overrides everything else. The techniques by which we will translate this principle into practical action all begin with the creative hypnosis session (Technique One) you have been practicing and go on from there. Which brings us to the next step, learning to do the entire process on your own. But, as I have already stressed, it is always prudent to precede action with evaluation and review. Let's review this chapter.

SUMMARY

This chapter has focused on your mind and the processes of mind. It has suggested that the term *mind* refers to what you do with your brain and, perhaps, the rest of your body and that there are many levels of mental processes going on below—maybe even above—your everyday consciousness. We have explored some important concepts regarding the nature of thinking, suggesting along the way that we make sense out of the world by means of *stories, symbols,* and *metaphors* and that clear thinking requires us to keep track of the difference between our images and understandings of reality and the reality itself. At the end of the chapter these ideas have been brought together to suggest that we don't need to think of hypnosis in terms of a *trance* state and that *creative self-hypnosis* involves using your entire mind to break out of automatic thinking and to take active, creative control over your *definitions of the situation*—which is actually the third step of the self-transformation process, *building new realities.*

New Key Principles developed in this chapter included:

SEVEN: You can do it by mindwork.

EIGHT: We make sense of the world by telling ourselves stories about it.

NINE: Things are rarely what they seem to be.

TEN: The map is not the territory.

ELEVEN: We respond to how we imagine things to be.

TWELVE: Physical sensation undercuts thought.

THIRTEEN: Imagination overrides everything else.

Technique Two: Basic Creative Self-Hypnosis I

OVERVIEW

On an index card write the following outline:

CSH Outline

1. Tense/relax.
2. Imagine place.
   "calmness . . . peace . . . energy . . . strength. "
   (Leave space to add your own words.)

3. Steer "up."
    "clear . . . flowing . . . more and more alive . . .
    awake . . . really waking up inside . . . supercons-
    cious. . . ." (Leave space to add your own words.)
4. Visualize present.
5. Visualize future.
6. Set mind.
7. Open eyes. Tell yourself, "That's it, end of ses-
    sion."

Notice that this is roughly the same outline as was employed in Technique One. You will use this outline as your
crib sheet for giving yourself a creative hypnosis session.
Carry it with you for easy reference.

HOW TO DO IT
The very first time you try creative self-hypnosis, it is
strongly advisable to first listen to your tape of Technique
One and then, using this outline, *immediately* give yourself your own session. Your initial self-hypnosis session
may take anywhere from five minutes to the length of the
taped session.
   Make yourself comfortable. If you can do it without
looking at your card, fine. If you need to open your eyes
at any time and find your place or suggestions on your
card, that's fine, too. Spend as long as you'd like on each
step; just go on to the next whenever you feel ready.
Here's what to do:

1. Read your card three times to help get the information
    into your short-term memory.
2. Read or remember step 1 in the outline. Close your
    eyes, take a deep breath, tense all your muscles, and
    then relax, letting yourself breathe in and breathe out
    naturally.
3. Read or remember step 2 in the outline.
    a. As you did in Technique One, let yourself imagine
        a scene or symbol or whatever feels right for you
        at this time. You can use the same or different

visualizations each time, perhaps whatever comes to mind, or a special one that works well for you. I'll refer to this metaphoric place as your "magical place" or "centerpoint," but you can call it anything you'd like.

b. To help you invoke this special image, you might want to say the words "calmness . . . peace . . . energy . . . and strength" over and over in your mind, or in a very quiet voice. You can imagine singing or chanting them, perhaps even visualizing them as you repeat them. Let yourself feel these words. As you become more comfortable with this technique, you might want to add or substitute some additional steering words; that's fine.

4. Now go on to step 3 in the outline. For now, you want to steer yourself in the "up" direction—more and more awake, and so forth. Imagine you are feeling this way, perhaps imagining appropriate images or symbols to go along with the feeling and repeating words such as those on your card to help guide you.

5. For step 4 in the outline, imagine yourself as you are right now. Perhaps envision a scene that best captures how you would appear to a completely objective observer. Focus on this scene for a little while. Although I use the term *visualize* as a cue, I will also describe this process more technically as *scanning your present*.

6. Now go on to step 5 in the outline. Imagine a future that you could feel good about. Perhaps set a time frame for yourself—one, three, five, ten, or twenty years. Perhaps think about the most important things that might tell you that you are where you would like to be in this imagined future and lead you to feel good about yourself and your life. But leave a lot of room for your creative imagination to fill in the details or even the entire story. Just let your imagination flow for a while.

7. When you are ready to return to normal consciousness, first think about how you would like to feel,
how you would like to be, and how you would like to
behave for the next few hours, or even days. Imagine
that you are already feeling that way, that you are
already behaving that way. Perhaps even tell yourself
in your mind that you *choose to* do a thing or *will* do
such-and-such, or feel thus-and-thus a way, and then
take another deep breath and open your eyes. Then,
to give yourself an unmistakable cue that now it is
time to return your attention to the everyday world
and to reassure yourself that you are in an appropriate
operating state, tell yourself (either aloud, under
your breath, or in your mind), "That's it, end of session."

Note: It might take you a few moments to shift
entirely back to normal consciousness. I sometimes
find that I feel a bit giddy or spacey for a couple of
minutes after a really intense session. Then I begin to
feel the energy and mental high.

INSTRUCTIONS FOR PRACTICE

Preferably begin practicing your basic self-hypnosis session two or even three times a day for the first week or
so. Morning, noon, or after work and evening before
bedtime are generally appropriate. Only the first or last
session of the day should be a full-length, intense session. The others can involve just zipping through the
pattern in a couple of minutes.

For the best results, it is advisable to continue to
listen to Technique One every two or three days and then
to do a quick run of Technique Two immediately after-
ward. Try this way for a week and then decide what
schedule works best for you—you can then practice Technique One as often or as little as you'd like, but you
should practice Technique Two at least twice a day until
you are ready for the next exercise.

SUGGESTIONS FOR TEAMS

You might want to postpone doing this technique until you meet. Go through the directions together and clarify them for yourselves. Then one of you might coach the other(s) through the technique. Discuss your experiences along with any problems you might have encountered and brainstorm ways to overcome the problems. Now do Technique Two again. Discuss your experiences.

TIP FOR TEAMS—HOW TO BRAINSTORM TOGETHER

For group brainstorming, you can work in teams of two or more. Each team should appoint a recorder. As in any brainstorming exercise, the idea is to generate ideas regardless of how realistic or silly they might be, and then to go back and evaluate them. So the group just calls out answers to the question under discussion as they come to mind and the recorder jots them down. For a large group, this can be done on a blackboard or with a marker on a large pad of paper. Keep listing answers until the group "runs down" and new ideas stop coming. You can pass the list around and have every group member vote by placing a check mark beside the two or three responses that now seem most appropriate to him or her (alternatively, have every group member go up to the blackboard/pad and check off the responses). See which ideas accumulate the most agreement and then discuss them.

It is also a good idea to make copies of these lists and all other written group activities and distribute them to group members.

THREE

Effective Action

Think about it all you want. Until you act, it's all theoretical—like Schroedinger's cat.

I suppose I had better explain. By around 1900, physicists had pushed the classical model of our universe to the limit. They were discovering things that simply didn't make sense in terms of the old *paradigm* (as the Harvard philosopher of science, Thomas Kuhn, terms our maps or models of reality). The New Physics of quantum mechanics defied common sense.

One of the leading lights of this Second Scientific Revolution, as we might call it, was the physicist Erwin Schroedinger. He worked out an equation (the Schroedinger wave equation) that permits scientists to describe mathematically the ways in which subatomic phenomena possibilities would actually occur. In fact, his model suggests that *actually occurring* means nothing until the moment somebody sneaks a look at what's happening; the act of observation causes all possibilities except the one observed to vanish.

What, this makes no sense to you? To give people a tangible metaphor for what he was talking about, Schroedinger came up with his famous cat parable: He places a cat inside a box. Also inside the box, is a device capable of instantaneously killing the cat in a way that nobody outside the box can detect without opening the box. This device will go off, killing the cat, if and only if a random event occurs in the first second after the experiment is started.

The box is now sealed. The experiment is underway; Without opening the box, tell me if the cat is dead or alive.

The answer is: either/or, both, and neither. Until you open the box, *you can't know*. There is no way of knowing. All you can state is that the cat is possibly dead and possibly alive. The moment you open and look into the box one of these possibilities becomes reality and the other vanishes. *Until* you act, neither *actually happens*. All you know are the possibilities.

Gary Zukav states in *The Dancing Wu Li Masters: An Overview of the New Physics*

> The commonsense view is also the view of classical physics. According to classical physics, we get to know something by observing it. According to quantum mechanics, it *isn't there* until we do observe it! Therefore, the fate of the cat is not determined until we look inside the box.

Key Principle Fourteen: *Reality is defined by action*. Life is like that: until you act, it's all hypothetical. You will never know how the story ends until it's over—and, to make matters even more complicated, your action itself becomes part of the story and shapes what has happened and what will happen next. Even if that action is to merely stand by and watch the show.

THE NATURE OF HUMAN ACTION

If our actions shape our lives—our very realities—then it follows that we would be wise to consider the question, "How do humans act?" Let's gather some data and see where it leads us.

Exercise 3-A: How Do Humans Act?

DIRECTIONS
1. Pay close attention to everything that happens as you follow this simple instruction: Do something spontaneous—anything.
2. Now, in your journal, answer these questions:
   - What did you do?
   - How did that behavior come about? What did you do inside yourself; how did you do what you did?
   - How spontaneous can human behavior be?
3. Compare and contrast the following:
   - An electric light going on when you flick the switch and close the circuit.
   - A houseplant growing toward the light.
   - A cockroach scuttling out of sight when you turn on the light (or, for country folk, a bug running for cover when you turn over a rock).
   - Your own responses if you were walking down a street at dusk, looked up, and saw a vast sphere of glowing light descending toward you.

SUGGESTIONS FOR TEAMS
Don't delay your experiment, but the next time you get together, repeat it. Count to three and on the count of three everyone should do something spontaneous. Then discuss the same questions.

The point of this experiment is to suggest that there is something special about the way people behave. They don't just respond—they *act*.

The concept of the act is so important that George Herbert Mead described it as the atomic unit of mind, self, and society. Not persons, not situations, not brains, not minds or causal forces, but *acts*.

What's so special about the type of acts in which people engage? Louis Wirth stated in his classic article, "Clinical Sociology":

> What distinguishes the action of men from animals may best be expressed in the word "conduct." . . . Conduct is self-conscious and personal, it is conventional behavior and consists of action that is oriented with reference to a goal which is not immediately present.

Clinical sociologists (and most other contemporary social scientists) take very strong issue with B. F. Skinner and other behaviorists who contend that human behavior, like that of cockroaches, can be described in mechanical terms of stimulus and response. Wirth is elaborating on this point. Let's consider the component parts of his definition of *conduct*. First, it is *self-conscious* and *personal*: "I" am doing it and, what's more, I am aware that it is "me" who is doing it.

Wirth is evoking everything we said in Chapter One about the self. He is also suggesting, as symbolic interactionists contend, that human behavior is *constructed* and not merely emitted. That we build up our lines of action in our minds, which is an entirely different kind of process than the mechanical glowing of a lightbulb's filament, the biochemical tropism by which a plant grows toward sunlight, or the reflex that prompts an insect to escape the light.

Wirth is also saying that conduct is *conventional* behavior—it follows rules we have come to share with others. And, what's more, it is *oriented with reference to a goal that is not immediately present*. It's goal-directed behavior. In other words, when we act, human beings behave in learned ways designed to attain objectives not present in the immediate situation, which may, in fact, exist at a level of logical type entirely different than the particulars of what is occurring in the here and now.

What may not be obvious is that even our spontaneous actions are conduct. Even when we are not trying to do so, we pattern our behavior according to learned rules for how a person like ourselves behaves. Sociologists describe this patterning as *internalization of norms*.

In the process of socialization, through the looking-glass self, we learn about how we are expected to behave in various situations. We learn about how our type of person is expected to behave. And we behave that way, even when we are alone (which is not surprising if, as discussed in Chapter One, we continually monitor our selves as if the whole world were there with us, inside our heads).

CONDUCT ALWAYS HAS A GOAL

The concept of conduct also states that our behavior is oriented toward goals not immediately present. Now, it does not say that these goals (or preferences) are clear to you or fully conscious or even conscious at all. Or even that they are goals you have chosen for yourself. They can be entirely outside your conscious awareness—subconscious, if you will—and they can be entirely counterproductive. These goals can also be forced on us by others; we can be "expected" into them.

EXPECTED GOALS

Think of all the parents who have expected their children to become doctors, musicians, lawyers, policemen, truckers, or scientists, or to be perfect "little men" and "little ladies." These are not goals you chose for yourself, but goals that have been chosen for you by parents, by your ethnic group, by your family's place in society, and so on.

These kinds of imposed goals can wreck lives, but they can also motivate accomplishment. For example, it is clear that family support—and family pressure—has been a key factor in motivating children of education-oriented immigrant groups to excell in school and surpass their parents' achievement by entering professions such as engineering, medicine, and law. This was true of Jewish immigrants in the early 1900s and is equally true of Asian immigrants today.

NEGATIVE GOALS

Another type of goal is almost always self-destructive. This is the *negative goal*. It is commonly associated with the effort to get rid of low self-esteem—as when a person tries not to feel worthless. I am not talking about manifestations of personal failings or psychological deficits, but, about situational problems. Such problems may have been dumped on individuals by others (or by society at large—we'll talk about such types of problems in Chapter Six).

Whatever the source of the problem, such a person has a negative goal. Since it is very hard to focus on negatives, one frequently converts the negative goal into a positive one by what I call a *means-to-ends transformation*.

Many people feel lousy about themselves. Some get the idea that they can remedy this situation by seeking respect and acceptance from peers. They might then seize upon some available means for getting social acceptance, such as being the loudest and most drunken party animal around. Or they might get the idea that they can make themselves feel like a million dollars by snorting a line or two of cocaine. Others try to do the same thing by clawing their way to the top of the social heap or by making lots and lots of money, or even by getting pregnant and having babies. These are only a few of the tactics that people employ in order to achieve the negative goal of *not* having low self-esteem.

The problem is that the means pretty soon become ends. Some of these means are patently self-destructive and others are socially approved, but they can all become a kind of addiction. You get hung up, in other words, and never quite attain what you set out to do. Instead of feeling good about yourself and your life, you are liable to discover that there are unexpected, long-term consequences of the means you have mistaken for the end. The results can be burned-out teen-agers, coked-out yuppies, women who feel trapped by their children, miserable middle-aged bullies who have been so preoccupied with intimidating and being one-up on everyone else that they never learned how to love or be loved and now find themselves stuck on an endless, joyless treadmill.

To some extent, the example of Paul in Chapter One illustrates this concept. It's as important to keep means and ends straight as to keep in mind the fact that the map is not the territory.

How do you deal with the problems just discussed? You act. How do you act? You make choices. You choose your own objectives.

ENVISIONING YOUR OWN GOALS

Ultimately, we all make up our own goals as we go along in life. However, there is a craft to setting productive goals. To orient yourself in a way that maximizes your chance of getting what you want out of your life, you need to work with the flow. You must learn to recognize how things work and make them work better for you.

If reality is defined by action, it makes sense to define goals in terms of action. Why? Because by acting in accordance with your goals, you can then define a reality you want. And it's a lot easier to affect your own actions than to try and change the world to conform to your desires.

There is always the off chance that the world might change (I warned you, I'm a bit of a mystic). But it probably won't. If it does, it will do so only because of the influence your actions exert on it, even if those actions are as subtle as thinking, imagining, wishing, or choosing. So it all boils down to what you do.

Key Principle Fifteen: Identify goals in terms of conduct, using "ing" words. This means to focus on action. Not just any action, but action that *exemplifies* what your objectives are and defines them in *present* terms. For example, if you want to stop smoking cigarettes or biting your fingernails or wasting time at work or blocking yourself from operating at maximum potential, I don't advise you to envision your future in terms of *not doing* these things.

You could conceptualize your goals in terms of *refusing* to do whatever you wish to cease doing, because to refuse or to block a line of action is in itself a creative action. But I suggest you go one step further and envision your preferred future by focusing on an imaginary scene in which you are doing or accomplishing the goal you *really* want to reach and *whatever it is you presently want to stop doing is not there in any way, shape, or form.*

Focus on being, feeling, and acting the way you prefer for yourself. Because you know that you have deliberately created a scene in which you are not engaging in the behaviors that are presently a problem to you, that meaning is associated with the image. Remember, you are also telling yourself that these old, unwanted forms of conduct are not part of this new self you are imagining, reminding yourself that you have left them behind and moved on.

Key Principle Sixteen: Envision positives; imply negatives. Part of the sneakiness of this approach is that it defines your preferred reality as taken for granted, as an implicit preference that you will tend to act out. Try this.

Exercise 3-B: Choosing Goals

DIRECTIONS

Proceed when you have read through these directions and feel that you understand them. You can do this exercise alone or in a group.

In your journal, number five lines (first line = 1, second line = 2, and so forth).

1. Close your eyes, take a deep breath, and breathe out, letting yourself relax.
2. Bring back your centering or magical place imagery from Technique Two. Let yourself float for a short while, letting yourself go.
3. Now, think about what you really want for yourself. As any goal or objective comes to mind, let yourself

feel it through—imagine that it has come true, that you have attained the goal, and see how it feels to you, if it feels right, if it makes you feel good.

4. If it does feel right, focus on that goal for a moment, let your imaginary scene exemplify the positive goal, and let any present negatives be conspicuously absent. (If you are trying to stop smoking, make sure your teeth are white in the dream, that the air smells clean and fresh, that there are no ashes or cigarette holes around.) Really build up the scene *as if you are there now*.

    Hint: How do you do that? Focus on whatever you would be noticing if you were actually there; then focus on action with whomever is there right now. It is often easiest to start with the trivial, background stuff—sky, wallpaper, what is seen through a window. Then fill in your image by scanning closer and closer in to where you are in the scene. Notice colors, shapes, textures, sounds, smells, movements, temperature, humidity, sensations on your skin. Let yourself really be there in your imagination. Just pretend you can feel, touch, see, smell everything as real as life itself. Allow your imagination to fill in details, let the story flow, if you'd prefer, like a daydream. (In fact, this is a *guided daydream*.)

5. Keep doing this, thinking of a goal and then feeling it through, until you're ready to proceed.

6. When you are ready, open your eyes. Now, reviewing your mindwork, list in any order (one item to each line in your journal), what seem to you to be your five most important goals *right now* for yourself and your life.

7. Now go back over each of these goals, close your eyes, and feel it through. If it feels right, acknowledge this to yourself and go on to the next goal. If it doesn't feel right, modify the goal or substitute one for it that *does* feel right.

8. When you are ready, open your eyes. You are done.

Consider this goals list to be a working record, nothing more. You can modify or amend it at any time. However, it would be useful to go through this list at least once a day for the next few days or weeks; read and feel through each of these goals. The best time would be immediately before your first creative self-hypnosis session of the day. You can have fun doing this. For example, you might play a game with yourself and try to imagine a future story that represents *all* of your goals at once. This is heartily recommended.

SUGGESTIONS FOR TEAMS

You can simply discuss your experiences. Better yet, one of you can coach the others or work in pairs with one partner coaching the other and then switching roles. Discuss your experiences, share any problems, and brainstorm solutions.

ASSERTIONS AND ASSUMPTIONS

One of the reasons people go to hypnotists or other therapists for help is that they have been unable to eliminate unwanted behaviors and still act in a way they feel is right for themselves and consonant with their goals.

Suzanne Powers, a clinical sociologist at the Cleveland Clinic, has dealt with many such problems. She feels very strongly that there is a better way to help people than trying to find out "what's wrong" with them and then seeking to "treat" or "cure" the underlying pathology:

Problems with "control" are typical of those brought to the psychotherapist by patients. The patient experiences lack of power over self, experience or behavior, often behaving in a "compulsive" fashion. Helping that person to attribute power in these matters to self and to act consistently with this definition of the situation is a major goal. . . . Often the therapist discovers that much of the problem lies in the actor–patient's inconsistency of stated and unstated preferences.

I am in full agreement with Dr. Powers, although I don't generally use the term *preferences*. Rather, as I see it, this type of problem with control can be attributed to a person holding contradictory definitions of the situation leading to diametrically opposed lines of action.

Trying to stop smoking cigarettes is a good example of this type of situation and it is this case that I have chosen to use to illustrate the concepts in this chapter. (Keep in mind that the example could just as easily be used for any number of situations, ranging from overeating to improving study habits or being more successful at work.)

At one level, the smokers who "cannot stop" feel, think, and imagine that cigarettes are something they need and want, that cigarettes make them feel better, relax them, taste good, give them pleasure, whatever. *Assumptions* like these are often so deeply taken for granted that people aren't clearly aware of having them. Rather, they tend to lie at the lower boundaries of conscious thought, serving to guide us when we take our attention off what we are doing and run, instead, on "automatic pilot."

Yet smokers have also come to hold a contrary definition that cigarettes are something they do *not* need or want, that cigarettes cause them harm by endangering their health. Otherwise, why would not stopping be a problem? This type of definition represents people's attempt to assert a new reality for themselves; it is something that people believe should be the way it is. We can call this an *assertion*. Notice that the assertion denies or attempts to supersede a preexisting assumption.

While some people appear to quit smoking by willpower alone, don't bet on it. As many of you have found out for yourselves, the more you try not to smoke, the more strain you inflict on yourself, the more conflict you provoke. For the majority of people, the strain eventually gets to them and they go back to smoking.

This is a pattern that counselors see again and again when working with conduct problems. When faced with a contradiction between the conduct dictated by one's assertions and one's assumptions, a person generally *increases* the unwanted conduct but does so involuntarily. The internal strain created by trying to enact contradictory definitions is resolved, in other words, by redefining the conduct you tried to change as outside your control, as being compulsive behavior. This does not, however, do very much in helping to cope with the social disapproval directed at people who can't control their own behavior. That, in itself, can cause a lot of stress (which only exacerbates our sense of needing something, like a cigarette).

In the past few years we have developed new ways to neutralize the consequences of value judgments and, in the process, to explain the out-of-control behavior. We label such behavior problems of mental health or problems of addiction. Both attribute the conduct problem to a principle inside either the person or the object of compulsion.

Gregory Bateson (whose theory of logical types we discussed in Chapter Two) calls this the *dormative principle*, a term he derives from a scene from a play by Molière, in which a candidate for a doctoral examination answers the question of why opium puts people to sleep, "Because, learned doctors, it contains a dormative principle." Bateson argues that a far better explanation would focus on the *relationship* between opium and people. To do otherwise, he contends, is to falsify the facts. I agree.

Compulsive smoking, compulsive gambling, compulsive overeating, compulsive drug taking, compulsive just-about-anything all tend to have the same anatomy. I am not denying that extreme forms of compulsive behavior exist that can run a lot deeper; psychiatrists term them obsessive-compulsive disorders. But labeling anybody and everybody's conduct problems as psychiatric deficits or, as in alcoholism, a physical disease, is downright absurd, as is blaming our conduct on the addictive properties of whatever we can't stop doing. As Bateson said, the problem lies in the relationship between the person and the object of compulsion, not in either alone. What I am saying might seem pretty cold-hearted and radical, but I am convinced that problems of self-control, both the psychiatric and addiction models, are cop-outs. I wouldn't go as far as some (like L. Ron Hubbard or Werner Erhard) to say that you are *entirely* responsible for your own behavior, but I feel that's a lot closer to the truth than saying that somebody or something else (including your unconscious mind) made you do something.

We all experience problems. That's life. Some of them involve what is now called compulsive behavior. I am convinced that most garden-variety problems or unwanted conduct which you have unsuccessfully tried to stop boil down to the fact that you are maintaining contradictory definitions of the situation. And the more you try to do what you consciously believe you should do, the more you end up fighting yourself, and that's a battle you can't win.

Of course, there *are* times when you might need professional help. Sometimes there are deep conflicts that are too hard to handle without competent professional help. If you ever feel that you are getting in too deeply, bail out immediately and get a consultation with a clinician of your choice.

At other times, it's not so much a matter of what the problem is but simply how complicated the situation has become. There are times and situations where you can't do it on your own, where you need a friend or a therapist to help you untie the knots. But you'll never know until you try. So ask for help. It's for your own well-being, so why not give it a shot?

To solve most problems, though, you can be your own personal change consultant and it doesn't require years and years of professional training. What it does require is a certain amount of smarts and what L. Ron Hubbard called "obnosis," taking a good hard look at the obvious.

Of course, the problem with our assertions is that they are not obvious but taken for granted and hidden from view. So to make them obvious, clarify what you really want for yourself and get on with what you choose to do. Whatever you might think about Hubbard and his Scientology religion, he was a practical genius who knew how to make things happen. One of the things you can learn from him is this:

Key Principle Seventeen: Confront it and it loses power over you.

Exercise 3-C: Confronting Unstated Preferences

DIRECTIONS

1. Make a list of three of your hardest-to-change behaviors or behavior patterns that really frustrate and/or annoy you.

2. Do Creative Self-Hypnosis (Technique Two) up through step 3, the waking-up sequence, but instead of continuing to visualize your present and future, proceed as follows.

3. Think about (or read) the first behavior on your list. Mentally rehearse going through that pattern; really feel it through. Run through it several times.

4. Now open your eyes and ask yourself the following probe questions, letting yourself brainstorm (that is, letting any and all answers run through your mind without censoring them on the basis of how reasonable or likely they are). Perhaps write your answers in your journal.

   a. How does this conflict with what I choose for myself?

   b. What unstated preferences does this reflect?

5. Close your eyes, bring back your "centering" place for a moment, and repeat step 2 with your second behavior on the list.

6. Repeat for the third behavior on your list.

7. Now take another deep breath, close your eyes, recall your centering place for a moment, and think about the unstated, hidden, or subconscious preferences you have uncovered during this exercise. As one of these preferences comes to mind, if you don't wish to keep it in your current agenda for yourself, tell yourself "I don't choose to feel this way, I'm free" (or

words to that effect). If you want to keep it as part of your conscious agenda, acknowledge it to yourself as one of your objectives. Keep on doing this procedure until nothing else worth bothering with comes to mind.

8. Now complete your usual Creative Self-Hypnosis routine, although you can do it very briefly, running through step 4 to step 7.

SUGGESTIONS FOR TEAMS

If working with a partner or a group, it would be valuable to work in dyads (two-person groups). One partner is the *practicer* (does the exercise) while the other serves as coach. Suggested approach:

COACH: "Okay, now do the self-hypnosis up through the point where you make yourself feel wide awake. When you get to that point, nod (or some other mutually chosen gesture) to let me know.

PRACTICER: (Nods)

COACH: Reads the first behavior on the practicer's list and reads/paraphrases the instruction in step 3. Then says "When you are ready to go on, nod to let me know."

PRACTICER: (Nods)

COACH: Asks the first question (changing "I" to "you"), records all of the practicer's answers, then does the same with the second question.

Continue in this way to the end of the activity; then switch roles.

CREATIVE SELF-MANAGEMENT

Whether you are primarily interested in changing unwanted behavior or in moving beyond a present high level of performance to an even higher level, the ultimate goal is the same: improving your skills in creative living. The approach around which this volume is centered is one that I call *creative self-*

management. This means you don't have to follow rules for living, particularly rules that you have not chosen or with which you do not agree. You can invent your own variations on old rules and you can make up new rules as you go along. I am not suggesting, by the way, that "nothing is true, everything is permitted." The corollary to the Thomas theorem is that "what people don't define as real can still affect them."

The term *self-management* is used in this book to mean two things at once. On one level, it designates the idea of giving you exercises to practice as well as other means to work things out on your own, without need of a therapist. It's not a new concept, but it's an effective one.

When I use the term in this way, I am also, at least partly, trying to suggest the concept of *liberation*—self-empowerment. The goal of this book is to enable you to break the trance of everyday reality and to gain control of your *self* and your *life* from the world and the things of the world.

Self-management is also used here in a technical sense of managing one's self. I am not talking about management by willpower or maintaining an iron grip on yourself and making yourself do this, that, or the other, but, rather, something more like self-cultivation.

"If it doesn't fit, force it" does not apply here. I urge you to go easy on yourself, to adopt a playful attitude, to allow yourself to grow into the person whom you choose to be. Creative self-management is rather like Montessori education in that it emphasizes spontaneous learning through activity. The Montessori school provides an environment in which all the toys teach the children about concepts and their application, so that the children discover how to spell or how to do arithmetic as they play with the things they find in the school environment. Creative self-management involves rigging your *internal* environment so that you learn new ways of using your mind and can allow yourself to spontaneously adapt your action to the situation at hand. While each of the steps can be "unfolded," so to speak, creative self-management is as simple as "ESP":

The Creative Self-Management Process

1. Evaluate the situation
2. Strategize
3. Practice, practice, practice

This same pattern applies regardless of the level of generality on which you are focusing, from your life as a whole to a specific problem, objective, or relationship. In the rest of the chapter, we'll look at each of these three steps in turn. To keep the discussion from getting too abstract, I will continue to use the example of the compulsive smoker. Keep in mind that this is only an example, designed to "stand in" for virtually any other case of trying to develop a new pattern of action for yourself.

EVALUATION VERSUS VALUE JUDGMENT

The reason I have highlighted evaluation in the creative self-management process is because the following is a basic rule of successful action, to be ignored at your peril:

Key Principle Eighteen: Stop and evaluate; then make your move. To get an idea that you want to change something or accomplish something and then to attempt it haphazardly is to invite disaster. While there is no substitute for action, there is also no substitute for intelligent action. You not only need smarts but you need *good information* (intelligence). The amount and depth of information you need and the time you should devote to the intelligence-gathering process will depend on the situation.

I am currently working as a marketing research consultant specializing in the health care industry. Before pharmaceutical companies introduce new drugs—something that can take years and cost millions of dollars—they come to us to evaluate the market. We interview physicians around the country to find out what they are currently doing, what they look for in a particular medical product, what they perceive their unmet needs to be, and how they evaluate our clients' new drug concepts. We analyze what we've learned and report back to our clients if it would be prudent to proceed and, if so, how best to meet physicians' perceived needs. Each major research project might take months and cost more than a hundred thousand dollars. But such companies have learned that ignorance can be far more expensive.

As an individual, you may need to do nothing more than stop for a moment, take a look around, and then proceed. This works, for example, when you want to cross the street.

Most things fall somewhere in between these two extremes of full-scale research and looking both ways before you cross the street. This evaluation is called *situational analysis*. As W. I. Thomas suggested over fifty years ago, a situational analysis should, ideally, take into account both the *objective features* of the situation and the *meanings* or subjective interpretations of those features made by participants in the situation (including yourself).

The discussion of smoking in the previous section focused pretty much on the latter part. A complete analysis should also include paying attention to the characteristics of the objects involved (e.g., the cigarette and cigarette smoke— put a tissue over the end of the cigarette, take a couple of drags, look at the tissue, also notice the taste and feeling of the smoke in your mouth and throat, how many cigarettes you smoke, what is the cost). Additionally, it is useful to look at what participants in the situation are doing (e.g., how you smoke cigarettes, when and where you smoke them, what triggers or determines when you smoke, what happens when and immediately after you smoke).

While there are many pitfalls to self-assessment, one of the most essential ones to avoid is making *value judgments*. When you make value judgments, you place a moral interpretation on what you observe and you react to this label. You jump to a conclusion based on the way things appear to be, based on flimsy evidence and, often, prejudices and a dash of anecdotes from your own or others' past experiences. It's the easy, lazy, commonsense way and it doesn't work.

How we tend to react to failure is an excellent example of what I mean by value judging. I am indebted to Professor Harry Cohen of Iowa State University for making this point.

> People often make mistakes. It is common in our culture for people who make mistakes to suffer problems of low self-esteem and a poor self-concept, a feeling that they are total failures. They value-judge themselves instead of evaluating their mistake and using what they learn from it for better living in the future. . . . They react to the *act* of failure with the perception—a value judgment—that they *are* failures. This is likely to become a *self-fulfilling prophecy*. . . . That is, they are likely to act as if they are failures, with the consequence of making that negative self-definition come true.

The situation of the person who has been unable to stop smoking is a good example of the *failure syndrome*. My analysis of smoking is an example of evaluation. The point both Harry Cohen and I are trying to make is that evaluation is a scientific, empowering process while value judgment is a reactive, self-defeating process. It is also part of the glue that keeps us stuck to the flypaper of postnatal suggestions.

The general solution to value judgment is careful *evaluation* of the situation. At minimum, evaluation calls for vigilance and "triangulation"—looking at the situation from as many different sides as possible, using as many different kinds of data as possible—and trying to build your understanding from the ground up (that is, inductively).

Throughout this book, I will be introducing concepts and techniques designed to assist you in evaluating situations as the first step to developing effective strategies to overcome problems and accomplish your desired objectives. However, we can't really do justice to the subject of how to do evaluation as a general skill. The notes to this chapter suggest some resources for learning more about this subject.

WHY UNDESIRED CONDUCT PERSISTS

In the evaluation I have made of compulsive smoking so far, I have omitted some key points in order to highlight the importance of our definitions of the situation. Let's remedy this omission.

I may have given you the impression that definition was all a matter of abstract thinking, a purely intellectual process. When I talk about ideas, concepts, or definitions, I do not mean to imply anything of the sort. Thinking, imagining, defining the situation—these are *acts*. As I have suggested, they are acts of the entire organism. I have already discussed this in passing, when introducing the tense/relax method used in Technique Two.

Here, let's turn to what is possibly a still more subtle point. What you are trying to change (or institute) is a *pattern of conduct*, not random behavior. As you might recall from our definition of conduct, it is learned or, perhaps more accurately, forged in your interplay with the social world in which you find conduct and it is always goal directed, which then tells us something concrete about our conduct problems.

Key Principle Nineteen: *If there wasn't a payoff, the conduct wouldn't persist.* A one-time act might be a fluke. There is no way to interpret it. But if we consistently act in a certain way, there is a reason for it. This is a basic sociological principle going back to Emile Durkheim, one of the founders of scientific sociology: Conduct (whether of an individual or a group) persists because it is *functional*, because it *serves a function.*

I am not saying that the objective or the payoff is necessarily rational or calculated or conscious; the objective may be a matter of avoidance or feeling or habit and the payoff might be symbolic or even perverse. But the objective and payoff are there. You can bet on it.

This fact is as true for unwanted conduct as for anything else we do. Unstated preferences and acts based on these preferences always offer *some* perceived benefit. These benefits may be symbolic, they may be illusory, they may be shortsighted and ultimately suicidal, or totally off the wall, but they are there. I made this point in my previous book, but I cannot make it too often.

Unless you learn to recognize and compensate for these benefits, you will continue to defeat yourself. So let's get to it.

Exercise 3-D: Hidden Payoffs

NOTE ON METHOD

This exercise involves *individual brainstorming.* I have mentioned this technique before but let me clarify it here. You think about or ask yourself the question and just keep writing any answers as they come into your mind, no matter how silly they might seem; if you seem to be running down, ask yourself, *Is there anything else?* until you feel empty of ideas.

DIRECTIONS

1. Review your list of problem behaviors from Exercise 3-C. Revise or change any item on the list as you feel appropriate.
2. Now, consider the first item on your list. Brainstorm the question, *What payoffs do I get from doing this?*
3. Repeat for the other two questions.
4. Then review your list for each. Which answers seem to be closest to the truth? For each item, rank the three answers that ring truest to you 1, 2, and 3.
5. Looking at all three lists, what generalizations or conclusions can you draw about your own personal problem behaviors and the hidden payoffs you get from them? (Write your answer in your journal. Perhaps share it with your partner/group when you get together next.)

Let's apply the concept of payoffs to cigarette smoking. For the purposes of this discussion let's assume that you are one of those people who have decided to quit but find that you have been unable to do so.

The first step in quitting is to stop smoking. The second step is to change your definitions of the situation to eliminate the unstated preferences associated with smoking and the identification of yourself as a smoker, but we'll get to that later. First I suggest that you assess what you are currently getting (or think you are getting) out of smoking.

In many cases, smoking seems to be a way of managing stress. There are also components of habit (what else do you do with your hands and mouth?), familiarity, and comfort (it's a stable part of your life whereas everything else is changing) and social norms for appropriate behavior in specific situations (many people find themselves automatically lighting up in bars).

A very few individuals might be trying to commit slow suicide with cigarettes, just as some overeaters might be eating because they are afraid of sex, but such explanations simply can't account for conduct in which at least a third of the people in our society engage.

Generally, you can find the payoffs for unwanted conduct in the here and now. It does something immediate for you: release tension, gives you a sensation, etc. The possible long-term consequences of the immediate act of taking, lighting, and smoking a cigarette are simply too remote to serve as a disincentive to that behavior.

Yet I've had clients come to me for a stop-smoking program who have already had a cancerous lung removed, who have been wheeled into my office attached to an oxygen tank because they have end-stage emphysema!

The problem seems to be that *consequences* is a concept, not an act or a stimulus (sensory experience or its imagined counterpart). Hence, consequences are of a different logical type than the act of smoking or the subjective experience associated with the act. That is, you obtain a here-and-now payoff from smoking. Whatever that payoff is, you have come to define it to be desirable.

Now, if you are trying to stop, that means you have also come to define the consequences of smoking as undesirable. This creates a mental conflict (technically known as *cognitive dissonance*), which in itself becomes a source of stress and triggers the need to smoke in order to relax.

Of course, you can probably convince yourself that you don't *really* like what you get out of smoking. This is one of the classic defense mechanisms described by Sigmund Freud, known as *denial*.

In fact, given the moralistic climate of the current anti-smoking crusade, you are likely to push your unstated preferences for the payoffs you get from cigarettes entirely out of your conscious awareness. This is technically known as *repression*. You convince yourself that your unstated preferences simply do not exist.

The problem, in either case, is that you are lying to yourself. The underlying definitions do not go away; they just go deeper into your unconscious thinking, placing you in the position of having to remember not to think about them, which gets really complicated. And stressful. There has got to be a better way!

STRATEGIZING

The better way is to make things easy on yourself by using your creative intelligence and letting the momentum of daily life to do a lot of the work for you. The trick is to finesse the situation, not to force it. Finesse requires deftness and the ability to recognize how things flow and when and where to nudge. *Strategy* is a well-designed program of action for accomplishing your purposes and overcoming any barriers along the way.

This book represents a strategy designed to help you out of powerlessness and into calm, easy, self-determined control over your life, thoughts, conduct, and relationships. The core around which creative self-hypnosis and self-management revolve is:

Key Tactic One: Use your creative imagination to resolve any underlying contradiction between your assumptions and your assertions. In order to quit smoking and never go back to it, you have to *literally* change yourself from a smoker to a nonsmoker. However you do this (that is, whatever specific *tactics* and *techniques* you employ) involves changing your definitions of the situation at a gut level, breaking the identification of cigarette smoking with pleasure or relief and eliminating the image of yourself as a smoker from your mental repertoire. Then you can stop fighting yourself and you can take your attention off cigarettes and do something useful with your energy and your life.

Do you see how evaluation leads directly to "strategizing"? A good assessment tells you what you need to do to resolve the problem and attain your objectives. It also enables you to spot subtle aspects of the situation that would otherwise continue to trip you up.

THREE GAME PLANS

Okay. You have a basic strategy. Now you have to work on your line of action.

There are at least three ways of implementing change—let's call them *game plans*—employed by therapists (or that you can employ yourself) to accomplish their objectives:

1. Direct
2. Indirect
3. Cooperative

By a *direct* game plan I refer to the tried and true method of attacking a problem head-on. This is the approach usually employed in hypnosis and self-hypnosis. While I will be showing you several direct strategies in this book, we will rarely use a pure form of this approach. If you want to learn more about it and the variety of techniques that can be used, consult my previous book *Strategic Self-Hypnosis*.

There are several drawbacks to this game plan, however. One is that it mobilizes all the forces of resistance to change within yourself and around you. Another is that it tends to commit you to one, limited line of attack. Not only does it limit your flexibility but after a while you can get trapped into continuing with an unprofitable line of action, because you have already invested so much of your time, effort, or, perhaps, money.

I have to admit that there is another reason why I have moved away from the direct approach: it's boring. I found a more playful way to go, one allowing for more variety.

Indirect game plans can fit the bill. By indirect, I mean that you don't grab the bull by the horns, but you figure out how to coax the bull to lie down and roll over. That's what I've been encouraging in this chapter.

Perhaps the most famous form of indirect game plan is that pioneered by Milton V. Erickson. The client is not told how to accomplish the desired change or objective but is guided to use his or her own innate creativity and inner resources. Erickson called this "relying on the unconscious."

Like Erickson, when I use an indirect approach, I do not expect clients to resolve deeply repressed conflicts, nor do I expect that conduct can be changed simply by guiding clients toward achieving "insight." Instead, as I am doing in this book, I try to prepare people for change, but recognize that the change itself must come from the individual's own actions. By acting in a changed way, the person literally changes his or her realities.

The beauty of an indirect approach is that it allows you to bypass resistance and dependency (either on a therapist or a specific "formula" for change). Erickson's indirect approach has been further applied and popularized under such names as neurolinguistic programming and strategic brief therapy. I am particularly fascinated and impressed by the latter, which is one of the names used for the work done by the Mental Research Institute in Palo Alto, California. For example, the therapist will very often tell clients not to change their behavior "too quickly." Think about that. Much of the time, the client returns for the next session sheepishly apologizing for having disobeyed.

The cooperative approach is less easily applied to self-hypnosis. This type of game plan is difficult for me. For most of my formative years, I was a loner. But I have come to realize that I missed out on a great deal and I am trying to remedy the deficit.

A cooperative approach involves using the power of social cooperation in our change efforts, working *together* rather than separately. It means giving up some of your independence and autonomy, letting some of your barriers down—and reaping rewards beyond measure.

I will show you a number of ways to take advantage of a cooperative approach. An obvious one is working with a partner or with a group, but I realize that most of you will be working on your own, which is perfectly fine.

The real power of a cooperative approach comes in mobilizing and enlisting the support of others to help you accomplish your objectives. We will spend more time on this subject in later chapters.

INTERNALIZING THE FUTURE

The concept of *internalizing* means that you take material from outside yourself and make it part of your mental reality. For example, we tend to internalize social rules; the process of everyday hypnosis is actually an internalization process. Sociologists call the internalization process *socialization*.

By internalizing other people's images of you, or what you imagine to be other's images, you engage in the socialization process that Cooley and Mead described as internalizing a self. Mead points out that when you internalize your *self* you simultaneously internalize your interpretation of *not-self*, of the world around you. Thus, he explained, you internalize the entire society at the exact time that you internalize an image of yourself in society.

We keep internalizing images of self and of the world throughout our lives. As we do so, we keep modifying and updating parts of our self-image.

Normally the material comes from our experiences in the world with other people, through our firsthand experiences, through experiences we learn secondhand from others, and, increasingly, through hand-me-down experiences we learn from television, radio, records, books, and magazines. We keep building up our own internalized definition of the situation—of what the world is like and of what we are like as its inhabitants.

Now, with creative self-hypnosis you are going to do something very tricky. You are going to create your own image of the world as you'd *prefer* it to be—if only that fragment of the world that is yourself—and you are going to internalize it as your taken-for-granted future reality.

You are *not* going to try to make that reality come true. You are just going to imagine it and imagine it and imagine it until you automatically imagine it whenever you think about the future.

Key Tactic Two: Define a preferred future and make it internalized reality. You can assist this process by also focusing on your present life as it actually happens to be. This creates what Robert Fritz calls "structural tension." He contends that you will automatically act to resolve that tension by acting in a way that actualizes your preferred future, *if you keep on envisioning that future and allow your present to change.* There are some excellent programs based on Fritz's work that are described in the notes to this chapter.

FRAMING STRATEGIES

Another way in which you can expedite the process of change and self-empowerment, generally, is to pay attention to how you *frame* your evaluation, goals, and game plan: in other words, the way you communicate to yourself or others your definition of the situation, particularly regarding what it means for you and how it fits into the whole; the "spin" you put on it.

Framing is a strategic move in its own right. In this regard, the late Nathan Hurvitz, a well-known radical psychotherapist and family counselor, developed an immensely useful concept. He drew a distinction between *instrumental hypotheses* and *terminal hypotheses*. An instrumental hypothesis is a cognitive map of the situation that focuses on action and suggests the possibility of change. An example might be, "I've gotten myself so used to smoking and to thinking of myself as a smoker that it's very difficult for me to really believe that I can be a nonsmoker and I have not yet been able to stop smoking."

Contrast this example with, "I am a smoker. I am addicted to tobacco and I can't stop." Terminal hypotheses are static ways of framing things which rule out change and very often involve value judgments. They define the status quo as inevitable ("that's how it is") and attribute behaviors to a person's character or personality. Terminal hypotheses attribute cause and control to uncontrollable forces or powers outside of (or inside of) the person.

As a family therapist specializing in poor, often minority families, Hurvitz was forced to abandon a lot of the intellectual baggage brought into the field by college-educated, middle-class practitioners. He had to get down to the nuts and bolts of things. Very often he found that interpersonal problems stemmed from the fact that family members had adopted terminal hypotheses about their situation and, consequently, felt trapped and unable to change. By helping them reframe their situation, Hurvitz was often able to start them on the road to change.

Key Tactic Three: Frame things instrumentally, not terminally. The example of family therapy suggests the other side of this same business, *reframing*. That is, focus on a problem situation and redefine its meaning or how it fits into the whole. Very often, you will discover that it has been framed by a terminal hypothesis so that this involves constructing an instrumental definition of the situation.

For example, in my discussion of smoking I was purposely seeking to reframe smoking behavior in your mind, from a habitual, out-of-control act (terminal hypothesis) to something you have set up yourself to do and can stop doing (instrumental hypothesis).

Similarly, Harry Cohen was trying to reframe the concept

of failure for you. This reframing begins with evaluation but you can extend it to visualization and through visualization into your background thinking.

Exercise 3-E: Instrumental and Terminal Framing

DIRECTIONS
1. Think about your present. Select one behavior that annoys you most and you have found difficult to change. Describe it in your journal, but do it two different ways:
   a. First describe it in a *terminal* fashion, identifying it as an inevitable, fixed, part of reality.
   b. Now describe the same thing in an *instrumental* fashion, focusing on action, identifying what is going on, what keeps it going on; getting at the "how" but not the "why."
2. Compare the two descriptions. Which gives you a better idea of how to change the situation? Which makes you feel more like you can do something about it?
3. Close your eyes and construct a mental image based on the description you choose, trying to "see" things that way with your mind's eye.

SUGGESTION FOR TEAMS
   If working with a partner or a group, why not share and discuss your terminal and instrumental descriptions. Perhaps have a contest: divide into groups of two, three, or four and see which group can produce a longer list of benefits of instrumental hypotheses and liabilities of terminal hypotheses, or of examples of each type.

RELAXATION AS A STRATEGY

Another major strategy is *relaxation*. By relaxing your muscles, you have already seen how you can "relax your mind."

By relaxing your mind and body very deeply for a relatively extended period of time (for example, at least ten to fifteen minutes), you can achieve what Herbert Benson called a *relaxation response*. This deep psychophysical relaxation apparently helps your body and mind to reset and recenter themselves, to normalize physiological processes and to generally restore and refresh you at every level of your being.

As you are also aware, hypnosis has long been associated with deep relaxation. Technique Three, at the end of this chapter, will show you how to use your basic creative self-hypnosis to achieve a deep relaxation state of this type.

It is recommended by Dr. Benson and many other authorities that you practice entering and experiencing a relaxation response at least daily, for fifteen minutes or more. You can do this by meditation, biofeedback, or self-hypnosis. The name changes; the miracle is the same.

If you want to learn more about relaxation as a strategy, read the discussion in my book *Strategic Self-Hypnosis* or in some of the references given in the notes to this chapter.

IMPLEMENTING ACTION

Don't try to change too quickly. Not yet. At this point, it is more important to focus on preparing yourself for successful personal growth, change, and goal accomplishment.

REINFORCEMENT

A final point before we end this chapter. Once is not enough. To make a new reality real for yourself you have to experience it over and over. This goes for new realities inside your mind and also in the outside world. Until experience is reinforced, and until imaginary experience is rekindled, again and again, it will not seem real to you; you will not respond to the experience as real and you won't be able to work with it.

At the same time, if you are trying to break out of the ordinary—including the ordinary for yourself—you are fighting the resistance of the whole world. It is going to gnaw at your inner realities, try to erode them away into more of the same. Your best defensive weapon, perhaps your only weapon, is to be stubborn and to keep on imagining over and over your chosen reality. Thus, the third step of the creative self-management process is practice, practice, practice.

SUMMARY

This chapter has focused on action and the concept of human behavior as *conduct*—self-conscious, goal-directed, and conventional action. Using the example of a person trying to quit smoking, it has suggested that many problems of control stem from a contradiction between two types of definitions of the situation: *explicit assertions* and *implicit assumptions*. We described the concept of *creative self-management* and the "ESP" formula, discussing each of its three components in turn: *evaluation*, *strategy*, and *practice*.

The following Key Principles were described in this chapter:

FOURTEEN: Reality is defined by action.
FIFTEEN: Identify goals in terms of conduct, using "ing" words.
SIXTEEN: Envision positives; imply negatives.
SEVENTEEN: Confront it and it loses power over you.
EIGHTEEN: Stop and evaluate; then make your move.
NINETEEN: If there wasn't a payoff, the conduct wouldn't persist.

Chapter Three also introduced you to three *Key Tactics*. These are designed to help you develop your own creative self-management strategies:

ONE: Use your creative imagination to resolve any underlying contradiction between your assumptions and your assertions.
TWO: Define a preferred future and make it internalized reality.
THREE: Frame things instrumentally, not terminally.

Technique Three: Basic Creative Self-Hypnosis II

DIRECTIONS
Identical to Technique Two except for step 3.

1. Tense/relax.
2. Imagine place.
   "calmness . . . peace . . . energy . . . strength. . . ."
   (Leave space to add your own words.)
3. Steer "down" (into deep relaxation).
   "calm . . . mellow . . . at ease . . . relaxing . . . deeper
   and deeper . . . dreamy . . . cozy . . . peaceful . . .
   drifting . . . more and more deeply relaxed . . .
   comfortable. . . ." (Leave space to add your own
   words.)
4. Visualize present.
5. Visualize future.
6. Set mind.
7. Open eyes. Tell yourself, "That's it, end of session."

RECOMMENDATIONS FOR PRACTICE
You do this technique the same way you did Technique
Two, except that in step 3 you think, feel, and imagine
yourself getting more and more deeply relaxed (and you
will). As recommended in Exercise 3-B, I suggest that
you mentally rehearse your goals immediately before
doing this technique for the first time each day. Then,
incorporate what you have learned in this chapter as you
go through the technique.

SUGGESTIONS FOR TEAMS
Same as for Technique Two.

FOUR

Strategic Interaction

Changing your actions is as far as most books on self-hypnosis or other kinds of self-help are likely to go. Possibly this is because they are generally written by psychologists and psychiatrists or those whose ideas are grounded in psychology. I am not a psychologist: I am a sociologist.

What is a sociologist? A sociologist is somebody who has studied sociology and, despite having taken classes in the subject, remains eternally curious about the patterns of life. But what makes one a *true* sociologist is discovering for oneself that, in human affairs, the part that defines the whole is what goes on *between* human beings.

A sociologist views *social interaction* as the central process of human life. Not individual human actors and not whole societies or cultures. As Cooley stated:

> A separate individual is an abstraction unknown to experience, and likewise is society when regarded as something apart from individuals . . . "society" and "individuals" do not denote separable phenomena but simply collective and distributive aspects of the same thing.

There are of course many schools of thought in sociology, each evaluating social interaction in its own way.

One approach to understanding social life looks at society as a kind of organism of which individuals are the cells. This approach is known as *macrosociology* and we will consider some of its implications beginning in Chapter Five. This chapter takes a complementary approach, looking at society as a sort of colonial organism (like corals and other ocean-dwelling creatures) built up by the interactions of individual social actors. This approach is known as *microsociology*.

Microsociology emphasizes individual human beings—but not as such. Classical psychology emphasizes individuals and their behavior. Microsociology emphasizes *interacting persons*, individuals in the context of social interaction, not in isolation like rats in a maze.

So far we have been exploring a microsociological perspective based on the works of Cooley, Mead, Thomas, and Wirth. This approach, not well known outside of sociological circles, is often referred to as the Chicago School, because many of its pioneers were associated with the University of Chicago in the 1920s and 1930s. For almost two generations, the leading advocate and elaborator of Chicago School sociology was Mead's student, Herbert Blumer, who died in late 1987.

According to Blumer, society *is* social interaction. He convinced us that we are creative actors who construct our world through social interaction; we are not passive objects of social, economic, biological, or environmental forces. Our approach, he wrote:

> ... does not merely give a ceremonious nod to social interaction. It recognizes social interaction to be of vital importance in its own right. This importance lies in the fact that social interaction is a process that *forms* human conduct instead of being merely a means or a setting for the expression or release of human conduct.

To understand and change human conduct, we need to take account of the fact that we don't merely act—we *interact*. Harry Cohen explains,

Every *act* of life is an *act*-ion (action). An action leads to a re-*act*-ion (reaction). A person acts; another person reacts to that act; the original actor reacts to that reaction. This is social life. Actions and reactions stand in relationship to one another. Action causes reaction. Actions and reactions make inter -*act*-ion (interaction).

Professor Cohen summarizes this concept in a useful equation:

Key Principle Twenty: Action ↔ ***Reaction = Interaction.*** The double-headed arrow is the crux of the equation. Human action is built by a reciprocal process of exchanges with others. Many social and behavioral scientists tend to take social interaction for granted, as a sort of medium through which social or psychological forces determine behavior.

Blumer argued that interaction was the *central* feature of human life. However, he felt that there was more to social interaction than meets the eye. He sought an answer to a question that must be addressed by any theory of society: How is cooperation possible?

Clearly, our actions ↔ reactions cannot be random. They must be coordinated, fit together in some way. Otherwise we'd be like a bunch of cockroaches scuttling around a New York City tenement.

At which point you may be thinking, "You sociologists are such dummies. I mean it's obvious to anybody over the age of two. People talk, they communicate. What's so mysterious about that?"

Exercise 4-A: What Is Social Interaction?

DIRECTIONS
1. Ask yourself these two questions:
   a. What are the key features of social interaction that permit human beings to cooperate?
   b. What are the key features of human beings that permit them to engage in social interaction?

2. Brainstorm your answers and record them either as lists of concepts ("pure" brainstorm) or in the form of a summary statement.

SUGGESTIONS FOR TEAMS
Do this exercise in a group. After brainstorming each question, see if you can arrive at a group answer.

There is no single "right" answer to these questions. In fact, Chapter Five will present a slightly different way of addressing this same issue.

There are a variety of clinicians and social scientists who now employ a language of social interaction. Most of us are of the opinion that life seems to have been constructed along the lines of the old purloined letter gambit: Hide the mysteries out in the open where nobody will look. Make it simple and no one will believe it.

Thus, we are united by a focus on the present situation and how participants interact within the situation. We don't try to reduce what is going on to social, psychological, biological, or other forces that are being manifested in people's interactions.

SYMBOLIC INTERACTION

According to Blumer, we are able to cooperate socially because we have (or are) selves and because we have the capacity to engage in symbolic mental processes. Now, perhaps, you can see why these topics were covered in Chapter One and Chapter Two. Other social and behavioral scientists using the concept of interaction have tended to focus on the behaviors themselves. For them, social interaction comes down to what individual acting units do in the presence of one another.

For Blumer and the generations of younger sociologists who work in his tradition, what matters is not what people do but rather the meanings that their actions ↔ reactions hold for social interactants. The name of the game is, literally, *symbolic interaction.*

One of the basic principles of Blumer's symbolic interactionist approach is that the proper function of social science is not to devise abstract theories about the world but to sensitize us to the ways in which human beings construct the realities of their lives. It is more a way of seeing than a systematic theory about the world.

While its name is definitely a barrier to popular acceptance, symbolic interaction offers a very practical kind of analysis. Specific to our present purposes, it suggests some useful answers to the questions raised by Exercise 4-A. Not only are the answers enlightening but they link together everything I have said to this point and provide a social scientific rationale for creative self-management.

Blumer contends that *symbolic interaction depends on creative imagination.* In order to coordinate actions and reactions with one another, human actors use their imagination to *take the role of the other.*

That is, for us to cooperate successfully, I must ascertain what your intentions and motivations are—what you *mean* by your actions. I do this by imagining what I would be thinking and doing if I were in your shoes. Nathan Hurvitz developed a highly successful approach to family therapy centering on the concept that most interpersonal problems result from difficulties in taking the role of the other person, and can be resolved by helping clients develop or regain this skill.

Of course, most of us are poor mind readers. So we coach each other through our words, gestures, facial expressions, body language, and so forth. This coaching amounts to something like a constant game of charades in which you try to guess what the other person means—what are his or her motivations and intentions.

Thus, we are continually exchanging messages with one another as we engage in the give-and-take of social interaction. In effect, what we are doing by our actions and by our words (which can be viewed as "speech acts") is defining the situation for one another.

Key Principle Twenty-one: A situation is defined by the interaction of participants. For all practical intents and purposes, the situation is what we are doing, period. That's what Chapter Three covered—only now I'm directing your attention to the fact that the situation is not a solo act. Rather, it is our collective production, our mutual accomplishment. Perhaps even more to the point, it is our ultimate work of art, an ongoing triumph of human creativity.

Blumer makes a second key point. He says that Mead's conceptualization of the self also implies a second process of *self-interaction* as

> . . . a form of communication, with the person addressing himself as a person and responding thereto. We can clearly recognize such interaction in ourselves as each of us notes that he is angry with himself, or that he has to spur himself on in his tasks, or that he reminds himself to do this or that, or that he is talking to himself in working out some plan of action. . . . One's waking life consists of such indications that the person is making to himself, indications that he uses to direct his action.

Which is, of course, precisely what we were talking about in our chapter on mind. Symbolic interactionism is really radical stuff, bordering on an anarchistic view of social life (in the sense that it denies the ultimate reality of the system or the necessity for any particular structure). Blumer is suggesting that you and I are free to change reality by changing the reality we define in our social interactions—and that we can start off by changing the reality we define at the level of self-interaction.

These changes would be a good example of what I described in Chapter Three as an *indirect* strategy. Actually, the strategy implies four different indirect strategies for changing the quality of our life experience and our situation.

- Changing my situation by changing how I define it in self-interaction (hence, predisposing myself to act and interact in new ways).
- Changing my subjective reality (self-interaction) by

changing our social interactions and, hence, the "objective" situation.

- Changing my situation by getting you to change your
self-interactions and, hence, your social interactions
with me.
- Changing my self-interactions by getting you to change
yours, hence your social interactions and the situation
you help to create for us both.

The bottom line in all four of these strategies is that
interaction and self-interaction are key levers for changing
our situation. By appropriate tactics of *interaction management*, we can modify our responses to the external situation,
modify that interpersonal situation, and even influence others' self-interaction and, hence, their own predispositions to
act.

***Key Principle Twenty-two: To change your life for the bet-
ter, change your interactions for the better.*** All material in
this chapter is an elaboration of this concept.

Exercise 4-B: Act ↔ React Analysis

DIRECTIONS
1. Close your eyes and recall an interpersonal situation
   or interaction for which you are sorry, preferably one
   you really hoped would go right but turned into a
   minor or major disaster.
2. Imagine that your memory is like a videotape and you
   are moving back to the beginning of this incident of
   interaction. Where was it? When was it? Who was
   there? What was happening? What was each participant saying and doing?
3. Now scan the incident from start to finish, replaying
   it in your mind's eye, so to speak. As you observe this
   imaginary videotape of the situation, pay close attention to the actions ↔ reactions going on between you

and the other participants. What did you do or say; what did they do or say in response?

4. Open your eyes and describe the situation and the actions ↔ reactions you observed, both on your part and on the part of the others involved.

5. Preferably going through the situation again in your imagination to help you with the details, analyze what you meant by the things you did and how you interpreted the things others did. Similarly, try to evaluate what the others *actually* meant by what they did and how they interpreted what you did. Look at the *symbolic* interactions. Write a summary of what you ascertain in your journal.

6. Now ask yourself how you could have interpreted the situation differently, acted or reacted differently, so as to help bring about the outcome you desired at the time. Write your answer in detail.

7. Close your eyes, imagine going back to the start of the incident, and "revise" it—imagine acting and reacting as you have considered in step 6 and let yourself feel and notice how the situation changes. Imagine how it could have gone if you had interacted more appropriately or more strategically.

SUGGESTIONS FOR TEAMS

One at a time, team members should explain their situations and what they observed about their interactions upon evaluation. Then, as a group, brainstorm how the sharer might have acted ↔ reacted so as to accomplish the desired outcome and prevent the outcome that did occur. Think of strategies of how the person might have actually dealt with the situation.

Perhaps keep a list of the ways in which some or all of you have made situations go wrong in the past and another list of strategic interaction tactics by which you could make things go right. Discuss your findings and, perhaps, all close your eyes and "revise" your personal situations, imagining what might have transpired if you had employed these tactics at the time.

THE DRAMATURGICAL PERSPECTIVE

This concept of *strategic interaction* owes a great deal to the late Erving Goffman, who even wrote a book by that title. While sharing the same basic perspective as Blumer, Goffman shifted the emphasis in analysis from the meanings that social actors exchange to the strategies by which they deal with their situations.

Goffman saw life as a kind of improvisational theater, taking as his theme Shakespeare's analogy that "All the world's a stage / And all the men and women merely players." His approach is consequently known as the *dramaturgical perspective* and employs the language of the drama when analyzing how people do social things.

We look at social interaction as a performance, a theatrical production. Consequently, we study the actors involved, the audiences to whom their efforts are directed, the roles they enact, the strategies, tactics, and other techniques they employ. We ask, "How do we perform this drama called social life?"

In contrast to Blumer's emphasis on the creation of situations through the exchange of meanings, Goffman adopted the premise that people and groups need to get certain kinds of things done in order to manage the business of living. He treated the context of action—the interpersonal situation—similarly to the way a fiction writer treats the characters' setting.

From this perspective, which is central to my practice of clinical sociology, we view that interpersonal reality is a fabric in which our interactions are the threads. Everything we do (or feel, or think, to the extent that feelings and thoughts are reflected in our social performances) becomes a new strand that changes the situation and, hence, alters the context for our next action or reaction. And for the other person as well.

The situation we create between ourselves is a joint production, but it is also a cause and an effect of our self-interactions (to the degree that a cause-and-effect analysis makes sense here).

While Blumer's type of analysis is enormously insightful and sensitizes us to key features of social interaction, it is also unwieldy and cumbersome. Consequently, most contemporary sociologists who identify with the symbolic interactionist tradition have adopted elements of a dramaturgical approach.

By directing analysis at the action itself, at the theater of social life, Goffman was able to get directly to the question of how people do social things. How do we manage impressions and elicit desired responses from our audiences? How do we enact our various social roles? How do we cope with the various types of situations with which we are confronted?

A lot of people, including social and behavioral scientists, mistakenly suppose that Goffman is hinting that we are all P. T. Barnum frauds and hypocrites putting on a show, that nobody is genuine and everything is a sham. I once asked Goffman about this, and he told me (to my relief) that making the assumption that what we do is "only an act" is nothing more than a methodological ploy. It is a means for making sense out of the ongoing action.

Nevertheless, as my teacher John Lofland has pointed out, it is easy to accuse Goffman and dramaturgical sociologists of going too far in this regard. Critics, he notes, might say that we see strategic consciousness, intent, and savvy where little or none exists. Professor Lofland defends this perspective by saying

> Actions have strategic consequences in, upon, and on a situation regardless of whether anyone in that situation consciously intends those consequences. "Unthinking," "mindless," "habitual," "routine" action does not necessarily lack strategic *significance* (consequence or import) simply because the person performing it does not consciously perceive or intend strategic significance.

What Lofland says is very appropriate for our purposes in this book. After all, one of the central goals of action is to open your eyes to the game of social life. You empower yourself to the extent that you acquire heightened strategic consciousness, increase your savvy, and become more adept with respect to both recognition and use of interaction management tactics.

The concept that the situation is defined by the interactions of participants is central to this approach as well as to Blumer's approach. However, our focus turns to how the social actors bring off their performances rather than the meanings they exchange in the process.

Exercise 4-C: Dramaturgical Analysis

DIRECTIONS
1. Review your notes for Exercise 4-B. Recall the situation you described in your journal. Possibly close your eyes again for a moment and recall an image of the situation in your imagination, just as you did earlier.
2. Go back over your imaginary video of this situation, but this time analyze it in dramaturgical terms: What is the script or story being improvised or acted out here? Who are the actors, what roles do they take, how do they perform those roles—and for which audiences? What strategies, tactics, or techniques are they employing in the course of their performances?
3. Again ask yourself how could you have altered the outcome by changing what you did, only focus on how you could have modified your actual performance. Pretend you are a playwright and rewrite the script in various ways until you feel that you've worked out how you could have been more successful.
4. Perhaps close your eyes and envision the situation again. Imagine going through it all again but, this time, creating a more desirable outcome by doing things differently, by a more strategic and appropriate performance.

SUGGESTIONS FOR TEAMS
Just as in Exercise 4-B, share your situations with one

another and brainstorm strategies and tactics that could more successfully manage such situations in the future. Perhaps everyone could then close their eyes and visualize making the situation go right. Discuss these concepts and how they can be applied to our daily lives.

SELF-FULFILLING PROPHECIES

A lot of sociological concepts have a way of passing into common usage without anyone being aware of their origin. We tend to give a lot of our intellectual stock away, in other words, and then wonder why nobody credits us with having anything to offer. The concept of the *self-fulfilling prophecy* is such a case. I have referred to this concept before in passing. It was introduced in the 1950s by Robert K. Merton, arguably the greatest living sociologist. Merton pointed out that we very commonly make a prophecy about people, events, or ourselves, and then tend to act in accordance with that definition of the situation, so that we end up making it come true by our own (often unconscious) actions.

Generally we think of negative examples of this process. Each of us can think of examples of how self-fulfilling prophecies caused personal and interpersonal disasters. In some ways, the example of Paul given in Chapter One is such a case. He became (at least in his father's eyes) the no-good low achiever he had been labeled. This theory also works at larger scales of social interaction, ranging from plays and movies that close because bad reviews say they won't succeed to the far more invidious examples offered by racism and sexism. Merton says:

> The self-fulfilling prophecy is, in the beginning, a *false* definition of the situation evoking a new behavior which makes the originally false conception come *true*. The specious validity of the self-fulfilling prophecy perpetuates a reign of error. For the prophet will cite the actual course of events as proof that he was right from the very beginning. . . . Yet the spurious evidence often creates a genuine belief. Self-hypnosis through one's own propaganda is not an infrequent phase of the self-fulfilling prophecy.

However, the identical dynamics can be used strategically—for better or worse.

Key Principle Twenty-three: People tend to make definitions of the situation into self-fulfilling prophecies. We have been making use of this principle all along. However, I am restating it to stress its strategic importance. If you can get people to believe that something is true, they will tend to act and react as if it were true, and thus they will tend to make it come true. The same goes for your own self-interactions.

Dramaturgically this is a crucial point. Other people will tend to behave toward you according to what they perceive your role to be. What you project, then, is what you *are* for them. There have been many reported instances of individuals posing as physicians who deceived everyone for years. They look like physicians, talk like physicians, carry themselves like physicians—and so they are accepted as physicians. Their patients and colleagues often have only the highest praise for them. Sometimes they are exposed only when they are nominated for awards or receive promotions.

A lot of practical wisdom supports the contention that the impression you convey to another person in the first few minutes of your first interaction has a lasting impact. How you conduct yourself creates an initial definition of the situation that can become a self-fulfilling prophecy.

There is an art to making a good first impression. I recently met a sociologist, Peter Jessen, who developed a highly successful career-change program based on this approach. His centers train clients in how to perform during job interviews, how to create desired definitions of the situation, and how to get the desired result of a high-level job offer. As Jessen and others have noted often, if a job seeker can establish the definition that he or she belongs in the firm, that he or she provides something that is needed and wanted, that he or she is compatible with the organization in question, the company may even create a position for the person.

Now, if you do not come off that well in your first encounters as a new employee or in a new relationship, this is not necessarily a fatal error. You can often overcome a first impression by an adept performance. I speak from experience.

However, if you trespass on the unstated rules of a social group you are liable to get yourself clobbered. A friend of mine was just invited to leave a position he had taken in a commercial firm for this reason. He'd given up a tenured professorship and moved halfway across the country to try his hand at applied research. But he didn't seem to recognize the importance of displays of loyalty and deference to one's superiors in the corporate world. Very quickly, it seems, he was defined as not being "one of us," so nothing he could do, subsequently, was deemed acceptable. He tried to deal with the behaviors flowing out of their definition of him in a rational way by trying to explain why he did what he did—which only proved that he didn't fit in. The colder and more critical his superiors' communications to him became, the more need he felt to justify himself. It was a losing proposition. A negative definition of the situation won.

In contrast, think of how elections are presently run. If a candidate can get defined as "having momentum" or being a contender, the mass media gives this person lots of attention. People talk about him. They say nice things about him to pollsters. The media pick up on the polls and report how popular he is becoming. Which can become a self-fulfilling prophecy—all the way to the White House.

NONCOMMUNICATION

This chapter has suggested that interaction is the central process of social life, that it shapes our selves and creates the situations with which we must cope. How inevitable is symbolic interaction? Can we go on strike, so to speak, and refuse to engage in a performance?

Can't we just be "genuine"? Can't we just be "ourselves," neither letting anyone else effect us nor affecting anyone else? After all, EST taught that we are only responsible for ourselves, that each of us is totally responsible for our own angle.

This chapter implies something very different. It suggests that we are linked together in a fabric of social communications. It suggests that you cannot opt out of the game, that there is no way to leave the stage. But can you *not* communicate? Can you not perform?

Exercise 4-D: Not Communicating, Part 1

DIRECTIONS
Do steps 1 and 2. Step 3 is optional, but informative.

1. Close your eyes. Try not to communicate with yourself. Don't think or imagine or make any other kind of indications to yourself.
2. Close your eyes. Imagine being in a room with one or more other people, or imagine two or more people in a room by themselves. Now try to visualize these people being together for at least five minutes but *not communicating* in any way—not by words, gestures, body language.
3. Recruit somebody to do this exercise with you. Be together in the same room or place (e.g., outdoors) for at least five minutes and *do not communicate* in any way—no words, no giggles, no facial or bodily gestures. If one of you loses it, the other does not respond in any way.

After each activity, or after completing the activities, think about what happened. What did you learn about the possibility of not communicating? What did you learn about the ways we interact with ourselves, with one another? Write a summary of your findings in your journal along with any implications or speculations you feel are worth noting.

SUGGESTIONS FOR TEAMS
This is a necessary activity. Perform step 3 as a team activity for a preselected time period. Discuss your find-

ings. Now make a list of all the ways in which you found yourself communicating.

Obviously, this was another setup. As Paul Watzlawick, John Weakland, Richard Fisch, and others associated with the Mental Research Institute in Palo Alto, California, have noted:

Key Principle Twenty-four: You cannot not communicate. In a social situation even silence is a message. It's part of the drama.

Exercise 4-E: Not Communicating, Part 2

DIRECTIONS

Do steps 1 and/or 2.

1. Imagine sincerely saying, "I love you" to a parent, sibling, child, or friend and getting the response of silence, no facial expression, and a rigid, "stoney" posture.
2. Recall a time when you reached out to another person with a communication that was important to you and got silence in return.

Answer the following questions for each step:

1. Is this—can this be—truly a nonresponse, or is this a form of strategic interaction, a ploy?
2. What is the meaning of silence and nonresponsiveness in this type of situation? What part does it play in the overall drama? How does it shape the ongoing action?

SUGGESTIONS FOR TEAMS

This is another ideal activity for sharing. For step 1 you might want to stage a "sociodrama." One person take the role of the sayer and the other of the recipient of communication. Decide on what your relationship is and act out step 1. Now, each person who participated should share what it felt like to act out a role in this scenario. Then others in the group should share what they felt and perceived. Discuss the two questions as a group.

If you would like, now share and discuss any experiences relevant to step 2. This can be a very empowering activity.

If you cannot *not* communicate, your communications help to structure our mutual situation—which, in turn, feeds back onto your life and quality of experience. Step 2 in Exercise 4-E was meant to sensitize you to the consequences of noncommunication by having you take the role of the other. Putting yourself in the role of the other is not entirely altruistic; it is also strategic since "what goes around comes around." You are stuck with the effects of your performances. It leads us to the golden rule, "Do unto others as you would have them do unto you."

This rule, by the way, is one of the arguments we can make for the scientific necessity of what is known as a humanist ethical system: putting human beings and human values first, before *instrumental* values such as profit or efficiency. That we consider this to be a *humanist* ethic might come as a shock to some.

At any rate, it is a major reason why I do not intend this book to be used as a manual for how to intimidate or exploit other people. If anything, this manual is intended to sabotage any such attempts.

MULTILEVEL COMMUNICATION

There is another level of social interaction that merits discussion. To employ a distinction drawn by Erving Goffman, whenever human beings are in the presence of one another they communicate at two levels. The messages they overtly express in their words and gestures is the first level.

They also emit a whole range of messages at an unstated

level: by means of intonations, facial expressions, posture, body language, even how they dress and the props they employ. In my studies of religious conversion, for example, new Christians told me how they carried around Bibles to discourage old dope-smoking friends.

Only some of the communications we convey are truly deliberate (whether or not they are strategic). For example, Condon and Sander have demonstrated the interaction phenomenon known as *entrainment*. Through microanalysis of sound films they have shown that when individuals converse, both the listener and the speaker are moving in tune to the words of the speakers. (I referred to their study earlier, with regard to maternal–infant interaction.)

This example suggests that the person who adopts a rigid posture and facial expression is actively blocking a normal response, which is why you are likely to perceive this and respond to it as a negative communication. In fact, noted social psychiatrist R. D. Laing suggests that interacting human beings are continually giving messages about their relationship to one another. We learn to pretend that we do not do this, to ignore this level of communication. Ignoring such messages is necessary in playing the role of a normal person in social life.

Gregory Bateson made a similar observation. He says that when we communicate we normally do so on at least two levels: We make a statement (verbal or nonverbal) and indicate how to classify the statement. This indicator is of a different logical type than the communication it modifies.

For example, I would have my introductory sociology students explore the tacit rules of everyday life by violating them. They might, for example, walk down the "wrong" side of the stairway between classes. Other people would bump into them, often becoming quite irate.

When one of my students was performing this experiment a huge gorilla type ran into him. This large young man didn't apologize or move. Instead, he initiated the sequence of behaviors that indicated he was angry.

My student smiled.

The gorilla type stared at my student for a moment, then exhaled and the tension left his posture. He smiled and walked up the stairs.

That little smile redefined the situation from a provocation into a prank or joke. It is a strategic communication at one level, and a classifier at another level. The smile told the gorilla how to interpret the situation. To employ this classifier was an example of what Goffman calls an audience management strategy.

Bateson feels that this concept of multilevel communication is crucial. He points out that it is a basic feature of all "play"—even among animals. When they play, puppies engage in fighting behavior but signal that "it is just a game," for example, by tail wagging. Kids do the same thing, by tone of voice, body language, and so on.

Exercise 4-F: Classifiers

DIRECTIONS

For working by yourself: See how many ways you can say aloud, "I love you." Alter tone, pacing, intonation, facial expression. What meanings does each way of saying these words convey to you? What do classifiers do in this regard? If you are really ambitious, why not jot down a list of classifiers and their effect on the meaning communicated by these words.

For working with teams: Working in groups of up to five, each person in turn should say, "I love you" in a different way; then everyone else should explain what they felt was conveyed by that particular way. Perhaps see who can think of the most ways to do this. Then discuss the concept of classifiers and perhaps compose a glossary or list of the ways one can modify the meaning of these three words.

This type of communication is generally known as *nonverbal* communication. Although the term most often evokes the idea of physical gestures, body language, and so forth, it is sometimes extended to include all the aspects of speech acts besides the words themselves.

Which brings us back to the point that interaction is a multilevel, multilayer process. The more aware you become of the structure of interaction, and the more adept you become at strategic interaction at these different levels, the more freedom and ability you have to create your preferred realities.

Key Tactic Four: Attend to what is expressed verbally and also to what is being given off nonverbally. One of Milton Erickson's "secrets" was his amazing adeptness at picking up and playing with the nonverbal messages being given off by other people. He sensitized therapists to the key importance of this level of communication, in particular the mixed messages our clients often give off.

For example, hypnotherapists commonly notice that their clients might be saying one thing at a verbal level and another thing at a nonverbal level. A subject may tell you she wants to lose weight but at the same time she is shaking her head as if to say "No." This indicates conflicting stated and unstated preferences.

Sensitivity to other people's nonverbal performances can give you an extraordinary degree of insight into their meanings and intentions. Particularly when you detect unspoken messages, this sensitivity can often give you strategic leverage over interactions. That is what body language is all about.

On the other hand, to the extent that you develop strategic control over your own nonverbal performances, you open new playing fields for yourself. A true master, like Erickson, could influence people to do things by strategic use of his nonverbal behaviors.

At the very least, by giving the right nonverbal signals you can almost instantly establish credibility or authority in your audience's mind. Those who train people in public speaking or business presentations stress the importance of nonverbal performance supporting verbal performance. How do you learn to become adept at this behavior? I don't know; that is something you will have to discover for yourself. What I can tell you is that the principle of "practice, practice, practice" is essential. Only by doing can you become able to do anything easily, naturally, effectively, and without having to think about it. It is only by focusing on the tacit "given off" parts of these communications that you can make them conscious and gain power over them. Which calls for this activity:

Exercise 4-G: Nonverbal Communication

DIRECTIONS

This exercise can be done privately or in a team. Ideally you should do it both ways, even if you are working on your own. First do the private form when you are reading this chapter; then do the team form at your next meeting or when you can find a friend (or several friends).

Individual form:
1. Stand in front of the biggest mirror you have.
2. As you watch yourself in the mirror, do silly and/or outrageous things with your body and your face. Get crazy! Be childish! Interact with your mirror image and have fun.
3. Continue to do step 2 for at least five minutes.
4. After you're done, write down your experiences and what you learned about nonverbal communication. (Yeah, I know you've got to figure out the connection. That's the whole idea.)
5. Variations: Repeat this exercise as often as you'd like. Perhaps try different types of body language, posture, demeanor, and so forth. See how each feels on you and what it "means" to you. Another variation I do, without mirrors generally, is to try on somebody else's body language—hold my face or body the way they do and see what it tells me.

Team form:
1. Good giver
2. Good recipient
3. Poor giver
4. Poor recipient

These are four roles. Teams can work in pairs or as a whole or somewhere in between. Preferably, list these four roles on a large sheet of paper or blackboard and post them where everybody can see them. Decide on some way to assign one of these roles to each team member to start, as long as there is an approximately equal division between "good" and "poor" roles. You may also want to assign a time-keeper or set a stopwatch to let everyone know when five, ten, and fifteen minutes have passed.

Rules for this activity:
1. Everyone must participate for the duration.
2. There is to be no talking, no vocal noises, no use of written words, and so on.

Instructions for play:
1. At the agreed upon start, everyone begin silently interacting according to your interpretation of your own role.
2. At the end of every five minute period, participants are to select different roles from those they have taken previously in this activity.
3. When you are done you can begin talking again. Discuss what the experience was like and what you learned about nonverbal communication.

NONCOERCIVE PERSUASION

Immediately prior to becoming involved in hypnosis research and practice around 1976, I had been doing graduate research on cults and new religious movements. I was struck by a perception that these groups were out there, on the open market, hawking proprietary technologies for personal transformation. "Come to my Guru, he's got the way." "No, no, join us, we've got a better way."

Toward the end of my graduate studies, I stumbled upon the hypnosis literature. In hopes of gainful employment (at a time when the market for new faculty had collapsed), I took a position with a franchise outfit that offered to train me in hypnotic techniques. I ended up with a bunch of unexceptional tapes that I could memorize but that taught me virtually nothing about hypnotic strategy or tactics. So I went to a medical school library and hit the stacks.

It was like opening a book and realizing that you've read the same story before. Here was good old symbolic interaction. The major difference was the strategic manner in which interaction processes were being managed. Hypnosis seemed to be a general case of the kinds of things I'd been observing in my cults research. Now, this phenomenon of hypnosis had been totally neglected in the sociological literature. No doubt, this neglect was because hypnosis is "obviously" a psychological phenomenon in which (as I suggested earlier) it appears that a subject is placed into an altered state of consciousness by a hypnotist. In this state, susceptible subjects may be guided by suggestion to do things we don't expect people to normally do: hallucinate on command, feel no pain in surgery, become unable to control body parts, or become able to perform what normally would be involuntary behaviors on cue.

I discovered that this asocial paradigm was no longer accepted by many psychologists. As early as 1950, Theodore Sarbin criticized the "state" model, arguing that hypnosis was best viewed from the perspective of social–psychological role theory. He continued to develop and expand this view until, in a 1984 review of his half-century's research career, Sarbin concluded that hypnosis can best be understood from the dramaturgical perspective discussed in this chapter. Sarbin views hypnosis as a social interaction in which the subject is being guided and coached by the hypnotist to give a convincing performance of being a hypnotized person. This behavior occurs within a specially structured social situation that is deliberately identified as *hypnosis*, in which the subject is asked to focus attention exclusively on what the hypnotist is saying.

This stream of ideas, images, and instructions from the hypnotist tends to rely on metaphors to a much greater extent than does normal conversation. Furthermore, in order to perform as directed, you are urged to "complete" these metaphors by engaging in a process of "as if" imagining. The hypnotist says, "You are becoming very, very sleepy" and you are supposed to let yourself feel as if you were falling deeply asleep. You are not merely to imagine feeling asleep but are to enact a performance of falling asleep.

At the same time, hypnotic communications imply that you are to ignore or suppress any of the usual classifiers by which you announce to yourself and your audience that this state is only make-believe, that you are only performing a role, or that the role you are performing is not your "natural" or "normal" self. The stage hypnotist tells you you're a rooster, and you strut around the stage clucking and crowing (assuming, of course, that you are "a good subject," which is a role in itself).

Ted Barber, another leading contributor to "nonstate," has conducted a thirty-year series of experimental studies demonstrating that the core phenomena of hypnosis are the subject's acts of thinking, feeling, and imagining along with suggested themes. For Barber, the hypnotist's role is primarily to elicit your active cooperation and to supply appropriate themes and images.

Putting this material together with what I learned about religious conversion and the broad range of contemporary psychotherapies, I realized that I was looking at a basic social process. *Noncoercive persuasion* not only accounts for what happens in therapy, hypnosis, and religious conversion but it offers a paradigm for how we can modify our own self-interactions and influence others to modify theirs. Which is, of course, why we are talking about it.

People don't have to be forced into believing things. They only have to be set up properly and given the right suggestions and they will proceed to make the beliefs real for themselves. That's how everyday hypnosis works, how therapeutic and stage hypnosis work, and how creative self-hypnosis can work. This same process is also seen in the types of religious conversion I studied, in effective stage and movie performances, in effective sales presentations and political rhetoric; that is, in virtually all cases of effective interpersonal influence and persuasion.

You can examine noncoercive persuasion on two levels. The first level is self-persuasion, which involves precisely what the exercises in this book have been training you to do more effectively: thinking, feeling, and imagining along with suggested themes, images, or words. If you do the exercises with enough involvement and for long enough, what begins as something you are aware of as only a possible reality starts to seem a tangible reality. This imagined reality then becomes one of the facts influencing your actions and reactions.

The second level is social influence. At its most general, this term refers to all the processes by which interacting individuals and groups seek to influence one another in order to adopt and act in line with their own definitions of the situation. This behavior can be deliberate and purposeful or it can merely be a by-product of everyday life conduct.

For our purposes here, we can concentrate on *strategic communications* used in deliberate attempts to bring about such influence. The most effective strategic communication strategies appear to be those that get you to automatically and compulsively think or fantasize about a suggested reality. For example, when a definition of the situation is so compellingly presented that you cannot (or do not try to) stop imagining how it would be if it were an objective reality.

Exercise 4-H: Persuasive Interactions

DIRECTIONS

1. Recall a time when you were persuaded by another person to do something you initially did not want to do. The more dramatic your "change of mind," the better.

2. Recall in as much detail as possible what that other person said and did in the attempt to "bring you around." Recall the things he or she tried that *did not* influence you in the intended direction (or turned you off or stiffened your resistance) and the things that *did* influence you.

    Hint: You might do better if you close your eyes and let yourself relive the situation in your "mind's eye."

3. Make a list of the tactics that were persuasive or effective for you and another list of those that were not persuasive and might have been counterproductive.

4. Go over your "persuasive" list and rank each tactic from most persuasive (1) to least.

5. Now ask yourself, in retrospect, whether you feel it was a good thing that you were persuaded to go along in this situation.

    • If your answer is "Yes," close your eyes and imagine or write down how you could have been persuaded more easily, effectively, and quickly.

    • If your answer is "No," close your eyes and imagine or write down how you could have blocked the attempt at influencing you so that you would not have been persuaded. Be as concrete as possible, considering specific strategies and tactics. Write these down for yourself.

6. Now repeat steps 1–5, but if you initially selected a situation in which you are now *glad* you were persuaded, this time choose a case in which you are now *sorry* about going along with it, or vice versa.

7. Write out your answers to these questions: What are your "buttons" with respect to persuading you to do things? What are your vulnerabilities in this regard? What steps can you take to avoid being persuaded to do things you will regret later?

SUGGESTIONS FOR TEAMS

This is another excellent group exercise. Each of you should do step 1. If you are a two-person team, one should select a "glad" and the other a "sorry." If you have a larger group, you can ask for volunteers, or in some other fashion select two or three cases, at least one "glad" and one "sorry." The person whose example is being used should relate the story using as much concrete detail as possible (perhaps have the others close their eyes and relate the story in a way that makes it real to them). Then do steps 3, 4, and 5 as brainstorms and discuss how these steps relate to the material discussed.

STRATEGIC COMMUNICATION

The goal of bringing about self-persuasion in oneself or in other people can be facilitated in many ways. One stratagem is use of sensory and sensual—suggestive—language of the sort employed in Technique One and in much contemporary hypnosis. By undercutting rational thought about a subject and going directly to imagining and experiencing a possible reality, the need for long, complicated hypnotic inductions is bypassed.

This same principle can be applied in your attempts to get. somebody to see things your way. This can be in the context of getting the other person to take your role, so that he or she better understands what you are feeling or doing and why. It can also be applied in the context of seeking to persuade the other person to engage in a line of conduct you are suggesting.

Key Tactic Five: To facilitate self-persuasion, focus on concrete, sensory images. A second stratagem is to build an image of what benefits cooperation with your proposed line of action offers the other person. What are it's *consequences* and what is desirable about those consequences? These consequences do not have to be built in, that is, part of the way the situation would actually work.

Key Tactic Six: You can create causal or associative linkages by suggestion. This tactic is a basic one of noncoercive persuasion. By defining the situation so that the person is convinced that if *this* occurs then *that* will be a necessary outcome, you can create self-fulfilling prophecy. Traditional hypnosis works this way: If you are hypnotized by me and I tell you that I am giving you a posthypnotic suggestion that you will not eat cookies, then, after I end the session, you are likely to enact the suggestion *because you believe that you have no other choice but to obey me.*

This same basic pattern can be used to make a specific future behavior more appealing to a person. Consumer advertising, of course, employs this device—often accompanied by concrete, sensory imagery. Notice how advertising can link things together by communication and presentation that have no intrinsic relationship. Television ads, for example, tend to insinuate that using virtually any kind of product from an automobile to a new laundry soap will result in sexual gratification and/or adulation from others.

Let's make a distinction between legitimate interpersonal influence and *manipulation*. Manipulation involves the use of covert techniques to trick a person into doing things your way without making a choice to do so and without awareness of being persuaded. Manipulation is the theater of political and social movement propaganda and underhanded interpersonal games of all kinds.

My bias against manipulative conduct should be clear, although it is sometimes difficult to draw the line between manipulation and (what I would consider to be) acceptable influence. I am more inclined to view conduct as manipulative if I don't like the person responsible for the behavior or the objectives toward which it is being directed.

I feel that it is proper to create linkages that create situations facilitating mutual benefit or that, at least, have no detrimental consequences for the other party. For example, you might define a desired line of conduct as leading to (or maximizing the probability of) a future situation that the other person would identify as meeting his or her own objectives.

One way to do this is to build up a detailed image of the future that implies cooperation in the past (which begins, of course, in the present). This can best be done by using suggestive language as discussed. Another way is to focus on *process* and allow the other person (or yourself if you are working at that level) to supply the details of what the goals are and what the preferred future might be. For example, I worked as a youth supervisor in a summer program designed to place teenagers in jobs and give them some successful work experience. I quickly realized that it was going to be difficult to inculcate proper work skills in my charges. I explained to the youths that it was not my place to tell them what they should do or what they should want out of life. But I could show them how they could get whatever *they* wanted out of life. And the first thing they needed to do was to learn how to hold down a summer job. They were able to relate to that.

Exercise 4-I: Persuasion

DIRECTIONS

This activity is best suited for teams, although it can be done as mindwork by oneself. However, if you are working on your own, it would be very valuable to borrow a friend.

This exercise should be done in two parts.

A. *Individual mindwork*
    1. Close your eyes and recall the last time you tried

to persuade somebody to do something you felt
was really important to you.

2. Remember—perhaps visualize—what you did
and said and what the other person did and said
in response. All the actions ↔ reactions.

3. Think about the outcome. Did you get what you
want? What did you get?

4. Are there other ways in which you might have
gone about it? Imagine that you are back in the
persuasion situation again and imagine trying
these different alternatives. What would be the
advantages and disadvantages of the various tactics and strategies? What would be their outcomes?

5. Open your eyes and write in your journal at least
five things that you have learned from this exercise.

B. *Team exercise*. Work in pairs. One takes the role of
the persuader and the other is the persuadee. You can
do this exercise in two ways. The most challenging is
to try to persuade your persuadee right now to do
something that your persuadee is going to try not to
do (for example, laughing or saying a certain phrase).
The other way is to recall a situation in which you,
the persuader, were unable to persuade another person to do something you felt was appropriate, important.

1. Make an agreement about the game rules—what
you will be doing, for how long, and what limits
apply (if any). The maximum length of time
should be about five minutes.

2. Either sit or stand facing one another at a comfortable distance.

3. When the persuadee says "Start," the persuader
begins the persuasion attempt, using any or all
available methods of noncoercive persuasion.

5. As soon as the persuader succeeds or when time
is out, the persuadee says "Stop."

6. The persuadee tells the persuader what the ex-

perience was like, which tactics or implementations of tactics were most effective, which were counterproductive, and so on.

7. The persuader then shares his or her perspectives on what transpired, what it felt like, what was easy, what was hard.
8. Briefly discuss ways in which the persuader could be more effective.
9. Repeat steps 1–8, although the discussion can be briefer this time.
10. Now switch roles, the persuader becoming the persuadee, and repeat steps 1–8 twice, as before.
11. If time permits, share what you have learned from doing this activity.

ASSERTIVENESS

The concept of *assertion* is implicit in the idea of empowering your interactions: You have the right to determine your actions ↔ reactions for yourself. You do not have to play along with any person's attempt to cajole you or force you into surrendering the right to have and to communicate your own definitions of the situation.

Key Principle Twenty-five: You have a right to your own definitions and performances. Assertiveness is not, however, the same thing as aggressiveness. Being aggressive involves encroaching on the other person's rights. The core principle of responsible assertion is *reciprocity*. That is, it involves standing up for your interactional rights (e.g., not to be interrupted, rushed, dominated, intimidated, imposed upon, or ignored). But assertiveness also involves being a responsible interactant who is respectful of the rights of others.

I suspect that a lot of the exercises in this chapter have illustrated ways in which a person can be nonassertive and the consequences. Nonassertion never pays. You don't get what you want; you only get hurt.

Exercise 4-J: Nonassertion

DIRECTIONS
1. Think about times when you have really wanted to express your feelings to another person but held back for any or all of the following reasons:
   - You wanted to be "polite."
   - You wanted to avoid coming off as overly aggressive.
   - You felt that you shouldn't have those feelings.
   - You were concerned about what would happen if you acted assertively in that particular situation.
2. What were the consequences of your nonassertion in each case?
3. How might you have acted assertively in each situation, and what might the outcome have been had you effectively and appropriately done so?
4. Now define and distinguish the following for yourself:
   - Genuine consideration for others versus being "polite."
   - Assertion versus aggression.
   - Genuine helpfulness versus nonassertion.

SUGGESTIONS FOR TEAMS
Do steps 1 through 4 together as a group exercise, perhaps splitting the examples among yourselves and brainstorming ideas for assertive behavior in steps 3 and 4.

Although nonassertion is almost always counterproductive, like noncommunication, it is often an interaction strategy. By not asserting yourself you attempt to make a hidden bargain with the other person. As pioneering assertion trainers Lange and Jakubowski state:

> A hidden bargain occurs when a person sacrifices some important rights or preferences, expecting that the other person will do something explicit in return, but without telling the other person what is expected in exchange.

They go on to suggest that you can check to see whether you are being genuinely considerate or striking a hidden bargain by asking yourself, "Will I feel used if the other person doesn't do what I expect him to do?" If your answer is in the affirmative, you are being nonassertive rather than polite.

Assertion training is worthy of a book itself; in fact, many books have been written and many courses and workshops are offered on the subject. Let's conclude this chapter with one of the best-known assertion techniques, one that has proven to be of enormous value in helping people communicate genuinely to one another without provoking disasters or stumbling over value judgments:

Key Tactic Seven: Use "I" messages to facilitate positive interaction. Perhaps the easiest way to explain this tactic is to contrast it with "you" messages, for example, "You really hurt me when you say that." Such a communication, in effect, paints the other person into a corner and forces him or her to either admit to an evil intention, defend what was done, or get angry and do something worse.

An "I" message referring to the identical situation might be something like, "I feel really awful when you say that to me." Notice that it places the responsibility for your own feelings on you, does not accuse the other person of harboring an ill intention, and points to the specific conduct that you are seeking to protest.

This strategy was first introduced around 1970 by Thomas Gordon in the context of parent assertiveness training. He suggests a somewhat more complex, four-part formula:

1. "When . . ." (you describe the other person's conduct)
2. "The effects are : . ." (concretely describe how the other person's conduct affects your life or feelings)
3. "I feel . . ." (describe how you feel)
4. "I'd prefer . . ." (describe what you want, instead).

Gordon, Lange, and Jakubowski suggest that you begin with this formula until you are comfortable using it and then tinker with it. Steps 3 and 4 can be optional. You can also play with this formula to make it better fit your own personal style.

This stratagem, by the way, also applies to your self-interactions. By phrasing things to yourself as explained, you can avoid getting into a mindset of blaming other people for your own feelings and responses. It creates appropriate definitions of the situation and keeps you focused on the parts of situations you are responsible for and can, therefore, creatively manage.

The major point of the "I" message technique is to convey your definitions and preferences without putting your foot in your mouth or putting your foot in the other person's mouth. It is an example of how you can strategically interact in order to communicate effectively and get your needs met. It also helps you put your relationship with the other person onto the right track, which is the topic of our next chapter.

SUMMARY

This chapter has extended our microsociological analysis to your interactions with other people. In fact, it has suggested that social interaction is the key to understanding and changing our lives. We have looked at Blumer's *symbolic interactionism* and Goffman's *dramaturgical perspective* and we have drawn their implications for creative self-management. Somewhat paradoxically, I have suggested that their basic implication is that the key to self-management is managing your social interactions. Toward this end we have looked in some depth at Goffman's concept of performance, at classifiers, and at nonverbal communication. I described my concept of *noncoercive persuasion* and explained how this concept relates to the ways in which you can employ strategic communication to better manage your interactions. We concluded with a discussion of assertion as a positive tool for creatively managing both your self and your social interactions.

Our discussion looked at the following Key Principles:

TWENTY: Action ↔ Reaction = Interaction.

TWENTY-ONE: A situation is defined by the interaction of participants.

TWENTY-TWO: To change your life for the better, change your interactions for the better.

TWENTY-THREE: People tend to make definitions of the situation into self-fulfilling prophecies.

TWENTY-FOUR: You cannot *not* communicate.

TWENTY-FIVE: You have a right to your own definitions and performances.

Four new Key Tactics were also introduced:

FOUR: Attend to what is expressed verbally and also to what is being given off nonverbally.

FIVE: To facilitate self-persuasion, focus on concrete, sensory images.

SIX: You can create causal or associative linkages by suggestion.

SEVEN: Use "I" messages to facilitate positive interaction.

Technique Four: Assertion and Creative Self-Hypnosis

DIRECTIONS
There are two parts to Technique Four.

PART 1. *Assertiveness.* Every day for one week make at least one of the following types of assertive statements and record your feelings before, during, and after making the statement. In your journal write what happened and what you learned. Be sure to perform at least one assertion of each type during the week.

Hint: You can use "I" messages for all three.

1. Make a request to another person to do or give you something you want.
2. Give somebody else an unsolicited compliment.
3. Assert a negative response to something another person says or does.

Directed CSH: Preparation for assertion. You should also begin to use your CSH directly, to prepare yourself for action in the outer world. We will call this *Directed CSH.* The only way in which Directed CSH differs from the Basic CSH exercise you have been doing is that it adds a step in which you can do *Tactical Mindwork.* For this week, you'll be focusing on assertiveness and strategic interaction, so you will be employing some tactics during your self hypnosis sessions that will facilitate this work.

Directed CSH

1. Tense/relax.
2. Imagine place.
3. Steer "up" or "down."
4. Visualize present.
5. Do tactical mindwork and/or scan future.
6. Set mind.
7. Open eyes. Tell yourself, "That's it, end of sesssion."

The tactical mindwork you will be employing at this time involves *imaginative rehearsal.* Before you try to use any of the assertive statements I suggest that you first *rehearse the performance* in your mind.

What you will do is pretty much the same as you have been doing up to step 5. Go through step 4 and briefly scan your present situation, omitting the future visualization. Instead do the following tactical mindwork:

1. Visualize a situation, preferably the real situation in which you anticipate making the assertion. Where would that be? Who would be there? What would be happening?
2. Imagine making an assertive statement. Practice doing so in the theater of your imagination.
3. How does it "play"? What happens? How do you feel about it? What did you feel? Did it seem right for you? Did it feel like it was going the way you intended?

4. Run through the assertive statement at least a few more times. Perhaps try different statements, different ways of presenting the statements. Imagine using different nonverbal presentations. Treat this practice like a real rehearsal or sports practice, trying out different "plays," settling on one or perhaps a couple of alternatives, and then practicing them until you feel *comfortable* and *confident.*
5. Now, as part of "setting your mind," tell yourself what you choose to do and how you intend to do it.

Note: It is normally only feasible to practice the first two assertive statements in advance. However, if you know of a situation in which the last one will be appropriate, by all means practice that one in advance.

PART 2. *Directed creative self-hypnosis and on-the-spot variant.* From now on, we'll refer to your basic self-hypnosis exercise as the CSH exercise. You have had experience using both an "up" form of the exercise and a "down" form. From this week on, select which form you'd like to use at the time of each session. Continue giving yourself at least a brief session in the morning to start off your day and one in the evening to relax yourself, to integrate what you learned and accomplished during the day, and so forth. It is a good idea to make this session last at least fifteen minutes in order to obtain a relaxation response.

On-the-spot variant [beginning quick CSH]. This week you will work with an introductory form of Quick Creative Self-Hypnosis. This is generally the same as your basic CSH exercise, only much briefer.

Introductory Quick CSH

1. Quickly tense/relax.
2. Flash place.
3. Steer "up" or "down."

4. Briefly scan present.
5. Mentally rehearse.
6. Set mind.
7. Open eyes. Tell yourself, "That's it, end of session."

Special instructions:
1. Rather than do a full tense/relax, you can simply tense and relax your bottom muscles (known as a *kegel* or *perineal retraction* exercise) or just squeeze your shoulder blades together and perhaps tense your back and fists for a moment. Then "flash" your magical place or centering point—think about it for a moment, let it fly through your mind, just recall it.
2. After briefly scanning your present, mentally rehearse what you intend to do and then end the session.
3. Use the Introductory Quick CSH *immediately before you enter the real-world situation and deliver the assertive statement.* Even at first, it should only take about thirty seconds to complete. It is particularly important and helpful to do this immediately before asserting a negative response to something the other person says or does. If necessary, just *imagine* that you are doing the Quick CSH for a moment or two before you respond to the other person; this is equivalent to counting to three before you respond.

SUGGESTIONS FOR TEAMS
Part I is great for group practice. Form pairs. One member is the first practicer. The practicer selects a situation and briefly sketches the scene and characters for the partner. Then role-play the situation: the partner taking the role of the object of the assertive statement and the practicer playing himself or herself giving the statement. Run through it once. Then share your responses, think about how the practicer can improve the implementation, and run through it once or twice more. Then switch roles. Ideally, each team should work through each type of assertive statement.

FIVE

Positive Relationships

Why don't *you* start this chapter?

Exercise 5-A: Ken and Barbie

DIRECTIONS

Read the following:

Ken goes to the health club and bumps into Barbie. Literally. Ken says, "Hey, I'm sorry. I wasn't looking where I was going."

Barbie, glaring, says, "You idiot, why don't. . . ." But then she recognizes Ken. "Oh, it's you. How's that little brunette, uh, Tammy?"

The jerk is smirking like the cat that ate the canary, she thinks.

"Look, why don't we go up to the juice bar and talk," he says. *Maybe I can get her to tell me why she stopped seeing me,* he thinks.

"Why?" Barbie sneers, *so you can try and talk your way back into my pants?*

I keep forgetting what a bitch she can be, Ken thinks and drapes his arm across her shoulder, feels her tension, massages her neck muscles. "But, baby, you know I love you."

"Be still my heart," she says, smiling sarcastically, flutters her eyelashes at him, turns and walks away. Ken is left wondering where he went wrong.

1. Evaluate what is going on in this story.
2. Define *relationship* in your journal.
3. Answer these questions:
   a. What is a good relationship?
   b. What is a bad relationship?
   c. What makes a relationship good or bad?

SUGGESTIONS FOR TEAMS

After discussing your answers to the questions above, you might want to do some *sculpture*. This term denotes silent, wordless role-playing:

1. Break into groups of two or three.
2. Model (either in pantomime or as if you were statues frozen in time) first a good/positive relationship and then a bad/negative relationship. Perhaps group members can suggest relationships to sculpt from their own personal experiences.
3. Discuss your experiences and what you learned from the exercise.

Obviously we've caught our protagonists somewhere in the middle of a story. As Harry Cohen would put it, we can see that their actions ↔ reactions are flowing along a well-grooved track.

Ken and Barbie have clearly interacted before. Their present interaction is merely the latest encounter in a series. The situation that their actions ↔ reactions define is another scene in a bad relationship.

Goffman termed a situation of interaction between strangers an *encounter*. As social actors encounter one another repeatedly, they build up a pattern or "track" of interaction. They begin to form expectations for how each of them will act and react. That is, they begin to negotiate and establish their respective *roles*. With repetition, they become accustomed to interacting in certain ways, along certain tracks.

Thus, tacitly accepted rules for conduct, known as *norms*, emerge. Norms are created in interaction but take on a reality of their own. They become social facts, which then influence the ongoing action.

Ken and Barbie are no longer strangers. If not exactly friends or lovers, they have become acquaintances. They have a *relationship*. We have gone a step beyond interaction, to the concept of relationships as grooved tracks of actions and reactions and of *social structure* as a general term for the web of relationships in our life situations. Social structure is viewed as a transpersonal reality (i.e., exists at a higher level of logical type than individual human beings and their interactions).

THE SOCIOLOGICAL IMAGINATION

What we have discovered here is that the personal troubles and triumphs of individuals are tied to larger, social, structural realities. This is an example of what C. Wright Mills (yet another famous, dead hero of mine) called the *sociological imagination:*

> The sociological imagination enables us to grasp history and biography and the relations between the two within society. That is its task and its promise. . . . By means of the sociological imagination . . . men now hope to grasp what is going on in the world, and to understand what is happening in themselves as minute points of the intersections of biography and history within society.

Like Blumer, Mills recognizes that we have a part in shaping our society and its history, but he stresses the far greater degree to which the variety of person we are, the situations we face, and the ways in which we deal with our situations are "made by society and by its historical push and shove." Thirty years ago he wrote:

> Consider marriage. Inside a marriage a man and a woman may experience personal troubles, but when the divorce rate dur-

ing the first four years of marriage is 250 out of every 1,000, this is an indication of a structural issue having to do with the institutions of marriage and the family and other institutions that bear upon them.

Let's get back to our soap opera starring Ken and Barbie. It raises a key question about relationships. Look at the story again. Does the social structure as it shapes and forms their ongoing relationship prompt them to interact in this way, or does their interacting in this way create and perpetuate a bad relationship? Or both or neither? Are we asking the right question?

I hope to convince you in this chapter that it is *not* the right question, that these are *complementary* perspectives and that our accustomed cause-and-effect analysis is generally not a useful way of approaching human affairs.

Blumer would argue that Ken and Barbie's interactions *are* the relationship, so they are free to change it. "Macro"-oriented social scientists would argue that their conduct flows out of their relationship, and that their relationship itself reflects what is occurring in the larger society. Both perspectives, I believe are true.

This evaluation strategy of accepting what appears to be mutually exclusive, contradictory definitions of the situation as true is a key principle of the New Physics, known as *complementarity*. Niels Bohr conceptualized complementarity as the only way to deal with the fact that, depending on the type of experiment you conduct and how you look at it, light can be described either as a kind of wave or as a kind of particle (photon). Bohr proposed that both statements were true; they were *complementary,* in that a complete description of how light behaves required looking at it from both angles, so to speak.

Key Principle Twenty-six: Complementarity often gives you the best handle on things. In evaluating the conduct of human beings, this translates into the idea that you need to look at people both as individual social actors and as parts of a larger social structure. Take another look at Ken and Barbie's interactions.

Notice the sexism permeating Ken's behavior: For example, the way he seeks to assert dominance over Barbie by putting his arm around her, invading her space. Of course, she's being hostile, giving off a lot of unspoken messages and making a lot of value judgments about Ken's intentions. This example may have something to say about the relationships between men and women today. Notice also that Barbie's aggressive behavior would have been far less likely in the 1960s than today. Her conduct has clearly been influenced by the Women's Movement of the 1970s. The fact that they run into one another at a coed health club is a direct consequence of the fitness boom of the 1980s.

Careful evaluation shows that you cannot naively blame the divorce rate on the selfishness of individuals, or the rising rate of teenage pregnancy on a lack of self-discipline. And you can't explain the drug epidemic of the late 1980s by saying that drug users have "addictive personalities" or lack willpower. The crucial question in all such instances is, "What is going on in the larger society that explains these things?" But how does this relate to self-hypnosis? you might ask. As I have stressed, effective problem resolution and effective action, generally, depends on an accurate evaluation of the situation.

By looking at the way in which historical and societal factors impinge upon your life and relationships, you can sort out what's happening. I am not suggesting that insight will cure your woes, but, rather, that recognizing the degree to which your troubles stem from your own and other people's response to the larger social world helps you avoid value judging the other person. It tips you off to the fact that it is senseless to get hung up about the meaning of another person's behavior and probably incorrect to imagine that he or she is specifically out to get you in some way.

To understand Ken and Barbie's story, you really need to have a grasp of Ken and Barbie's world and times. By placing the specific situation into its context, you get a far better idea of what is occurring.

By attaining a deeper understanding of the situation, you get a sense of perspective that allows you to empathize with the people in it. By getting into their heads, so to speak, you can better understand why *they* think they are doing what they are doing. This, in turn, gives you a better sense of where the points of leverage are and about what you can do that can make a difference.

In our example, it would be easy to label Ken as a male chauvinist pig and assume that everything negative about his and Barbie's relationship is his fault. However, he's been hypnotized by postnatal suggestion (and probably by hearing his own lines too often). He means no harm, whether or not he has caused any, and he is genuinely puzzled as to why Barbie no longer wishes to be intimate with him.

And, what is more, Barbie is not totally free from responsibility for their negative relationship, either. As I suggested, she comes on a bit too heavily to describe her as assertive. Rather, her interactions with Ken are at once aggressive and nonassertive. This reflects some of the confusion many women feel about relationships today, in part because they were raised to be nice little girls and find themselves in a society where they are expected to compete according to the old boy rules. The sociological imagination teaches us compassion, even for those we detest. It shows us that we are not responsible for the situations that shape us, nor are we to blame for being shaped by our social lives. We, like the people in the movie, *Network*, can open our windows and shout, "We're mad as hell and we're not going to take it anymore!"

Key Principle Twenty-seven: You're not to blame for becoming a victim, but you are free to stop being victimized. Barbie seems to have decided that enough is enough, that in her best judgment she has no alternative but to break off her relationship with Ken. She has decided to take control of her life.

Ken's behavior certainly suggests that he is not about to change his act. She may be far from perfect, but who isn't? Whatever her faults, she seems to be handling the situation with some finesse. Notice, for example, that she doesn't cause a scene or try to change him or show him the error of his ways. She understands that people virtually never solve their relationship problems by "having a discussion" or "talking them out." They only start fights that way. So she just shrugs and walks away.

THE TWO HUMAN FLAVORS

I did not randomly select the example of a male/female relationship to begin this chapter. Many social scientists believe that male/female relations are *paradigmatic* of all other relationships. That the way men and women relate provides one of the primary metaphors around which we construct our images of how the world works and which, we, in fact, concretize in our social structures.

Exercise 5-B: Gender Change

DIRECTIONS
1. Close your eyes.
2. Imagine yourself in any three or more of the following situations, one at a time, *but imagine that you are of the opposite sex.* Imagine being in the body of the opposite sex; imagine thinking, feeling (mentally, emotionally, and physically), acting like a person of the opposite sex. Really build each fantasy:
   - Walking down a crowded street in the middle of the day and running into a friend of the same sex you are imagining yourself as being.
   - Being on a crowded public beach, wearing a bathing suit.
   - Being at work or at school and dealing with somebody with a great deal of authority and power over you (e.g., a boss, a professor).
   - Being at a party and flirting, dancing, just having a ball.
   - Being married, spending an evening at home after you and/or your spouse have had a hard day at work.

3. Open your eyes and write down your experiences. What did you learn about yourself, about the other sex, about your knowledge of the other sex?
4. What can you learn from this exercise about your relationships with members of the opposite sex? About how to improve these relationships? About troubles you have had with them?

SUGGESTIONS FOR TEAMS

You might want to try a variation of the Gender Change Game I developed for my sociology classes: Spend at least ten minutes pretending you are at a party, but that each of you is of the opposite sex. Set up the room with props—empty cups for beer, designated areas for the men's room and women's room, music. Someone can videotape this exercise so you can analyze your behavior. Be as creative as you'd like. Discuss not only what you learned but how easy or difficult it was to accurately perform as the opposite sex.

In the next part of this chapter we want to consider four aspects of male/female relationships and how they relate to creative self-management:

1. Hierarchy and authority
2. Power and exploitation
3. Intimacy and trust
4. Love and commitment

HIERARCHY AND AUTHORITY

Hierarchy refers to the fact that we organize our social statuses in layers, with one person being "above" or "superior" to another. The person in the higher or *superordinate* position has *authority* over those below, meaning that, by the rules of the social game, the *subordinate* individual is supposed to defer to the higher-status person. That is, if I have authority over you, you are supposed to do what I tell you to do.

Why?

Because. Because that's the way it is. Because that's how things are—or are supposed to be.

Many social scientists believe that the basic model for authority relationships is the historical relationship between men and women. Men are almost invariably in a one-up position over women. They tell women what to do.

I don't want to get into a discussion of cultural anthropology, so I'll stick to the example of our own society. We train boys and girls to accept the premise that men have authority over women. We show them in our family lives, on television, in work situations, and in school. We hypnotize ourselves into believing that this is how it is.

Sure, there are times and situations when women end up in a position of authority. The Women's Movement involves a collective effort to redefine sexual hierarchy. Hopefully, we are seeing the emergence of a new pattern of relationship between the sexes. I do not believe that there is anything necessary or anything right about male dominance.

But the fact of hierarchy remains. And perpetuates itself. And lays down the template or paradigm for all other authority relationships in which one person agrees to be subordinate to another person because of the kind of person he or she is, because their social world is hierarchically organized.

To the degree that we play along, hierarchy and authority are real. To the degree that we ignore them, however, we will violate other people's realities—and they won't like that. Creative self-management, consequently, requires delicate handling of the hierarchical relationships in your life.

POWER AND POWERLESSNESS

Authority slithers right into our second issue, *power*. Power is somewhat different from mere authority. Power is the ability to get your way, to get what you want regardless of what the other person might want. Ultimately, power is backed up by the threat of force.

Clearly, the fact that male human beings tend to have larger, stronger bodies has a lot to do with the fact that men tend to have more power in relationships and in society than women. Boys practice fighting and winning, whereas girls tend to practice nurturing and caring (playing house). And so on.

The power disparity between men and women has many important implications for our lives. First, because power usually translates into *control over scarce resources,* it means that men tend to control economic resources and have the power to withhold those resources if women don't grant them the authority they expect. While this, too, is being somewhat eroded by women's rights and the increasing prominence of women in the work force, the fact remains that when couples divorce, the woman usually ends up with the short end of the deal financially.

Women are paid less than men are paid for similar work, and the concept of comparable worth is a politically hot issue, suggesting that it goes against the grain of what we have come to define as how things are. Men continue to have more access to economic resources, such as high-paying jobs.

This not only affects the lives of men and women but it means that people tend to get confused or bothered when the situation doesn't fit our programmed expectations. When wives start making more money than their husbands, they both tend to have problems with their respective roles. Men are supposed to be the breadwinners, right? If you're not, then you're not a real man. This is another value judgment to watch out for. It can be a real killer of self-esteem and of relationships.

Power becomes a major issue, then, between men and women. It also becomes a major issue in the family—some social scientists believe that it is *the* major issue in the family. A family is really a power structure within which we train our children to accept, recognize, and defer to the authority of those of higher status. Some major family therapists, such as Jay Haley, see most family problems as power struggles in which family members form coalitions (teams) to get control over the others and get their way. This struggle, of course, extends through the rest of our lives, to our work and to the larger society.

The powerful control the resources that count, whether these are sex, money, goods, salaries, or promotions. Those with less power have to exert wiles to get their way; they employ strategies of sneakiness, deceit, sexual leverage, and manipulation to "manage" the powerful in such a way that they get what they want, but the powerful think it was all their own idea. It's a dance—one that can dehumanize both parties.

Powerlessness is an especially devastating condition. If you feel powerless, you tend to lose self-esteem, to feel that your life isn't worth living. To feel frustrated, hopeless, and helpless. To resort to liquor or drugs to make you feel better. But once again, as attempts to attain negative goals, these are nonsolutions that can only make things worse for you.

For well-socialized men, there is an added horror to powerlessness in that it "feminizes" you. It takes away your manhood and places you in a one-down position. For women this part is generally easier since women are trained to accept powerlessness.

There is a major school within sociology that focuses on this issue of power. Commonly known as *conflict theory*, it analyzes social structure as a definition of the situation emerging not from consensus as Blumer would have it but from the struggle for dominance and power among groups and individuals. C. Wright Mills was a major influence on modern conflict theory.

Mills was especially concerned with the fact that our modern "mass" society allows powerful groups to go beyond crude force to get their way. The technology of mass communications and mass media (advertising, television, newspapers, magazines, and so forth) make possible a new dimension of manipulating people without their becoming aware of being controlled. Call it a game, for it is a game, albeit an often deadly and humorless game, of "I win, you lose and if you don't like it, tough."

Part of the game of controlling other people either individually or on a collective level is "hypnotizing" them into believing that they are relatively powerless. That they can't do anything about it. And if you can get them to accept that definition of the situation, they *are* powerless because they will act that way. And let you walk off with all the goodies.

Exercise 5-C: Powerlessness

DIRECTIONS

This exercise introduces a special form of quick CSH for use with exercises:

CSH for Exercises

1. Close eyes and inhale deeply.
2. Quick tense/relax.
3. Flash place/imagine awakening ("up" direction).
4. Follow directions for exercise.
5. Take a deep breath and open eyes.

Note: When using this CSH for exercises, feel free to open your eyes at any time to check directions, and so on. After you have done so, just close your eyes, "flash" your magic place/centering point, and continue.

1. Do CSH for Exercises through step 3.
2. Remember a time when you felt powerless. Really build it in your imagination.
3. Analyze the actions ↔ reactions to see how you were made to feel powerless, how you made yourself feel powerless, and how you played along with this situation. Look at this situation as theater and see how the various participants played their parts in the drama of your feeling (and being) powerless.
4. Recall a time when you felt that you had power over others. When they felt relatively powerless compared to you.

5. Repeat step 3 above for this situation.
6. Imagine a situation in which you feel empowered. By this I do not mean that you have power over somebody, but that you feel free to create your life as you choose, free to move and to act, free to make things work out right. To accept and give authority without being controlled by it—as play, as give-and-take. Most of us will have to make up a fantasy situation of this type, but if you can remember one, all the better. But build a real or imaginary situation of empowerment in your mind. Really let yourself get into it.
7. Now repeat step 3 again for this situation.
8. Tell yourself you choose to be empowered in your life (if that is, indeed, what you would like for yourself. If not, skip this step).
9. Do step 5 in CSH for Exercises and jot down notes in your journal on what you did, felt, and remembered.

SUGGESTIONS FOR TEAMS
Steps 2, 4, and 6 are ideal for "sculpture." Try them.

EXPLOITATION

Exploitation is another aspect of power relationships. *Exploitation* occurs when those with power over other people use that power to set up a social situation in which they use the others in an unfair manner. This exploitation can be economic—of which the most extreme example is slavery, interpersonal, or sexual.

Everybody is aware of economic exploitation. Most of us are aware of interpersonal exploitation, where one person uses another to the first person's advantage and the second person's disadvantage. A lot of the time this boils down to a combination of power, raw physical force, and the abusers' confusion, fear, and responses to having been similarly abused themselves. Recently, a shocking amount of information has come to light about the number of married spouses who are locked into violent, abusive relationships. If you are either a victim or a channel of spouse abuse, you really should seek outside help. Your relationship needs intervention on the part of a skilled professional. If you don't know where to get help, contact your local community mental health center or social service agency for a referral.

Even more shocking is the amount of sexual abuse within families. There is very little that is more devastating to one's self-esteem or more crippling to one's ability to develop positive relationships than being sexually exploited by family members.

It is not always the parents or even the adults who abuse power in this way. And it doesn't only happen in the boondocks or inner city. When I taught sociology at Alfred University, one of my students was a young woman whose older brother had sexually abused her for most of her teenage years. Like many victims of incest, she assumed that it was her fault and told nobody. Her brother, of course, exploited her guilt and shame; in fact, he fed from it. She finally confronted her parents with the situation, but they couldn't accept it.

They sent *her* off to a psychiatrist to get her fantasies cured. She didn't get much out of the psychotherapy, since the problem was not inside her own head. It was in her relationships. However, she found my clinical sociology courses very helpful. She recognized what was occurring, worked with me on her self-esteem, learned creative self-hypnosis, and began to get her life together.

EXCHANGE AND RECIPROCITY

When we speak of exploitation, it is almost impossible to avoid making reference to fairness and justice. We have an innate grasp of what sociologists call the *exchange perspective*. Harry Cohen outlines this perspective as follows:

> Social life may be viewed as a series of *exchanges*. Exchanges involve mutual *gives* and *takes*. *Reciprocities* develop in the gives and takes and become part of exchange *relationships*. Exchange relationships involve *balances*. The gives and takes create the balances. *Imbalances* create the feeling of *unfairness* or *injustice*. This creates impetus to give more or less

and/or take more or less to maintain balance. A relationship, based on exchanges, strives for *equilibrium*. . . . Where a *disequilibrium* (because of perceived imbalances) occurs the participants in a viable relationship engage in a process of "working out" the problem so new balances can be made, and the relationship continues to grow. It moves ahead. Then another disequilibrium occurs. This too is worked out. It moves ahead again. . . . Relationships without movement stagnate. Relationships without resolution of states of disequilibrium tend to wither and to die.

People exchange all sorts of things: goods, money, favors, compliments. There are some social scientists, such as the great French anthropologist, Claude Lévi-Strauss, who believe that the principle of reciprocity is the central "glue" of social life. What do you think?

Exercise 5-D: Balanced Relationships

DIRECTIONS
1. Do CSH for Exercises through step 3.
2. Think about two relationships in which you are currently involved or in which you have been involved: a relationship with which you feel/felt satisfied, and a relationship with which you feel/felt very dissatisfied, very unhappy. These can be any types of relationships in any aspect of your life: family, friendship, work, love, school.
3. Evaluate the "good" relationship. Ask what are the exchanges, the "gives" and "takes"? What is the *currency* of the exchange? How *balanced* or *unbalanced* are the exchanges? How do issues of *power* affect the exchanges? To what extent is this exchange relationship a matter of mutual benefit? What kind of equilibrium is there and how is disequilibrium resolved? Is this relationship growing? Where is it heading? How did/do you react to this relationship with respect to your own feelings about *it* and about *yourself*? How do other participants seem to feel?

4. Do the same with the negative relationship.
5. Thinking about this negative relationship, whether it was in the past or is ongoing in the present, ask yourself what would you really like? What changes in the pattern or balance of exchanges would make it a satisfactory relationship from your perspective? From the standpoint of others involved? Is a mutually acceptable balance realistically possible? Whether or not you can envision striking a new balance, what are your options with respect to coping with the situation?
6. When you are ready, do step 5 in the CSH for Exercises. Write down your experience and what you have learned from it or have resolved to do. Perhaps brainstorm your options and evaluate them. But don't do anything until you are truly ready to act.

SUGGESTIONS FOR TEAMS

This is another opportunity for sculpture. Also for sharing successful practices. Share with one another what you have done that has worked for you with respect to resolving and dealing with unbalanced relationships. Perhaps compile a list of strategies and tactics.

Certainly, the sense of participating in a balanced relationship is a key to our willingness to commit ourselves to continuing in the relationship, whether it is one of work, love, marriage, friendship, or reading a book. If you don't feel that you are getting a fair exchange you are unlikely to feel that it is worth your time and energy to keep going.

Key Principle Twenty-eight: Balanced exchange is a necessary condition for positive relationships. Sometimes, however, we feel trapped, unable to act. Creative self-management is a key here, or at least a starting point. Also, in your exercise you may have discovered how feelings of guilt, shame, blame, and anger may originate in your responses to perceived imbalances in relationships—not from the workings of your unconscious mind (or at least not entirely).

In fact, it is not at all uncommon for people to experience so much distress from the lack of perceived reciprocity in their relationships that they feel they cannot continue in the relationship. Sometimes this is because one feels exploited by the other person, that one is doing all the giving and the other is doing all the taking. At other times it works in the opposite direction, that one feels that one is taking too much without giving, that one can literally not "take it any longer."

Neither situation is a healthy relationship. While there are times when breaking off a relationship—whether a friendship, a marriage, or a work relationship—is, indeed, the most appropriate way to deal with a lack of reciprocity, it is always worth remembering to "look before you leap."

Key Tactic Eight: Before committing yourself to a line of action that will terminate or drastically change a relationship, evaluate the exchanges and brainstorm your alternatives. This tactic suggests a direct approach to resolving the situation. You can also adopt an indirect one as suggested by Exercise 5-E, which is to evaluate the situation and then visualize what you prefer. Particularly when no options appear satisfactory or there appear to be no options, you are far better off not trying to change or *tinker* with the situation.

Key Tactic Nine: A generally useful indirect tactic is to focus your preferred future visualization in CSH on having overcome a current problem and decide to allow yourself to resolve it. By focusing your preferred future visualization in CSH on the specific relationship or situation while continuing to accurately scan your present, as you learned in earlier chapters, you employ Robert Fritz's strategy of *structural tension*. By defining the situation in this way—to imply or explicitly tell yourself that you will solve the current problem—and by deciding to allow yourself to resolve the situation, *but not trying to do so*, you mobilize all levels of your creativity.

Exercise 5-E: Envisioning Change

DIRECTIONS

You will practice implementing Key Tactic Nine.

1. Do your regular CSH, using the "wide awake" direction.
2. When it is time to scan your present, focus on whichever relationship in your life currently presents the most problems for you (i.e., is least satisfactory, most painful, most frustrating or disheartening) and symbolize the pain and imbalance of this relationship in your visualization.
3. Similarly, focus your preferred future visualization on having resolved this problem. Visualize a situation implying or showing you that you have *already* handled it and moved on to something else in your life; it is no longer a problem for you. *But do not focus on actually resolving it or how you might do so.*

   That is, imagine that you are remembering this once-negative relationship from the perspective of the future and you have resolved it in the best way possible for you, so that it is no longer a problem. You feel you are balanced and that your relationships are balanced in a way that is right for you. Build up a visualization of what the situation might be that makes you feel this way. Let your creative imagination go to work.
4. Before ending your session, imagine deciding that you will allow yourself to resolve the situation but that you will not try to do so until it is time to act. Perhaps say these words to yourself and let yourself feel them: "I will allow myself to resolve this relationship (name it) and move on to the next thing in my life, but I will not move too quickly or try to do anything about it until I am ready to act."

INTIMACY

One of the biggest issues in any relationship, particularly between men and women, is how much intimacy is tolerable to all participants. At what point do we feel encroached upon, put upon, invaded, or threatened? How much exposure are we willing to risk? How many of our social masks are we willing to put aside? How much of our real self-interactions are we willing to reveal?

This issue seems to mesh directly with reciprocity, since our unstated preferences regarding intimacy in our relationships tend to place a hidden set of demands or conditions on what we can accept as a fair exchange. How often do we act out or see acted out in others what Lillian Rubin calls the *approach–avoidance dance?*

Exercise 5-F: The Approach–Avoidance Dance

DIRECTIONS
1. Recall the last time you became (or were becoming) involved in an intimate relationship, whether or not it lasted any length of time. If possible, choose a case where the relationship was with a member of the opposite sex.
2. Do CSH for Exercises through step 3.
3. Close your eyes and remember what it was like as your relationship spiraled into more and more intimacy, as you came closer and closer to one another and began to reveal more and more of your inner selves. I may be asking you to remember the last time you fell in love, although falling into intimacy may not be exactly the same thing for you.
4. Recall how you felt as you experienced yourself letting down your masks, letting go of the boundaries you normally maintain around yourself. What did you do and say as this was happening? What did the

other person do and say? What did he or she reveal about what was happening to and for them? What did he or she do as you spiraled closer and closer? Was there a point at which one or the other of you "put on the brakes"? How did each of you manage your growing intimacy? What problems did you feel or have? What happened?

5. Do step 5 in CSH for Exercises and make your notes. What, if any, generalizations can you make about the similarities and differences in the ways in which men and women experience and deal with growing intimacy or love relationships? About the problems, fears, and concerns that each experiences?

SUGGESTIONS FOR TEAMS

This is another exercise where sharing may involve taking some heavy emotional risks but can pay off beyond your wildest expectations, particularly if sharing with a member of the opposite sex (or even among men or women only). But why not go ahead and share your experiences, fears, hopes, and problems with one another?

He says "Come closer." She says, "I want to be close to you." They get involved, then more involved, then one or the other flinches and backs away, leaving the partner mystified as to what he or she did wrong.

Dr. Rubin is a sociologist and marital therapist near San Francisco. In 1984, she published *Intimate Strangers*, a book that has influenced my own thinking a great deal. Like myself, she is convinced that there are few, if any, intrinsic differences between men and women to account for the way we behave toward one another. Many years of family counseling and research have convinced her that there is, however, *something* that must account for the persistent nature of the differences between the conduct of men and women and the problems each faces in their relationships.

Her answer is that the manner in which men and women deal with the issues of *separation* and *unity* lie at the root of the problem. The key to the riddle of why men and women have such different angles on intimacy, she believes, is that our society assigns the role of infant caretaking to women, and that *only women mother*.

This means that the human infant develops its initial attachment to and dependency on a woman. A woman is our most significant other, to borrow Cooley's language from Chapter One—the single most important influence on our self in the first year(s) of life.

This arrangement is not a necessary one. There is no reason why men do not care for infants equally with women. None, that is, outside of thousands of years of custom built into the social structure. The idea of giving men paternity leave to help care for their new babies is considered radical in this country. There have been many studies showing that fathers, even "liberated" fathers, do not generally engage in the mundane, often unpleasant, caretaking tasks such as diapering, burping, holding, comforting their infants as much as the more exciting tasks such as playing with the baby.

The baby experiences its most intimate attachment with a woman, normally the mother. Every infant and toddler experiences moments of anxiety, panic, and terror. And mommy is there to comfort and to hold and to do all the emotional stuff we collectively term "mothering."

As the toddler matures, he or she must face two painful but critical developmental tasks. The first is to develop a sense of self—to carve out a boundary, to separate one's self from the selves of the others in one's life. This is what psychologists call developing one's *ego boundaries*. At the same time, more or less, the boy child must learn what it means to be a *boy* and the girl to be a *girl*. This is known as developing one's *gender identity*.

Rubin shows us that the process by which boys and girls go about these twin developmental tasks is fundamentally different. For the boy, the process means renouncing and relinquishing his initial identification with a female mother, learning to see father as a role model "like oneself." This means that the boy must, in effect, block or cut off his emotional attachment to the mother and create a separation, a boundary across which he must now learn to relate and interact.

For the girl, the problem is quite different. She does not have to achieve as dramatic and thorough a separation from her first greatly loved one, but she has to define and maintain a sense of self independent from the person she identifies with so closely. This results in far less rigid boundaries around the self, and with a greater concern or even preoccupation with emotional relationships (which the boy, in developing his sense of maleness, is called upon to block off or somehow neutralize).

This process results in a lifelong difference in relationship style between men and women and in a different set of problems that each experiences with their relationships:

> In adulthood, when we find ourselves in an intimate relationship, we each experience again, even if only in highly attenuated form, those early struggles around separation and unity—the conflict between wanting to be one with another and the desire for an independent autonomous self.

For a man, this conflict results in a sense of anxiety about letting go of one's boundaries, of feeling too much attachment, of allowing one's emotions to rule one's conduct, *of allowing another person, especially a woman, to come too close.* In contrast, for a woman, the problem is more one of maintaining herself as a separate person while remaining connected to the other. As Rubin states, "For a woman, the problem of finding and maintaining the boundary between self and a loved other is paramount."

Remember, appropriate action must be based on evaluation and not value judgment or irrational responses to your own self-interactions and your social interactions with others. Certainly, positive relationships require mutual understanding.

Consequently, what Rubin has to teach us about the problem of intimacy goes a long way toward helping us manage our relationships. Awareness of the approach-avoidance dance helps us deal with our own feelings. It also helps us understand rather than value-judge the other person struggling toward intimacy.

On a third level, it also helps us understand what happened. I cannot tell you how many times I have been consulted by people—males and females, young and old—who are troubled by the perceived disequilibrium in their relationships or the collapse of intimacy. How many women blame themselves for pushing too hard or asking too much so that men slam the emotional door in their faces and cease to communicate? How many women accept the definitions of what is wrong with them that men express in their attempts to rationalize emotional reactions that they themselves are unable to accept? And how many men have come to me hurt and confused, blaming themselves for situations where women suddenly turn men off because they feel dominated or controlled, or that their boundaries are being ignored, or that men are willfully ignoring their feelings?

Not to mention all the men and women who do not seek help, but who act out the scripts dictated by these internal dynamics. The men who hop from relationship to relationship, walking away the moment intimacy or love is in sight. Or women who wall themselves off and try to keep intimacy away in order to prevent themselves from being hurt. Or people who use *nurturance* as a mask or a screen, as a strategy by which to avoid true intimacy. Rubin says:

> Nurturance is not intimacy. . . . Nurturance is caretaking. Intimacy is some kind of reciprocal expression of feeling and thought, not out of fear or dependent need, but out of a wish to know another's inner life and to be able to share one's own. Nurturance can be used as a defense against intimacy in a relationship. . . . It can be used manipulatively—as a way to stay in control, as a way to bind another and ensure against the pain of loneliness.

All those joyful, growing relationships that never blossom. All those aborted possibilities. Use creative self-management in your own relationships and give yourself a chance.

TRUST

Given our problems with intimacy, we seem also to have problems with trust. The crucial fear for both men and women in relationships seems to be, "Can we trust one another? Should we trust one another?" Or will we be exploited?

I do not, of course, have any easy solutions to this issue. Every time you open yourself to intimacy and to the possibility of caring, you experience what I call the *clam's dilemma*. A clam is very safe with its shell closed. Nothing hurtful can get in. But while it is shut, *nothing* can get in—not food, not nurturance, nothing. Nor can the clam move. It can just sit there and be safe. The moment the clam opens its shell, it opens itself to infinite possibilities, including the possibilities of being hurt, of making a mistake.

We have all been hurt. No one can decide if you should open your shell but you. I don't think, in fact, that I have *consciously* made this decision for myself. There are decisions in which you seem to have no choice as long as you are true to being you. This may be one of them. But I don't think life would be worth living as a clam.

I do have some strategic pointers to share. One is simply:

Key Tactic Ten: For positive relationships, allow yourself to trust and be trustworthy yourself. Trust may be a matter of faith. However, I am convinced that if I don't stick my neck out and take the risk of being trustworthy and open myself to trusting others, I'll never have the opportunity to find out whether it was worth it. If I don't do my part to create a situation in which others can trust, who else is going to do so? And how can I demand that others be trustworthy themselves?

Key Principle Twenty-nine: Creativity means that you have to be open to experience, to allow things to flow.

LOVE AND COMMITMENT

Love is our final issue; perhaps it is *the* final issue. We use this term to refer to a number of concepts. The Greek of the New Testament offers several different terms: There is physical love or lust, brotherly love, and *agape,* usually taken to mean the love of God or "charity" in the King James version of the Bible.

Certainly, there is a difference between lust and caring so much, so passionately for another person that one is willing to sacrifice everything for the beloved's sake. Yet in English we make no distinction between the words we use for these very different concepts or relationships.

Exercise 5-G: Imagining Love

DIRECTIONS

In this exercise, you are to recall all the different things the word *love* has meant to you and all the different feelings and relationships you have come to associate with this term or concept.

1. Close your eyes and meditate on this topic. Let yourself remember all the situations you have labeled as love, all the feelings, relationships, ideas, images, sensations, interactions, and experiences you have come to associate with or refer to as love. All the different ways in which you have used the word in a conversation, in a line, in your thoughts and fantasies. Just spend a few minutes reviewing these things and letting yourself remember and feel everything love has ever meant to you or you have ever meant by love.
2. Now, in your journal, list all the different meanings, feelings, uses of, and uses for love you have been remembering. Brainstorm the uses and meanings of love.
3. Review your list, then try to pin down what this word

means to you and what love *really* is. It is perfectly permissible to decide that it means several different things and define each of them.

4. If you could have only one form of love in your life, in its most perfect form, what would that be? I don't expect you to have a logical, rational definition but, rather, just close your eyes and imagine having it, being it, doing it, or whatever. Imagine having that one form of love in its fullest expression, in its ideal, most perfect form. (Later on, we'll refer to this as *idealized love.*)

SUGGESTIONS FOR TEAMS

This exercise is a good opportunity for a group brainstorm and discussion. Vote on which form of love you would most want in your life. Discuss your hopes and fears and yearnings for love, if you dare.

The ambiguity of the term and concept *love* opens all sorts of tactical possibilities that relate directly to our discussion of intimacy. I cannot speak from a woman's perspective, but I have plenty of experience as a male.

To the degree that one adopts the classic "playboy" mindset, love connotes the feelings of lust, desire, and wanting to be submitted to, cared for, and pleasured. Let's call this *sensual love.* It's one of the more pleasurable aspects of life, but it's nothing cosmic. Nor does it require intimacy in Rubin's sense of the term. In fact, obtaining merely physical intimacy without opening one's self to emotion and calling that "love" is probably the male counterpart of avoiding intimacy by nurturance.

Sensual love is coupled with the concept that a real man should be a sexual athlete, should not exhibit too much caring or affection, and even if he fails to actually implement this fantasy self, he should present himself this way to others; in other words, rock star sexuality.

This brings us to a second connotation or style or flavor of love: *romantic love.* Romantic love is full of deeper-running feelings, a fearsome proposition for most of us males, but one to which we find ourselves attracted like moths to a flame. Falling in love involves tumbling toward intimacy, stars-in-the-eyes, accelerating involvement; a risk-taking proposition with promises of "forevers" writ large in them.

Falling in love can hold more promise than a man (or woman) can bear to fulfill. It is sort of like skiing, in that you trudge to the edge of the cliff, take a deep breath, push yourself over and let yourself begin to slide, feeling yourself accelerate faster and faster, exhilarating in it.

Unlike skiing, if it all gets to be too much, too fast, too scary, too threatening, you can slam on the brakes. Unlike skiing, romantic love is a *fantasy*, a sort of waking daydream.

When a man (or woman) begins to see what this mad slide is going to cost him, could cost him, very often he pulls out of the dive, turns, and vanishes.

Notice that both of the types of love I have been discussing center around *intense feeling*. This is critical.

Intense feelings are lovely. Intense feelings are like drugs—they give you an unutterably pleasurable rush, they are euphoric, they get you high, but they also wear off. And while you're high on them, you're liable to act intoxicated, do things you wouldn't do otherwise, make a choice on the basis of how you feel in the immediate present. That's not a good way to build anything that you're going to have to live with for the rest of your life. Yet we make or break relationships that way; we even make babies.

Sensual and romantic love do not offer very satisfactory bases for making decisions about relationships. They can lead you in the right direction, but, like any passionate feelings, they can also tear you and your life apart.

THE FEELINGS SOCIETY

However, our contemporary society seems to have accepted the idea that *what feels real is real*. We talk about reason and we act on the basis of feelings—how we feel now, since later we might feel differently.

We live in a *feelings society*. A world based on the impermanent sand of our transient feelings. Basing relationships and decisions about relationships on feelings seems to rule out commitment, although if the feeling is strong enough we might believe that we are always going to feel that way. It also makes a mockery out of trust: If we feel that this is really and truly it, we should trust ourselves and go with the flow.

Commitment is a concept that transcends the feelings of the moment. Commitment involves staking everything on relationship. It is something that Americans younger than fifty seem to fear and dread.

Making a commitment. Three words that inspire fear wherever they are thought. Think about it. Commitment is an act. It is an affirmation of relationship, an agreement to create something and keep it there. It is easy to promise commitment, of course, but the follow-through is not easy. To make commitment really work requires discovering how to create self-renewing relationships.

For commitment to be meaningful, it must be mutual. It must be an agreement among social actors to stake everything on an ongoing, reciprocal relationship. The details of what that relationship is are not the point, nor is the type of social relationship we are talking about—there can be commitment in friendship, in family relationships, in business relationships, in group memberships.

Yes, I am talking about another meaning of *love*. This meaning comes closer to the spirit of the Greek *agape* or what most world religions mean by the term. It is very likely that when you thought about your highest dreams of love you really meant something like this. I will let you define this higher sense of love for yourself. For, in the end, it involves placing your self on the line, staking everything and risking everything on a creative relationship.

This leads us to a final point about love. A clinical sociological evaluation suggests that for any social structure to be stable and offer true reciprocity it needs to be based on commitment to a positive relationship and not on feelings. A truly healthy, positive society must be based on relationship.

It is the quality of the relationships we create, not the biological and psychological individuals we happen to be, that bring promise of freedom and fulfillment.

I am suggesting that our contemporary values are based on sand, that the "me" generation had the wrong idea, that there is a direct linkage between love and humanist values, between love and empowerment.

Key Principle Thirty: Positive relationships are the key to our human potential.

TWO RELATIONSHIP MANAGEMENT TACTICS

We have already considered how you can envision the future with a focus on the quality of your relationships. This is a basic indirect strategy.

Now, let's briefly consider and practice two further strategies of relationship management and repair that will help you create and maintain positive relationships and change the track of existing negative relationships. In the end, these strategies for positive relationships involve changing your actions ↔ reactions and redefining the interpersonal social structure you are creating or perpetuating.

- Stop trying so hard.
- Take the role of the other.

Stop trying so hard. One of the basic patterns that therapists and counselors discover is that the more effort people throw into solving interpersonal problems, the worse the problems get. Each attempted solution tends to result in new problems that only make matters worse. By taking your attention off of solving the problem, you can devote your energies to doing whatever it is the problem is blocking you from doing.

Exercise 5-H: Trying to Fix Relationships

DIRECTIONS
1. Do CSH for Exercises through step 3.
2. Remember a relationship you once had that you tried unsuccessfully to salvage. This can be any kind of relationship: friend, co-worker, lover, family member. For this exercise, choose an intense relationship that you tried desperately to save.
3. Go over your memory videotape of this relationship, moving quickly over the beginning when it was a satisfying relationship or it seemed to be solidifying into a satisfying relationship, and then, still scanning through it quickly, recall the relationship going sour. Observe the interactions, the exchanges, the performances.
4. Now, begin paying close attention to *what you did to try to save or salvage the relationship* and what the result of each attempted solution was. Pay close attention to the interactions and performance when you tried to make things better, to heal things, to save the relationship. Also focus on what you felt was at stake, what you felt you were losing, and how you tried to minimize your losses. Play it through to the end. Open your eyes.
5. Ask yourself whether this relationship was, in fact, either salvageable or worth salvaging. Sometimes we simply don't want to give up the investment in time, resources, self-image, and effort we have put into something that really has nothing positive to offer us any longer. And ask yourself whether the ultimate outcome was as bad as you feared it would be.
6. In your journal, make a list of the *attempted solutions* and what the outcome of each was for you and for the relationship. See what conclusions you can draw about different kinds of attempted solutions and their effects. For example, how many times did your at-

tempted solutions ultimately become or create *new* problems?

7. Close your eyes and imagine that you can mysteriously or magically talk to yourself at the time when you were most troubled by the relationship you have examined. Imagine comforting your younger self and telling yourself how it all worked out in the end, that you survived and that you ultimately learned and grew from the pain, that you will be okay and that you are okay. Really feel yourself receiving this message.

8. Do step 5 in the CSH for Exercises.

SUGGESTIONS FOR TEAMS

This is another good group exercise. First, perhaps, share your attempted solutions and put together a master list of attempted solutions and the kinds of outcomes each tends to create. Then you might do some two-person role-playing, first simulating a bad relationship and one or both players trying hard to fix that relationship with some of the attempted solutions you have discussed, and then trying alternative ways of resolving the situation and switching the relationship onto a more positive track. End with a brainstorm about how we can help to switch negative relationships onto more positive tracks.

Probably the *worst* way to try to solve a problem is to attempt to "talk it out." From a male perspective, this usually involves trying to reason with the other person. From the female perspective, it usually involves trying to get the other person to understand feelings and to honestly communicate about them. In either case, you are more likely to end up with an argument in which you are responding to what you infer the other person's tone of voice or facial expression or choice of words to mean. That is, hidden messages or hints you detect and, very often, project to be there in the first place.

Honest communication about a problem situation is certainly not a bad thing, but generally you don't get that result when you talk it out. Rather, you end up making value judgments, placing blame, trying to explain to the other person what he or she is really feeling or meaning. And getting it all wrong (at least insofar as the other person is concerned). If you can find neutral ground and use "I" messages and focus on the *structure* of the interpersonal situation, you might have a chance. Maybe if you scream and shout and verbally fight you have a chance. But you are better off not trying to talk it out.

Take the role of the other. As you might have noticed in the gender change exercise, you can get a lot of insight into a situation from imagining yourself in the other person's position. There are many ways in which you can imaginatively take the role of the other, but one of the best is to do so within the context of creative self-hypnosis.

You can do this by imagining the problem situation or a typical problem situation, but imagine being the other person in that situation and the other person being yourself. Taking the role of the other in your mind can be facilitated by role-playing the situation with a partner, but we rarely have this opportunity. If you are working with a partner or a group, you can devote some time to helping one another by role-playing problem relationships or situations. We'll discuss some possibilities of this sort at further length in Chapter Six.

Now, role-playing will not change what the other person does. However, combined with other strategies and tactics that you are learning here, and with CSH in particular, you may find that you automatically—even "unconsciously"—change your own actions ↔ reactions to the other person in such a way as to change the pattern of social interactive exchanges and redefine the interpersonal situation.

One hint for making role-playing work for you:

Key Tactic Eleven: When taking the role of the other, "ape" the person's physical expressions, postures, gestures, and language. You may need to study the other person in real life and then (even if you are doing CSH) physically imitate the person as you imagine being him or her. The more realism you can bring to the performance, the better your understanding of the situation will be and the more impact the imaginative role-playing will have for you.

Exercise 5-I: Taking the Role of the Other

DIRECTIONS

Sit or stand in front of a mirror. Think of a person with whom you currently have a relationship of any kind. Try to mimic that person's facial expression, gestures, posture, muscle tension. Feel what it feels like. Then repeat this for other people in your life, including people you like and people you dislike, people you care about and people who care about you, people with whom you are having relationship problems.

SUGGESTIONS FOR TEAMS

This can be done as a two-person exercise. Each of you "ape" the other; try to be the other person. If you want you can share some information about yourselves first. Perhaps, if you are working in a larger group, you might want to switch partners and repeat this exercise.

By placing yourself in the other person's perspective, you can often achieve a breakthrough in your evaluation of the situation. You can imagine what he or she might be meaning by the actions or words that trouble you and you can often spot the pain and distress that the other person may be hiding behind aggression, nastiness, or emotional withdrawal. By gaining a genuine understanding of the other, you may find that you cease to respond to your own value judgments concerning the other person's behavior and, rather, free yourself to act creatively and freely to bring about your goals for the relationship.

It is not the insight that is important, but rather liberating yourself from thoughts, feelings, and imaginings based on a misconception of the situation. Sometimes this misconception extends to *projecting* your own hurt, fears, guilt, or anger onto the other person, reading your own feelings into his or her actions.

We have all acted this way, particularly when we feel our own feelings are unworthy, unthinkable, unacceptable. You commonly see these actions among victims of abusive relationships. Remember the woman who felt for many years that she was the rotten one, that it was her seductiveness that encouraged her older brother. And then, when she confronted her parents with the facts, they refused to accept the possibility that they could have been blind to this abuse for so many years, that they could have raised a son who would do such things.

Therefore, they projected their own sense of guilt and shame onto their daughter, defining her as needing therapy, and almost irrevocably alienating this loving, talented, wonderful young woman. It was partially by helping her to take the role of her parents and understanding this concept of *projection* that I could help her find some ways of redefining her relationship with them and achieving a degree of long-overdue healing. So take heed:

Key Tactic Twelve: Be alert to the dangers of projection and make it a practice to own your own feelings.

SUMMARY

This chapter has dealt with relationships. It has gone beyond the microsociological approach of previous chapters to introduce the concepts of *social structure* and the *sociological imagination*. It also introduced the concept of *complementarity*, the idea that there may be several equally valid ways to describe something and that each way of looking offers information other ways cannot supply. We then looked at the paradigmatic example of male/female relationships to investigate some basic principles, issues, and problems found in all types of relationships. We concentrated on four sets of issues:

1. Hierarchy and authority
2. Power and exploitation
3. Intimacy and trust
4. Love and commitment

We also looked at the *exchange perspective* and the concept of *reciprocity* as it relates to positive relationships. Finally, we discussed and explored three strategies for creating positive relationships and switching relationships onto more positive tracks: envisioning positive relationships, stop trying so hard (attempted solutions), and taking the role of the other. We ended with a brief discussion of projection and owning one's own feelings; I leave it up to you to think about this and apply it to your own life and relationships.

We discussed the following Key Principles in Chapter Five:

TWENTY-SIX: Complementarity often gives you the best handle on things.

TWENTY-SEVEN: You're not to blame for becoming a victim, but you are free to stop being victimized.

TWENTY-EIGHT: Balanced exchange is a necessary condition for positive relationships.

TWENTY-NINE: Creativity means that you have to be open to experience, to allow things to flow.

THIRTY: Positive relationships are the key to the human potential.

Five new Key Tactics were also introduced:

EIGHT: Before committing yourself to a line of action that will terminate or drastically change a relationship, evaluate the exchange and brainstorm your alternatives.

NINE: A generally useful indirect tactic is to focus your preferred future visualization in CSH on having overcome a current problem and decide to allow yourself to resolve it.

TEN: For positive relationships, allow yourself to trust and be trustworthy yourself.

ELEVEN: When taking the role of the other, "ape" the person's physical expressions, postures, gestures, and language.

TWELVE: Be alert to the dangers of projection and make it a practice to own your own feelings.

Technique Five: Directed CSH for Empowering Relationships

DIRECTIONS

For at least the next week focus your CSH practice on improving and renewing your relationships. The following approach is recommended:

A. *Directed CSH with relationships mindwork.* At least twice a day, do Directed CSH using either the "up" or "down" approach through step 4. You can scan your present very briefly. Then do the *imaging supportive relationships mindwork* in step 5. ·

Directed CSH

1. Tense/relax.
2. Imagine place.
3. Steer "up" or "down."
4. Visualize present.
5. Do tactical mindwork and/or visualize future.
6. Set mind.
7. Open eyes. Tell yourself, "That's it, end of session."

1. In step 5 of Directed CSH, imagine social support. Imagine feeling caring and cared for. Imagine feeling that other people are with you and for you. Imagine that you are part of a web, a network

of caring and sharing relationships. Don't even try to visualize individual people, but, rather, focus on this concept and feeling of relationship. Perhaps visualize a web of warm, glowing light connecting you to other people, connecting them to you and to one another. Let yourself imagine that you can feel the connection and the positive energies flowing through that connection, supporting you, soothing you, making you feel like part of something greater than yourself.

2. Think about your *current* relationships and select one relationship that you want to *improve* or *renew* (revitalize or make even better). Whichever relationship comes to mind this time is perfectly okay; you may surprise yourself by settling on a relationship you would never have consciously chosen. Envision a situation that exemplifies how this relationship is for you right now. Really build it up so you can feel as if you are actually there now, being in the situation, experiencing it in present time. Visualize the relationship, feeling and focusing on the actions ↔ reactions, norms, social structure, and other elements discussed in this book. Be alert to projections and let yourself recognize and accept *all* of your own feelings about the other person and your relationship.

3. Now imagine taking the role of the other. Literally, imagine how it would feel, imagine what it would be like, what you would think and feel like if you were the other person (or one of the other persons) in the relationship. Keep focusing on the interactions but let yourself fantasize how it might be for the other person in this positive or negative relationship. If you were this other person, what would you be thinking, feeling, imagining as you interacted? What would your intentions be? What would you be trying to accomplish? What would be your goals, your

dreams, your hopes, your fears regarding this relationship?

4. Shift your focus in time and imagine seeing from the outside (as if you were watching a video recording) a future scene that tells or shows any problems in the relationship that have long since been overcome or worked out, or that symbolizes this relationship has worked out beyond your wildest hopes and dreams and fantasies. Do not focus on solving any problems but focus on enjoying the fruits of your success. Feel the connections between yourself and the other people in this scene; feel the positive exchanges, the positive energies you are getting from your interactions. Really build this preferred future.

5. In step 6 of Directed CSH imagine deciding that you choose to improve the relationship but that you will not try to do so until it is time to act. Perhaps say these words to yourself and let yourself feel them: "I choose to make this a truly positive relationship, but I will not try to improve it too quickly."

6. End your session.

B. *Quick CSH for on the spot.* If you are in the middle of interaction and feel that a relationship is moving along the wrong track, in order to change the track, do the advanced form of Quick CSH.

Quick CSH

1. Close eyes (optional). Inhale deeply.
2. Quick tense/relax (optional).
3. Flash place.
4. Set mind.
5. Open eyes. Scan situation.
6. Breathe deeply. Go ahead and do it.

1. If you can, close your eyes briefly (at least blink) and take a deeper-than-usual breath. You can do an optional quick tense/relax as described in Technique Five if you have time and opportunity.
2. Flash your centering point or magical place in your mind's eye.
3. Tell yourself that you refuse to act and react this way and very quickly visualize how you prefer for the interaction to flow. Perhaps tell these things to yourself in your mind at the same time.
4. If your eyes are still closed, open them. Scan the situation briefly. Observe what is actually happening right *now*.
5. Don't try to change anything but simply take another breath and allow yourself to perform as closely to what you have told yourself as possible.

SIX

Optimal Performance

This chapter is about *optimal performance.* I am not talking about peak performance. That concept involves the idea of pushing something to the limit. Of always pressing past one's previous limits to running as fast and as high and as much as you can. It suggests beating the competition, leaving them behind in the dust. No, I am speaking from a more gentle metaphor.

By *optimal performance,* I am borrowing a concept from my friend, Steve Smith, an applied physicist and inventor. He taught me years ago that *optimization* means specifying a set of goals (not just a single quantity to maximize) and then letting your system seek a way to achieve the best *balance* among those objectives.

In previous chapters, we considered the dramaturgical perspective that views life as a performance. We *do* our lives. We *do* ourselves.

This same perspective sees our lives as a series or chain of miniperformances. Every interaction with another person (or even our selves), every dealing we have with social groups and organizations, every task we undertake and challenge we meet can be viewed as a situation in which we strive to give the best, most skillful, most effective and persuasive performance that we can.

For every performance, there will be a *preferred outcome*, that is, your overall definition of what it is you wish to bring about through the specific performance, what you want to create by it. As we discussed with respect to stated and unstated preferences, it is important to ensure that the preferred outcome toward which you are aiming furthers your overall goals for your life and yourself. Only then can we say that optimal performance means a performance that results in the preferred outcome. But that remains abstract. More practically, we need to identify some criteria for what would constitute a successful performance. I believe we can identify at least four dimensions or *parameters* in this regard:

1. Attaining your specific objectives (the desired effects).
2. Meeting the demands being made of you by others (audience demands).
3. Achieving the response you want from others (audience management).
4. Maintaining your sense of calmness, clarity, comfort, and control (stress management).

An optimal performance, one that leads to your preferred outcome, involves achieving as much as possible of all four of these parameters, not just maximizing one of them. Achieving a *balance*.

To achieve your specific objectives while alienating your audience and raising your blood pressure is not a truly successful performance—nor is keeping cool but getting defined as an uncaring lout who ignores all the rules. To do so would not, I expect, be in line with the preferred outcome you have in mind.

It is important to understand the difference between a *preferred outcome* and *desired effects*. A preferred outcome can be considered to be the whole and the desired effects are elements that when taken together result in the preferred outcome. They are more concrete and exist at a more immediate level of reality than the more abstract preferred outcome. However, when you visualize the preferred outcome, you are also establishing the parameters for optimizing your performance.

In life and in any specific performance in life we always have many goals, many needs, many demands being made of us. The idea of optimal performance is to meet them *all* as best as we can. In this chapter, we are going to consider how you can optimize your performances.

Key Tactic Thirteen: For optimal performance consider the preferred outcome, the audience, and the desired effects. To mobilize your emotions and feelings and your entire creativity, focus on the preferred outcome, but when analyzing the specific demands of the performance, it is wise to look at the desired effects you wish to produce. You should also evaluate your audience. When you focus on the desired effects, you should remain sensitive to how they relate to both audience demands being made of you and of how you need to manage that audience in order to bring about a successful performance. However, once you have gotten the idea, you probably do not need to be explicit about these other two parameters except when they have a direct bearing on the desired effects you need or wish to achieve. Just scanning your audience will probably be all you need to do in most cases.

Exercise 6-A: Performance Analysis

DIRECTIONS

CSH for Exercises

1. Close eyes. Inhale deeply.
2. Quick tense/relax.
3. Flash place/imagine awakening ("up" direction).
4. Follow directions for exercise.
5. Take a deep breath and open eyes.

1. Close your eyes; do CSH for Exercises.
2. In step 4, after flashing your centering point or magical place, focus on scanning your present with an emphasis on the things you feel will be most important for you to do, deal with, or accomplish in the near future—say, no earlier than four days from today but no longer than two weeks from today.
3. Do step 5. As soon as you open your eyes, write in your journal all the things you identified as important to do or bring off successfully in this near-future time frame. Can you see how they amount to *performances?*
4. Now identify no more than three performances to focus on as you work through this chapter. Circle your listing or description of each of these in your journal.
5. Choose one of these.
6. Write the heading: "Preferred Outcome." Under this heading write a brief description of what you want to get out of this performance, how you want to feel, what you want to have, what you want to have set in motion, what you want it to be like.
7. Now write a second heading, "Desired Effects." Under this heading just list or describe in a couple of sentences what *effects you want to cause* with respect to each stage, part, cycle, or aspect of the total performance. What, in other words, you want to make happen, in concrete ("operational") terms.
8. Write the heading: "Audience Demands." What do you anticipate your "audience"—the others participating in the forthcoming situation—will expect of you? Not only in terms of actions but also in terms of symbolic behaviors—*expressions* of loyalty, command, obedience, sensitivity, strength, affection, authority, fellowship, whatever. Add what *you* expect from *yourself.*
9. You guessed it; write "Audience Management." What do you anticipate you will have to do in order to get

the response you want from this particular audience? To convince them that you are meeting or exceeding their demands but also in order to bring about the effect you desire. These considerations may be at odds. What kind of problems do you anticipate with respect to audience management? What do you know about your likely audience that gives you clues as to how best to manage them? What does your audience need to know to "set the stage" for your desired effects?

10. Write "Stress Management." What types of stress or stress responses can you anticipate in this type of situation? How have you dealt with this type of stress in the past? What problems have you had in dealing with this type of stress; what successes have you had? We will focus more on stress management later.

That's it. You can continue. Feel free to use this five-part basic assessment scheme with the other performances you identified and with any future performances. You will probably want to integrate some additional elements discussed later in this chapter, but the four parameters listed earlier offer a useful starting point for evaluating what needs to be done.

SUGGESTIONS FOR TEAMS

In addition to sharing, you might want to do a "team fiction" case study. Select a kind of performance that is important and has been a problem for all of you. Now make up a fictitious example for the near future. You can do this in round-robin fashion, someone starting by saying something about what the performance situation will be like, then each of you in turn adding to that—making up details about the audience, about the situation, then elaborating and fleshing out these details until you have something very realistic. Now go through the four steps above together as "brainstorms." Perhaps add more evaluation material from the rest of this chapter. Then, again in round-robin fashion, make up the story of how you deal with the performance successfully, so as to exemplify an optimal performance.

We will consider types of performances that may be relevant to various readers. We will discuss matters in *generic* terms—meaning from the perspective of a category or class of similar type rather than concrete instances—but you should keep in mind the specific performances identified in Exercise 6-A and always ask yourself how the material relates (or can be related) to them.

To begin, we must consider two key principles. Understanding them provides the key to optimal performance. Both concern the structural realities of our lives.

Key Principle Thirty-one: *Human development moves in a helical progression.* Our lives move both ever onwards down the one-way stream of time and also around and around in a series of cycles. For example, this chapter is about *optimal performance*—that was my starting point. But are we back where we began? When you read that last sentence, was it a repeat of what you experienced when you read it the first time? Or was there something added this time? Did the sentence conjure up some additional associations, images, or ideas?

In the past few pages, two things occurred. We came round in a cycle, from "twelve o'clock" around and back to "twelve o'clock." But in the process of getting there, by virtue of the process of getting there, both the context of the identical statement changed for you and *you changed*. Your interactions with me via this book and the exercise you completed provided new *information* that to some small degree altered your perception of the identical six-word sentence.

The distance of a couple pages and the time it has taken you to read them and do the exercise (plus any "down" time between the moments when you have been reading this book) separate the first and the second time you read the sentence.

So there was both a linear component of elapsed time and the events, actions, and reactions that occurred during this span and also a cyclic component of returning to a starting point. By virtue of returning to that point, however, you underwent change because you incorporated new experiences, new information.

You have completed many exercises in the course of working through this book to this point. Each tells you about the method, then gives you a set of directions. Each exercise itself has a start, a middle, and an end. You can consider the process of doing any individual exercise a cycle. Each chapter also has a start, a middle, and an end. All end, for example, with a summary and a technique. You have gone through five of these cycles so far and are into your sixth.

I hope you have experienced many changes in the quality of your life as you have worked through these six chapters. Perhaps you no longer feel as hypnotized by the world as you felt when you began this book. Perhaps you have felt yourself moving ahead in your life according to your own choices rather than according to those dictated for you by others and by events. Perhaps also "I" have shifted in your experience from a formless "auctorial" (author's) voice to almost a real person. You may be feeling a sort of relationship with me.

This happens. You have an encounter with somebody. You have another encounter and then another and, as we suggested in Chapter Five, a relationship crystalizes. As you begin to interact within the context of a new relationship, your roles solidify and a social structure emerges. As you keep moving through cycles of interaction, the social structure develops and your relationship develops.

That is, there is a dimension of change as time moves on. Notice how, in your social life, the direction of motion is commonly one of *moving inward,* toward deeper, more intimate, more involved social relationships. The others, once strangers, become more and more important to us. We begin to see ourselves as members of an "in group," from which most others are excluded because they do not participate in this deepening relationship. We begin to speak of "us," implying a "them."

I am sure that you have been familiar with this type of happening in your life many times before. Perhaps it was when you moved into a new house or apartment. You met the strangers who lived next door; they became your neighbors and you, yourself, became a part of the neighborhood and then of the larger community. Perhaps you entered a new school, or class, or took a new job and met new people, some of whom have become your friends, or maybe even your lover or spouse.

We tend to visualize the pattern of our lives either in terms of lines or of circles. You can think of your life (or all of history) as being like the line of a graph in a business presentation, now rising, now sinking, but always moving onward through time. Or you might think of a ray of light shining through the clouds, like a bridge into the sun. "The arrow of time"; it makes intuitive sense.

Alternatively, you can envision all things moving in a circular motion. This, too, makes intuitive sense. The circular clockface of time, the wheel of karma, or the rhythm of the seasons. Everything comes round again; up and around and down and up. Birth, growth, decline, decay, and birth again.

What I am suggesting is that *both* of these ways of looking at life are valid, but that they are partial, complementary descriptions. We now need to take on an expanded frame of reference. We need a way of thinking about the progression of our lives that recognizes both the way in which we continually move through little cycles and through big cycles. I find that the easiest way to envision this is to think of a helix, such as the spring of a ballpoint pen. Our lives involve a succession of cyclic activities or *rounds*. We wake up, go to work or school or whatever, go to bed, sleep, and wake up again. We go to work on Monday, do the same thing for five days, and then the weekend comes again. We start a job, a task, a relationship, we go through its natural cycle, it ends, we start the next cycle. Yet with every completion of a cycle, we're farther along in time. We have developed, changed, grown, or at least become more of something and less of another, but we never find ourselves back where we once were.

This concept of helical progressions can be applied to understanding the overall pattern of our lives. But we can also apply it to the practical structure of our performances. Any single performance can be viewed as having a beginning, a middle, and an end. The "end" is, of course, arbitrary in that each performance leaves you at the start of another, and where to draw the line or even where to say one particular performance starts is a matter of *labeling* more than anything else.

Key Principle Thirty-two: *Everything in our lives is connected into a whole.* We will consider other implications of this principle shortly. But for right now it is of primary importance to recognize that our performances flow into one another and that *we can select what we choose to be the starting point.* We already touched on this point in Chapter One, with Key Principle Three, that the best time to start anything is right now.

Big cycles link with other cycles and are themselves made up of lesser cycles. You can start anywhere and work your way toward where you want to go. The trick is to *redirect* the trend that your life's performances are taking by redirecting the small performances that lie directly before you. You don't have to take on the whole thing at once.

THE ART OF REDIRECTION

Redirection can be considered an art. I can't, alas, teach you art, but I can help you foster your own creativity and I can teach you something about technique. It is only by practice that you will acquire the requisite skill to deftly accomplish the things you want. This is another reason why I urge you to take things slowly.

Now, there are actually two ways I know to manage a performance. My previous book *Strategic Self-Hypnosis* teaches you one of them, the art of nudging events along by the craftsmanlike application of specific techniques and strategies. This book teaches you the other way. The art of redirection. Of *creative performance.*

Key Tactic Fourteen: For creative performance focus on process and redirection, not details of what, when, and how. This approach is one that I resisted much of my life; I was always under the impression that the way to get things done was to master the details of how to do them. And for that reason I have all too often held myself back, avoiding the temptation to overextend myself or step beyond my knowledge into the unknown. Which means I have lost out on a lot of possibilities and have made life harder for myself. This lesson was not an easy one!

The *process* part was no trouble. That was preaching to the converted. By *process* I mean focus on *what is happening*, what the action is, who's doing what.

Redirection means to then take creative control over the cycles of which your life's performances are made, and by dealing with them one after another, redirect the larger trend so as to bring about preferred outcomes. By dealing aptly with the concrete cycles before you, you gain control over the entire helical progression. That certainly made sense to me. Deal with the here and now, because that is all you can do anything about, anyway.

But *how* do you do this?

This is where it gets difficult. We all learn how things work—make plans, and execute those plans. When something breaks, we figure out what happened and fix it. Right?

Creative performance says, "Wrong."

In fact, I cannot tell you how to practice redirection. Furthermore, neither you nor I *need* to know. Not if we choose to follow the method of creative performance.

But, you say, that's *irrational*. It runs counter to everything we've been taught.

Okay. Let's consider why I am suggesting that you might want to learn the creative approach. Assume that I load you up with techniques and instructions. Assume that you practice and practice and become skillful in their use. Then you must deal with something.

There are three major pitfalls to attacking the problem directly with your arsenal of strategies and techniques according to a well-designed game plan:

1. You can't plan for every contingency.
2. You are liable to become self-conscious and trip yourself up.
3. You may create performance anxiety and stifle yourself.

The first pitfall is obvious. If you are dependent on a set of how-to techniques, your flexibility is limited and you are in trouble if something occurs for which you have not prepared. How many times have we all studied and studied for that big exam only to find that the teacher has asked for everything other than what we had studied!

Training yourself in creative problem solving keeps you flexible. This method of redirection allows you to improvise as the need arises rather than bind yourself to a technique that may be be right for the moment.

Exercise 6-B: Redirecting Performance

DIRECTIONS
1. Do CSH for Exercises through step 3.
2. Close your eyes. Remember a time when you were called upon to do something difficult and important, one in which you tried your best to do everything right and were doing fairly well, but then you found yourself suddenly becoming intensely self-conscious. Relive this performance situation in your imagination and experience again what happened. Open your eyes.
3. Close your eyes. This time remember being very anxious about a difficult and important performance or interpersonal situation. Remember such a situation and feel again that anxiety; recall imagining all the things that could go wrong, imagining what might happen if you were to fail. Run this imaginary videotape to the end of the performance and experience again what happened. Open your eyes.
4. This time you are going to imagine an alternative

history of yourself. You will go back in your imagination to one of these two situations you have just
visualized and you will imagine successfully redirecting your performance. After you close your eyes,
imagine yourself at the beginning of the situation and
doing the following:

a. Entering the situation and taking a breath, flashing
   your centering place in your mind, then, with your
   eyes open, *quickly scanning your actual present—*
   just taking a clear look at what is occurring, who
   is there, sensitizing yourself to the audience demands and feeling out your audience with an eye
   toward audience management.

b. Then, perhaps blinking your eyes shut for a moment, think about the preferred outcome and
   imagine experiencing that outcome.

c. Now go ahead and deal with the first cycle of
   performance at hand, letting yourself identify the
   desired effect you want to bring about and then,
   concentrating on the present moment, allow yourself to *just do it.*

d. Then quickly scan the situation once more and
   focus your concentration on the next cycle of
   action, identify the desired effect, and just do it.
   And the next cycle, and the next, until you have
   completed the performance.

e. Imagine what might have occurred, what you realistically might have accomplished by proceeding
   in this manner. Then open your eyes.

4. Now close your eyes again. Recall something you do
   well. Something you feel you do *really* well. It can be
   anything, from the mundane (putting on makeup,
   knotting your tie) to the extraordinarily complex performance of creating a work of true art, analyzing a
   complex market, or conducting cardiovascular surgery. Remember doing it, whatever *it* happens to be.
   Open your eyes.

5. Now, see if you can write in your journal *exactly* how
   to do this last performance in such a way that a total

ignoramus would be able to replicate what you did, down to the last detail. When you have tired of trying to do this, consider whether you really noticed the details of how you did what you were doing at the time when you actually did it, or whether your attention was focused on something else entirely. If so, on what?

6. Do CSH for Exercises step 5 and continue with this book.
7. Write down some things you have learned about optimal performance from what you imagined in step 4 and what you did in steps 1, 2, and 3 above.

SUGGESTIONS FOR TEAMS
Just a reminder—if no suggestions are written for you, either make up your own exercises or at least discuss your experiences.

MASTERY

The way in which you do the things you excel at doing and can do almost automatically, with your eyes on the larger goal, is the way of *mastery*.

Key Principle Thirty-three: The ideal way to do anything is to be there and just do it. A master of any art, science, or craft knows exactly what to do and can just focus on the overall *process* of bringing together more and more complex preferred outcomes. The master has transcended the earlier stages of development and no longer needs to perform the task step-by-step.

That is the epitome of creative performance. A method such as the one outlined in step 3 of the exercise is merely a way of bringing yourself up to speed in new and unfamiliar performance situations.

Wouldn't it be nice to be able to live our lives like that? I believe this is, in fact, what the ancient Taoist philosopher,

Chuang Tzu, viewed as mastery of the Way. In his essay, "The Secret of Caring for Life," he tells the story of a master butcher, Cook Ting. When complimented by his lord, Cook Ting lays down his knife and replies:

> What I care about is the Way, which goes beyond skill. When I first began cutting up oxen, all I could see was the ox itself. After three years, I no longer saw the whole ox. And now— now I go by spirit and don't look with my eyes. Perception and understanding have come to a stop and spirit moves where it wants. I go along with the natural make-up, strike in the big tools, guide the knife through the big openings, and follow things as they are.

When you act with mastery, you automatically seek the optimal performance. When you act with effort, you tend to block yourself from achieving that balance and, in fact, you might even ruin the outcome.

This chapter is really about two meanings of the word *performance*. Most important, it is about using creative self-hypnosis to optimize your skillfullness at performing. Second, it is about showing you some strategies for optimizing specific performances in life. In line with the overall method and theme of this book, I will not provide "how to do it" instructions for management of specific types of performance (but you can consult my previous book *Strategic Self-Hypnosis* for some ideas along those lines). Here, I want to focus on the more general problem of how to optimize any or all of your performances in work, life, and relationships.

So far, this chapter has really focused on the first performance objective. After the next exercise, we will shift gears and direct our attention toward this second objective. However, I urge you to keep in mind that learning how to do specific performances well, while certainly valuable and important, is only a step toward learning how to do *all* your performances well.

One note: In this section I have only talked about half of the principle of mastery, the "just do it" part. The "being there" part involves learning how to be sensitive to the knots and blockages in the flow of things, to instantly evaluate what's going on and to be able to focus intently on each situation as you work through it.

The secret is being there and being awake. This, too, was part of Chuang Tzu's secret of caring for life. Cook Ling goes on to say:

> However, when I come to a complicated place, I size up the difficulties, tell myself to watch out and be careful, keep my eyes on what I'm doing, work very slowly, and move the knife with the greatest subtlety, until—flop! the whole thing comes apart like a clod of earth crumbling to the ground.

Exercise 6-C: Mastery of the Way

DIRECTIONS

1. Do CSH for Exercises through step 3. Spend a little extra time on shifting into the "up" direction of expanded consciousness.
2. Open your eyes and reread the section above on mastery.
3. Close your eyes and recall your centering point.
4. Now, imagine that you, like Cook Ting—or perhaps, like Milton Erickson—have mastered the Way. Just imagine; just let it flow.
5. Whenever you're ready, do CSH for Exercises step 5 as you normally do and continue reading or whatever.

SUGGESTIONS FOR TEAMS

Although it's a bit of a detour, you might want to do some library research on this mastery stuff and discuss it. Then all of you should do the above exercise at the same time.

You might check different religious, philosophic, New Age, or humanistic psychology writings. I suggest going to original sources, which may include Buddhist sutras, Hindu texts, Zen sayings, Taoist texts, books by Jewish and Christian mystics and philosophers, by Sufis, Native American shamans, and so on.

HUMAN SYSTEMS

Let's get back to something I only touched upon in Chapter Five. I asked whether the social structure causes people to interact in a certain way or whether the way in which they interact creates a certain kind of social structure.

At that time, I suggested that we might be asking the wrong kind of question. That cause-and-effect logic might not be the most fruitful way of understanding human conduct. Let me show you what I mean. Imagine an alternate universe in which Ken and Barbie got married and we're taking another look at them twenty years down the line.

Exercise 6-D: Ken and Barbie Revisited

DIRECTIONS

(This incident is loosely based on a real couple who came to me to help the wife stop smoking. That's what they said at the time. But I discovered the following.)

Barbie drinks because she feels she is trapped in a rotten relationship and she is economically and emotionally dependent on Ken (who is, by now, a rich toy tycoon) who gets mad at her and maybe even hits her. She guesses that she still loves him; there are times when she loves him so much that it hurts. But it seems that no matter what she does for him it's never good enough. It was different when Tammy and Jimmy were little. She really loved being a mommy. She really hates being a nobody stuck all alone in a big empty house with nothing to do, no one to talk to, nobody to care for. It's just no fun anymore. She wishes she were thirty pounds lighter, twenty years younger, and a model again. Come to think of it, she wishes the same were true of Ken.

But if she thinks about that kind of stuff too much she just get's too wound up. Maybe she pops a few tranquilizers. Or makes herself a cocktail or two. Or both. And then a few more and when she sobers up the guilt sets in. Where did their lives go wrong?

Ken can't cope with the embarrassment of having a wife like Barbie, who used to be so glamorous and so much fun and who, ever since the kids went off to college, just sits around the house moping all the time, reading those stupid romance novels and complaining that Ken doesn't pay enough attention to her. Not that he doesn't try. He doesn't run around on her, although the thought has certainly crossed his mind. Maybe she should pay *him* a little more attention. Of course, sometimes, although more and more rarely, she's a pleasure to be with, almost like the good old days. That's usually after he's bought her a present. But most of the time, he gives her whatever she wants and still it's not enough; she's never happy.

She sits around the house and gets herself all worked up and starts to drink and cannot stop and ends up getting sloppy drunk and making a fool of herself in front of his friends and business associates. He tries hard to control himself, but the moment they're alone she nags him and he tries to ignore her, but eventually the nagging causes him to lose his temper and then the screaming begins and sometimes he just loses control and maybe he even hits her. And then the guilt sets in.

Where did their lives go wrong?

1. Which is the "real" Ken and the "real" Barbie?
2. Consider and evaluate each of these hypotheses about Ken and Barbie's relationship and what approach is most likely to salvage it.
   - These guys are messed up. She's an alcoholic and he's a wife abuser. They need in-depth psychotherapy badly. They've got to get themselves together before they can expect to get their relationship together.
   - They've gotten themselves trapped in a relationship that's driving them crazy. The problem is *between* them and not *within* either one or both of them. They need to get their interpersonal act together

and then they will have a chance of getting themselves together.

3. Have you ever been involved in, observed, or known about a situation that was in some way like this? What was going on? What, if anything, was done about it or what did the participants try to do about it? What happened?

SUGGESTIONS FOR TEAMS

Discuss this situation in light of the material presented below. If you were asked to be Ken and Barbie's therapist, what might you do or suggest? Share any experiences you are willing to share about similar situations in your own life or experience.

This is an old, old story. Every counselor has seen it again and again and again.

We've got a two-person group here, a family experiencing the "empty nest" syndrome when the kids have grown and left the house, leaving two strangers stuck in a bad dream.

There are two complementary sociological approaches for working with people who are trapped in a bad relationship. One is to take the perspective developed in the past couple of chapters and look at this problem as a sort of family drama. Perhaps we might use some of Nathan Hurvitz's methods—help each person to take the role of the other, negotiate a more satisfactory exchange relationship, change those negative interactional tracks.

There is, however, another approach on which I want to focus in this present chapter because it offers some key insights into how you can "debug" and improve your performance in any area of your life. I am not talking about magic.

I am talking about the *human systems* perspective that focuses on the whole rather than on the part. A while ago we said, "You are your act." The systems perspective suggests that your act is largely determined by the network of relationships in which you are embedded, so that who you are in any relationship is more an expression of that relationship than of the real you.

The key concept is that of a system. A *system* is any set of mutually interdependent elements organized into a whole. The properties of the system emerge from how the parts are connected and cannot be predicted from the nature of these parts in and of themselves. In fact:

Key Principle Thirty-four: In any system, the behavior of the part is shaped by its relation to the whole. This is the principle of *wholeness*. Our modern approach to systems was pioneered by a biologist, Ludwig von Bertalanffy, and represents an image of the world based on biological organisms. His *general systems theory* was soon taken over by engineering types involved in the birth of the computer age and, today, systems theory often comes across as pretty mechanistic.

Some of my humanist colleagues don't like systems theory because they believe it is based on the model of the electronic computer. But I think they miss the point in three ways. First, one of the exciting things about computers is that the way in which they operate is modeled after the way living organisms operate.

Second, the whole point of von Bertalanffy's science of systems was to show that all wholes made up of interdependent parts—that is, all *systems*—follow similar general systems laws regardless of what *kinds* of parts they happen to be.

Third, systems theorists *do* recognize that human beings are different from diesel engines and IBM PCs.

All systems exhibit certain properties. One is wholeness, the idea that they are made up of interacting parts. Another is that they have boundaries separating them from their external environment. Living systems, however, are seen as presenting an array of properties not shared with other kinds of systems.

They are *open* systems, meaning that they are dynamic, always in a state of flux and interaction with their environment. They maintain themselves through processes of mutual adjustment such as *feedback*, the arrangement by which they detect and adjust to any changes in their internal state or external environment.

For our purposes, a very important characteristic of living systems is that they are coordinated by *information* rather than by mechanical linkages. And, finally, living systems can use information about their environment and about the results of their actions to modify subsequent behavior. They can learn.

SOCIAL SYSTEMS

Although many systems thinkers approach an individual's performance problems from the perspective of changing intrapersonal systems, I believe that this is stretching a metaphor to the snapping point. I am convinced that you can get a better grasp on your behavior as an individual social actor by adopting the microsociological analysis we have been discussing.

When it comes to a relationship or a small group, such as a family, a group of friends, or a work team, then it becomes useful to employ elements from *both* an interactionist perspective and a systems perspective as complementary alternatives. As you move beyond to larger-scale *organizations*— businesses, schools, agencies, and so forth—then the human systems perspective really comes into its own.

All such *social systems* consist of human actors in identifiable relationships, linked together by exchange of information into an interdependent whole. Each participant in the system plays his or her role as part of a larger acting unit, which can then interact with other systems at a higher level of organization (or logical type). One can identify systemic relationships between systems and in a phrase coined by my colleague, Tom Leitko, can view society as a whole, as a complex of "nested social systems."

When analyzing social systems, you need to know about two things. First, you must know about the structure or *configuration* of the system—of what *units* the system is composed, how they are *organized*, and second, what *link-*

ages tie them together into a whole. Let me introduce some descriptive concepts you may find helpful when thinking about or analyzing social structure.

As I have suggested, you can look at various levels of scale:

- *Primary Groups:* small and informal, characterized by face-to-face interaction, intense, emotional relationships, strong interpersonal bonds, and a strong sense of mutual belonging, such as families.
- *Secondary Groups:* larger and more businesslike, based on getting things done rather than just being together, with members relating to one another primarily in their formal roles, such as a college class, a club, or a small congregation.
- *Organizations:* on a still larger scale, formally structured with several layers of hierarchy, often composed of smaller groups, such as corporations and agencies.

We also need some terms to describe the internal structure of social systems. I introduced you to these terms in Chapter One:

- *Roles:* the set of expectations for conduct, defining how a person within the system is to function relative to others in the organization; the emphasis is on the relationship between roles—boss and worker, manager and subordinate, teacher and student, and so forth.
- *Positions:* a formalized social location within a social structure for which the task or function is determined by the group or organization's nature or goals, such as head nurse, secretary, or receptionist.
- *Status:* the unique place held by any position in the social structure with respect to the hierarchy of authority.
- *Hierarchy:* authority structure within the organization or group; positions can have statuses that are lower, equal to, or higher than other positions, generally based

on who has the right to make decisions for or give directions to others (in most work structures this translates into higher and lower pay).

You also want to know about how the system *functions*, both *how it works* and *how it flows*. For example, how inputs enter the system, how they are processed within the system, and how or what the system outputs. Some of the issues associated with this process level of social systems include how the activities of social systems are coordinated and executed, how decisions are made, how problems and conflict within the organization are resolved, how well the system detects and responds to internal changes and changes in external environment, and, of course, whether the social system is growing, maintaining a steady state, or declining. The beauty of this approach is that the same basic approach can be employed whether you are evaluating a family, a workplace, or an entire community.

Exercise 6-E: Social Systems Analysis

DIRECTIONS

You are undoubtedly involved with at least one organization such as your workplace, your school, your club, your church or synagogue. If you are not currently involved with something of this sort, you certainly have been involved in the past. For this exercise select one organization you know well, preferably the one in which you spend the largest amount of your time.

1. Analyze the *structure* and *functioning* of this organization by answering these questions, paying attention to how it *really is* rather than how it is *supposed to be*.
    a. Of what *units* is this system composed? (If there is more than one level of organization, ask this of each level structure; for instance, a department

can be composed of units and each unit of several positions, such as secretary, file clerk, supervisor, analyst, and assembly-line worker).

b. How are these units and/or roles *related* or *organized*? (Look at what kind of *hierarchy* there is, at the official and unofficial reporting and working relationships between different parts of the system, and at what holds this particular system together—contracts, pay, loyalty, shared purposes, what?)

c. What is the pattern of *flow*? What are the *inputs* (such as information, material, or personnel), the *outputs* (products, services, or information)? What are the *activities* that occur within the organizations?

d. And the big question: How well is this organization *working*? (Is it effectively adjusting to changes in its environment and to internal conditions? Is it growing, staying the same size, shrinking? Are there any special bottlenecks or problem areas in flow? Are there any special areas of strain, dissatisfaction, or conflict within or between units? How satisfied, healthy, motivated, or productive are the people in this system?)

2. After analyzing this organization, can you draw any conclusions about how the configuration and flow of a system affect the people who participate in that system? Affect their performance as members of that system? About how your participation in systems like this one might affect your performance in other areas of your life?

PERFORMANCE AND SOCIAL STRUCTURE

When we talk about social interaction, we talk about persons or social actors. However, when we talk about social systems, we normally talk about the roles and positions, how individuals assigned to positions perform their roles, the consequences of the way the social structure functions for people in the organization.

There is a definite and crucial link between the social systems in which you are involved and the quality of your life. I mean this both in the sense of the type of person you become and your degree of satisfaction, well-being, and effective performance in all areas of your life.

For example, the English clinical sociologist and organizational consultant, Elliott Jaques (who first described the concept of midlife crisis), feels that the ways social systems are organized produce powerful effects on human behavior and relationships:

> The structure of relationships between roles has a decisive effect upon . . . the people who occupy them, and upon the quality of their social interactions. Change the nature of this structure of social relationships and you change the behavior and the quality of social life. The same people act and go about life differently.

While we are rarely in a position to change the social structure of the larger groups and organizations in which we are involved, this insight can be crucial to understanding why we are feeling and behaving as we do and suggesting what we can do about it.

Goffman and others have identified a number of problems relating to the roles we play in our social systems:

- *Role strain.* We find it hard, unpleasant, or painful to perform certain roles.
- *Role conflict.* We feel pulled apart by the demands made by the different roles we play in life.
- *Role overload.* We feel we just have too much to do.
- *Role ambiguity.* Our roles (and positions) are poorly or not at all defined and we are placed in the position of not knowing what is expected of us or what will be expected of us next.
- *Role disenchantment.* We feel we cannot stand our roles any longer, prompting us to feel trapped or burned out.

- *Multiple roles*. Curiously, researchers have found repeatedly that taking on multiple roles seems to have a buffering effect, reducing strain and increasing well-being.

Other aspects of roles and positions that affect people's performance include:

- *Status discrepancy*. When there is a conflict between the official and unofficial social structure, as is often the case, situations arise wherein those in higher status positions are placed in the role of taking orders from those in lower positions, causing strain and conflict.
- *Status incongruity*. Sometimes the statuses that individuals hold within a social structure are out of whack with their skills or status in other social systems; examples would be a highly skilled Ph.D. holding a low-status data processing job, or, in the opposite direction, a totally unqualified person holding a high-status job by virtue of connections.
- *Structural strain*. Sometimes, particularly in times of rapid growth or decline, the social structure becomes inadequate or inappropriate to the tasks those within it face, bottlenecks occur, roles become confused, and the old rules no longer work.

There are also process-level issues that affect those within a social structure or organization:

- *Control*. The amount of control over one's time, work, and activities appears to be a key variable in well-being and job satisfaction; the more control, the better.
- *Conflict*. Interpersonal, interunit, and intergroup conflicts may arise over issues of who does what, who gets what, who gets to decide these things, and how others are affecting one's own situation. While conflict may be therapeutic—a way of identifying issues and working out contradictions within the system—unresolved

or uncontrolled conflict can be devastating and disastrous for all involved.

- *Conditions.* The social, physical, and psychological conditions associated with life in the social structure present have a clear effect on how well activities are executed and how well individuals in the organization function. In this respect, it is important to consider the pacing of work and of changes and the amount and rate of demands made on those in the system.

When any or all of these issues become problems, it is essential to recognize that they are problems of the system, not problems of individuals or caused by individuals. And while these systems problems really require systems-level solutions, they become a problem for those within the system.

STRESS AND STRAIN

In C. Wright Mills' terminology, these problems of social structure become *predicaments* for individuals holding those roles, in those positions and statuses. Analytically, these predicaments all revolve around the issue of *strain*. The ambiguities, demands, or conflicts in the system become too much for those within the system to deal with them comfortably, overloading their coping mechanisms, which results in frustration, sometimes depression, and, almost always, stress.

In my previous book, I focused on stress from the perspective of the individual experiencing it. I continue to think this is a valid approach, but my systems-thinking friends and colleagues have pretty well convinced me that stress is less a matter of an individual's experience of too much or too little input from the world in general than it is a response to the specific *stressors* in the individual's social systems. I would like, consequently, to take a social systems perspective in this book.

I already have. This is what the last section covered. The reason I want to raise the matter of stress at this point is:

Key Principle Thirty-five: Unresolved strain and unmanaged stress are barriers to satisfactory performance. The first step in creative problem solving is always evaluation. So let's consider some of the *stressors*, sources of strain, and, hence, stress in our social systems.

And, as I have been doing to keep things concrete, I am going to focus on the relationship between stress and the social organization of work and the workplace. Now, I am aware that many of you may be students, homemakers, or others who do not work in an organization, per se. The fact of the matter is, however, that the school is a complex organization just like most workplaces and, in any case, there comes a time when we all must graduate. And then go to work. Homemakers and retired people face many of the same types of problems as those in the paid work force—perhaps more.

Being a housewife and/or mother is hard work. Sociologists have noted that the stress many women feel in their lives is commonly due to the demands made on them by their unpaid employment within the home. While problems of work structure are a major source of stress for paid workers, homemakers must deal with a *lack* of structure and of accepted means for setting a limit on one's tasks. Psychologically, this lack of structure appears to often prove more devastating than the problems caused by a faulty structure.

Retired people, then, seem to have both the theoretical opportunity to structure their lives as they please and the reality of having been forced to quit working—exiling them, in too many instances, to their homes, apartments, or retirement communities to spend the rest of their lives doing nothing in an unstructured environment.

There are alternatives. Individuals who are involved in creative or intellectual pursuits—musicians, artists, writers, philosophers, and scientists—are generally exempted from the rule that you are supposed to pack up and go home after age sixty-five. Societally, the increasing numbers and the vitality of older Americans have begun to force some long-overdue changes, such as new challenges to mandatory retirement. And other societies have long recognized the fact that our older citizens have a lifetime of wisdom and skill to share. In China, for instance, older people are expected to take an active and honored role in raising and teaching children.

You will notice that I have not mentioned unemployment. Losing a job can be a severely stressful event not only because of feeling invalidated and losing income but because of being structurally prevented from working. This is a terrible blow to the human spirit.

I have just described several of the structural issues that can provoke *strain* and result in perceived stress. These are the tip of the iceberg. Kenneth Pelletier, for example, describes some additional sources of stress for managers: work overloads, erratic schedules, job instability, cut-throat competition, dealing with "stress carriers" (which he defines to include workaholics, passive–aggressive subordinates, and anxious, indecisive individuals), sexual harassment, and being in a position of responsibility for other people.

Clinical sociologist Art Shostak has devoted a great deal of research and thought to the problems of blue-collar workers. He identifies not only the above stressors but also monotony, restrictions on freedom and motion (e.g., being permitted to go to the bathroom only during designated breaks), restrictions against talking, rigid work tasks, a general structural powerlessness.

These problems are only multiplied for women and minorities in the work force. Particularly when they are breaking into new, higher levels of status from which "their kind" has previously been excluded. I had, for example, a client in Sacramento who had been the first woman promoted to supervisor in a ceramic tile plant. The "old boys" did everything they could to drive her out—dumped paperwork on her, harassed her verbally, excluded her from their socializing during breaks and after work. She kept fighting, although I had to help her lose the weight she had gained by using eating as a stress-management tactic.

Now that I have given you some ideas, I want you to apply them.

Exercise 6-F: Sources of Strain and Stress

DIRECTIONS
1. Focusing, if at all possible, on your work or other complexly organized social systems in which you are presently involved (school, other types of organizations), think of what is currently the most stressful and/or most frustrating, strained, or conflict-ridden situation in your life right now.
2. Do CSH for Exercises through step 3.
3. Then recreate the situation in your mind, but from the perspective of an outside observer.

    Hint: Imagining that you are watching a situation on a memory videotape is really a strategy for bringing about this sort of detachment and getting your viewpoint external to the scene. That is why I've been having you use this metaphor.
4. If necessary, open your eyes and reread the material in the last two sections. See what role level, other structural level, or process level of sources of strain and specific stressors you can identify in this situation. Be a sociological analyst, not a psychoanalyst (don't interpret *why*, just observe *what* and *how*).
5. Think about how this situation is affecting your performance outside of work, in your relationships, in your family, or other aspects of your life. Also look at what is happening in the reverse direction—how and to what degree are strain and stress from these other areas of your life affecting your performance and tolerance for strain at work.
6. Now, think about what you want out of this situation, what it could be like for you if these sources of stress or strain were either resolved at a structural level or somehow you made yourself invulnerable to them. Perhaps literally imagine that you are wrapping around yourself a *cloak of invulnerability* to stress and strain. Just imagine what it would be like.

7. Do step 5 of CSH for Exercises. In your journal, brainstorm what possible actions you could take to either change the structural situation or give yourself, in effect, that cloak of invulnerability. Really brainstorm—let ideas flow, no matter how wild or silly.

8. Now review your brainstorm and then make a list of three to five *initial steps* you could take to resolve the stress and strain, or, at least, immunize yourself to them, so that you can perform at your best both in this work (or other) situation and in all aspects of your life.

SUGGESTIONS FOR TEAMS

This is another exercise I leave up to you, but take a hint from the idea of a brainstorm. Also consider the possibility of sculpture, circle discussion, or role-playing exercises.

HARDINESS AND STRESS MANAGEMENT

Claire was one of the first women to be certified as a helicopter pilot, participated in transcontinental air races, and had, almost single-handedly, run half of the family business, which was delivering spare parts to mining and similar companies by airplane. When her husband died everyone assumed she would sell the firm or find a man to manage it for her. When she didn't, she found herself plagued with constant, often well-intentioned advice from family, friends, business acquaintances, all to the effect that this kind of thing was too much for a middle-aged woman to handle alone. I helped Claire to ignore those voices and develop some more effective stress management strategies, and she prospers to this day.

What was it about this woman that gave her the strength to carry on and to do all these things? In retrospect, I find that Claire exhibited a pattern of stress resistance that has become the focus of much recent literature on the subject.

Suzanne C. Kobasa, a University of Chicago social psychologist, studied 259 executives over two years and found that those who remained healthiest exhibited a pattern of three characteristics that she termed *hardiness*:

1. A positive orientation toward challenges and reasonable risk taking.
2. A positive commitment or sense of embracing the different aspects of their lives.
3. A belief that they had control over their own lives.

Claire had these three traits and they helped her succeed. Why not have a goal in your creative self-management program to make this list a description of yourself as well? If you haven't already noticed, from Technique One forward, I've been sneaking in these attitudes and orientations as part of what I've asked you to do. Now you know why.

Another facet of this new approach to dealing with strain and stress is that we are no longer speaking of stress *reduction* as much as stress *management*. Strain and stress are unavoidable in life. Just like bureaucracy and taxes. Consequently, you've got three choices: You can complain all the time, you can try to keep yourself very relaxed and minimize stress, or you can thumb your nose at stress and ride it like a surfer.

Actually, there can be a degree of relief in taking the role of a *kvetch*, a complainer. At least you feel better, although those around you may want to throw things at you. Some people get away with it and seem to do fairly well. But I really don't suggest making this your goal!

There is also much to be said for the strategy of relaxation. I believe that periodic practice of deep relaxation exercises (such as CSH in the "down" direction) are highly beneficial, but only a small part of the total solution.

Rather, I suggest you consider the third alternative: surfing. If you can't avoid stress, learn to ride it, to make its energy work for you. Of course, do what you can to adjust to the social structures in which you live and work, to fit your needs as a human being and also to suit your individual preferences. But also make the stressors you can't avoid your allies in creative self-management.

How can this be done?

Key Tactic Fifteen: Keep a sense of humor about yourself, your roles, positions, and statuses. Remember that at a higher level, it's all just a game. This is something that it is very easy to forget when we become so wrapped up in the details and dramas of our daily lives. But as religious, spiritual, and satirical authorities have been telling us all along, there's nothing to gain and everything to lose from taking life too seriously.

Key Tactic Sixteen: Don't worry about it, just do it. This tactic is one that works well for me. If I stop to think about it I begin to get stressed out and tensed up, and it all gets difficult. If I do my CSH and keep my sense of humor, I find that I can deal with very high levels of demand and stressors without falling prey to them. Instead, I get kind of turned on by the challenge. This is part of the reason why people tend to do well when taking on multiple roles—if we just deal with challenges, we find we create more energy, we expand ourselves to fit. If we hide from stressors and challenges, we shrink.

Key Tactic Seventeen: Spend some time every day doing something completely different. This is absolutely and utterly essential. If you are to manage stress you must make a point of breaking the flow every so often. Now, I know this is a heretical statement, and while I recognize the benefits of exercise, I suggest that much of the demonstrated stress-managing benefits of regular jogging or other aerobic activity come from the fact that they are a way to break the flow of the day's stream of stressors. It's hard to concentrate on that report on your desk when you're busting your buns doing some kind of exercise. However, some studies have found similar benefits from gentler pursuits, like gardening.

I personally make it a point to read some science fiction

or fantasy every day. I also like to watch television. Doing CSH, of course, is another way to break the flow.

All of these examples involve taking your mind off of real-world problems and demands. There is a bonus to doing this: By taking your mind off of the problem, you let your creative imagination work on it. When you do that, the solution often comes to you in the form of an insight, or, literally, as a sudden flash of inspiration.

All of these tactics are, in effect, steps toward realizing hardiness. As I said before, it's all connected.

PERFORMANCE ENHANCEMENT TECHNIQUES

Let's wrap up this discussion with a brief consideration of three useful tactics for enhancing and optimizing performances and then a fourth tactic for shifting performances back onto a desired track.

Key Tactic Eighteen: If you are having a problem with performance, do the problem. By this, I mean to literally do the problem as a voluntary act. Whatever it is you are doing and have been doing (attempted solutions, again) has not worked. Furthermore, if it is a problem to you it is persisting. Consequently, anything you do to disrupt what you have been doing is likely to disrupt the interactional system that has developed around the problem. This creates an opportunity for change.

Now, it is not always prudent or even possible to literally do the problem openly in the world of other people. But you can get much, if not all, of the same effect by doing it in your head.

Exercise 6-G: Doing the Problem

DIRECTIONS
1. Select a problem you are currently having with your performance at work, school, or, alternatively, in your intimate groups (family, friends).

2. Do CSH for Exercises through step 3.
3. Now, visualize a concrete example of the performance problem you have selected as it might occur in the near future—what kind of situation would it be, who would be the audience, what would be happening, what are the demands, and so forth. Really build it up. If you feel very uncomfortable about this performance situation, use the memory videotape technique; otherwise imagine yourself really being there. *At this point, just set the scene, set the stage, but do not yet start the action.*
4. Start the imaginary action but *make yourself lose it.* Do everything you are afraid you might do wrong, but do it deliberately and do it consciously. Go through to the end of the scene in this way.
5. Start again and do the scene again until you feel ready to stop doing it this way.
6. Do step 5 of CSH for Exercises.

SUGGESTIONS FOR TEAMS

Either in two-person teams or larger groups, select a performance problem (preferably one that is shared or relevant to all of you) and do the problem in a role-playing simulation. Ideally give everyone a chance to do a problem.

Hint: You may find that it is useful to recruit a team and work through problems in this way when they occur in real life.

Key Tactic Nineteen: Rehearse and re-rehearse until you know you're ready to perform optimally. Master systems consultant Ron Lippitt stressed how we tend to get an idea about changing something—our own act, the way our organization should operate, anything—and then jump right into action. And land on our faces.

After we get the idea that we need to change and want to change, we need to carefully explore our alternatives. Then we need to practice in a rehearsal mode until we have developed the skill and comfort to act effectively. Lippitt called this action a *skilled performance*. While most consultants would have clients and client organizations practice in small groups, this practice can also be done in our minds.

Exercise 6-H: Rehearsal for Skilled Performance

DIRECTIONS

For now, use the same problem or performance you worked on in Exercise 6-G.

1. Do CSH for Exercises through step 3.
2. Imagine a typical future example of the situation, seeing yourself there and seeing all the others who should also be part of the scene. Focus on the social structural aspects of the situation—the roles, positions, statuses, issues, and so forth.
3. Tell yourself what the situation is and what you are going to try to do (the performance).
4. Start the imaginary interaction. Try to perform as best you can, and as realistically as possible, imagine the probable response based on what you know of the realities of the situation. *Do it in real time, as if you were actually dealing with the other people right now, as if they were actually responding to you right now.*

   Hint: Use the Quick CSH technique you've been learning to set your mind for optimal action and break the flow so as to clear your mind. Even do this in your mental rehearsal.
5. As soon as you have a feel for how it's going, stop. Evaluate how it went.
6. Brainstorm or at least think about alternatives: How else could you "play" this scene; what changes could you make in your conduct, demeanor, words, pacing, whatever?
7. Repeat steps 4, 5, and 6 above until you feel comfortable with your performance and feel that you can

realistically and skillfully deal with all likely contingencies.

8. Visualize the very end of an optimal performance, just the last few moments when you are feeling really good, feeling the whole thing flowing your way.
9. Tell yourself you can do it and end your session with step 5 of CSH for Exercises.

SUGGESTIONS FOR TEAMS

You might want to form practice trios as Ron Lippitt would do. One person is the performer, another is the audience or the individual who is the most important part of the audience, and a third is the observer who starts the action, cuts the action once he or she sees where it's leading, debriefs the others, shares observations, and leads the brainstorm.

Key Tactic Twenty: Celebrate completion of every major cycle, every successful performance. This tactic is truly a key that most of us ignore. Lippitt and other systems consultants emphasize that it is enormously important to reward progress and successful performance. More than merely reward it, *celebrate* it. Celebrations can be as uncomplicated as getting an ice cream cone, or you can develop rituals of celebration (which might include going out to a good restaurant, having a celebration party, whatever). Preferably do not just celebrate by yourself, in a covert fashion. Rather, involve your significant others, or, perhaps, your work group in celebration of important performances or milestones.

It is, in fact, a good idea to plan for celebrations when you begin a creative self-management campaign. Decide what the important *milestones* are that will tell you that you are moving, progressing, getting somewhere. Keep them realistically near-term, so that you can expect at least a small celebration every couple of weeks. Decide on how you will celebrate each kind of milestone and with whom you will celebrate.

Exercise 6-I: Celebrations

DIRECTIONS

Although it is somewhat late to start, think about what your remaining goals for your creative self-management program are, what would be a reasonable choice for the *small* and *big* milestones of your progress, and how you will celebrate at least the first few of them. What will you do and with whom will you do it? Write these things in your journal. That's the exercise!

SUGGESTIONS FOR TEAMS

Do the same thing as a team, planning joint celebrations.

Key Tactic Twenty-one: To switch performance tracks, use Quick CSH but reverse steps 4 and 5—scan the present and then choose your preferred outcome. This is a way to break the flow and change tracks. It looks deceptively simple but it is really very powerful—see for yourself by doing the following exercise.

Exercise 6-J: Switching Tracks

DIRECTIONS
1. Do CSH for Exercises through step 3.
2. Imagine the problem performance on which you have been working in this chapter *as if you are really there.*
3. Imagine things are going wrong for you, or that you are feeling the strain and are worried that things are about to go wrong for you.
4. Do Quick CSH but reversing steps 4 and 5 and just imagining that you are doing step 6. When doing this, scan the imaginary situation as if it were your actual present-time reality, envisioning your preferred outcome and telling yourself that *this* is what you choose for yourself.

Quick CSH for Switching Tracks

1. Close eyes (optional). Inhale deeply.
2. Quick tense/relax (optional).
3. Flash place.
4. Open eyes (optional). Scan situation.
5. Choose the outcome *you* prefer.
6. Breathe deeply. Go ahead and do it.

> 5. Now do step 6 above for real.
> 6. Repeat this entire exercise at least three times without stopping.

SUMMARY

This chapter discussed the nature and facilitation of *optimal performance*. Performance analysis was then introduced, discussing the *preferred outcome* and how it relates to optimizing *desired effects, audience demands, audience management,* and *stress management*. We then looked at how our lives develop through *helical progressions* and how this pattern relates to the indirect performance optimization strategy of *redirection* and the concept of *mastery*. The chapter then shifted emphasis to *systems theory* and *social systems*. You were shown how to analyze social systems in terms of *structure* and *process*. Discussion turned to the workplace and the principle that stress is primarily a result of experiencing *strain* in our social systems. We considered *hardiness* and several tactics of *stress management*.

Five Key Principles were discussed:

THIRTY-ONE: Human development moves in a helical progression.

THIRTY-TWO: Everything in our lives is connected into a whole.

THIRTY-THREE: The ideal way to do anything is to be there and just do it.

THIRTY-FOUR: In any system, the behavior of the part is shaped by its relation to the whole.

THIRTY-FIVE: Unresolved strain and unmanaged stress are barriers to satisfactory performance.

Nine Key Tactics were presented:

THIRTEEN: For optimal performance consider the preferred outcome, the audience, and the desired effects.

FOURTEEN: For creative performance focus on process and redirection, not details of what, when, and how.

FIFTEEN: Keep a sense of humor about yourself, your roles, positions, and statuses.

SIXTEEN: Don't worry about it, just do it.

SEVENTEEN: Spend some time every day doing something completely different.

EIGHTEEN: If you are having a problem with performance, do the problem.

NINETEEN: Rehearse and re-rehearse until you know you're ready to perform optimally.

TWENTY: Celebrate completion of every major cycle, every successful performance.

TWENTY-ONE: To switch performance tracks, use Quick CSH but reverse steps 4 and 5—scan the present and then choose your preferred outcome.

Technique Six: Optimal Performance

There are no new techniques for this week, only some new ways of working with the form of CSH you learned in Chapter Five, and one other thing.

DIRECTIONS

1. For this week, when you visualize your preferred future, focus on optimal performance generally, and in terms of specific goals and objectives.

2. At least once a day, focus the working part of your CSH on a performance that is either a problem for you or that you wish to optimize. Using any or all of the

techniques and tactics you have learned in this chapter, do some mindwork designed to help you optimize the performance.

3. Use Key Tactic Twenty-one whenever necessary.
4. Now for the "other thing": *Go out and celebrate completing Chapter Six!*

SEVEN

Creative Living

Two of the most extraordinary things about human beings are our persistence and our optimism. Whatever the conditions with which we must cope, we find a way to get by. More than just get by—we find a way to squeeze some hope and joy and dignity and beauty from the most wretched of circumstances. We go on despite the fact that science and logic and reason all tell us that life is ultimately futile, that there is a universal tendency toward the degradation of order. Human beings and, in fact, all living systems manifest a stubborn tendency or compulsion to grow and reproduce and build elaborate sand castles on the beach of time.

This has a great deal to do with the concept of optimization. In this chapter, I am going to elaborate on this point and take our discussion of optimizing performance a step further, around the bend to the next turn of the helix into creative living—and I do not mean merely surviving. What I mean is making your life your masterpiece. Doing your life as a creative work. So, let's backtrack.

When my friend Steve Smith first described the concept of optimization to me, he explained that the only way a system can find and maintain an optimum balance is if it is continually in a state of disequilibrium. It cannot stand still. It must keep juggling the desired parameters, always seeking out an optimal balance.

Key Principle Thirty-six: Optimization depends on a moving equilibrium and, hence, on change. This principle is not merely a luxury that permits a person, system, or relationship to prosper but a basic necessity of survival for all living systems. Over fifty years ago, the Harvard physiologist Walter B. Cannon described this concept of a moving equilibrium as the key to *homeostasis,* the process by which organisms maintain the necessary internal balances for life. He pointed out that living organisms balance themselves through a set of self-correcting mechanisms that depend on continual fluctuations around the desired central point.

For example, your body measures the amount of sodium in your blood. If you were to gobble down a couple of bags of potato chips and the salt entered your body, it would break down into its component elements (technically, into ions) of sodium and chlorine. When your salt intake raises the amount of dissolved sodium in your bloodstream beyond a certain point, your body will act to bring the sodium concentration into line by increasing the volume of fluid in your bloodstream. Assuming that you don't jam in more salt than your body can handle, this response will dilute the salt in your blood to a tolerable level.

But how does your body know when to stop? It doesn't. What happens, instead, is that there will come a point where another internal switch will be triggered by a sodium-to-blood ratio that has now become *too low.* This causes your kidneys to work harder in order to pump out some of the excess fluid. They'll proceed until your body signals, "Whoa, too salty!" And that signal will trigger another cycle of dilution, triggering another cycle of excretion to keep your body within its design tolerances.

Thus your body is never actually at a point of equilibrium. There are no "points" in biology, only ranges! Your body doesn't hold to a set value for anything—not salt content, not body temperature, not blood pressure, not anything. Rather, it is constantly off balance, trying to bring itself back into balance by means of *feedback* mechanisms such as I have just described.

While your body or any other living system can only

withstand a certain amount of stress, within its range of tolerance it continually optimizes its internal relations and adapts them to new conditions in order to survive. Mere survival, however, is a far cry from creative living.

Things that depend on a tightly specified system are threatened by change, but *things that seek to evolve and develop in new ways require change*. And change is what creative living, creative self-management, and realization of your preferred outcomes are all about.

Key Tactic Twenty-two: *To optimize your performance, play with it; try never to repeat yourself exactly.* We are free to explore new possibilities for ourselves. We are free to explore new social arrangements at a collective level and new patterns of action ↔ reaction at an individual level. How is this possible for us?

Because humans are creative beings.

We *do* our lives rather than respond passively to internal or external forces. We organize our lives on the basis of our imagination and not by empirical necessity. Thus we can dream about possibilities. We can choose our preferred outcomes; we can choose what we want to become.

But you don't get your preferred future by charging ahead and forcing it to happen. You get there by a long-term process of optimization, which in turn depends on constant variation. Which is nice since all our evidence tells us that our universe is a dynamic one in which change and novelty are ultimate and irrevocable facts of life.

It makes sense to work with the way things flow naturally; creative living means that you learn to ride the dragon rather than let it step on your face.

Virginia Satir, a pioneer of family therapy and cofounder of the Mental Research Institute (who died as I was writing this book), expressed a similar philosophy in a speech she gave at a 1986 meeting of mental health professionals:

> Life is not the way it's supposed to be. It's the way it is. The way you cope with it is what makes the difference. I think that if I have one message, one thing before I die I would like

the world to know, it would be that the event does not determine how to respond to the event. That is a purely personal matter. The way in which we respond will direct and influence the event more than the event itself.

Surfing is a good metaphor for what she and I are trying to convey. Living in time, we all exist on the precarious forward edge of a changing world. We'll all drown eventually—for none of us are physically immortal—but until that time we might as well ride the wave and have some fun. Perhaps even create something bigger than ourselves, something we can be proud of that will survive us. To be sure, you don't really have much of an alternative—you can live positively or you can live negatively.

Exercise 7-A: Creative Living

DIRECTIONS

CSH for Exercises

1. Close eyes. Inhale deeply.
2. Quick tense/relax.
3. Flash place/imagine awakening ("up" direction).
4. Follow directions for exercise.
5. Take a deep breath and open eyes.

1. Do CSH for Exercises through step 3.
2. Remember a time when you felt you were living creatively, even if just for an instant. Just let it come back to you and let yourself remember and feel what it was like.
3. Imagine what creative living could be like for you. What it could mean to you and for you. Just let yourself meditate or fantasize or whatever for a couple of minutes.
4. Do step 5 in CSH for Exercises.

CHANGE AND OPTIMIZATION

Creative living involves consciously optimizing your life's performance and opening yourself to the possibility and the necessity of change. But this is really too passive a statement of what I mean.

Key Principle Thirty-seven: Creative living means that you actively invite and use change to optimize performance. There is both a strategic and a tactical implication to this principle. The strategic implication is that the only way to discover a better way is to try something different. A *habit* is something you do on automatic pilot, something you do as close to the same way as possible, again and again. It is the path of minimal effort.

Habits have their value. They make it possible for you to focus your attention on preferred outcomes and do whatever you have to do as you work your way toward them. They are just like socialization in that respect—they empower you to operate in the world, they provide structure, and they provide tools. Habits, we might say, are to the individual what socialization is to society.

However, habits and socialization alike are also coercive. That is why I liken them to being hypnotized into following postnatal suggestions. They restrict you to a set way of doing things. They are antievolutionary.

In theory, that is. In actuality, the force of both habits and socialization tends to be less than truly compulsive. As sociologist Dennis Wrong has explained, it is erroneous to assume that people behave only as they are socialized to behave. It is equally mistaken to assume that we are entirely creatures of habit.

This is a good thing, as every living system requires some randomness, some variation in conduct. Otherwise, there could be no change, no learning, no progress, and, ultimately, no survival. But the fact remains that sometimes both our socialization—our internalization of the roles, rules, positions, norms, and values of the social systems within which we have made our lives—and our habits become problems to us. They get in the way of change. We discover that they no longer serve our needs and purposes because either we or our situations have changed. Or we discover that the unanticipated long-term consequences that have begun to pile up are becoming a real drag and we want to stop pursuing this old line of conduct.

And we find we can't change. We are stuck on automatic pilot. Then we have a problem. It can be a problem of performance, of relationship, of action, of reaction. It can occur on any or all levels of our social participation, from a compulsive personal ritual to a public performance failure or an inability to operate within the social structure of our groups and organizations. It can be a real mess.

The main thing you need to know about habits and habit patterns is that *a problem of conduct, on whatever level it happens to operate, is a problem of blocked optimization.* It is a problem in living, not (at least in the vast majority of cases) an outcropping of psychopathology, the effect of some genetic cause, or the result of what anything or anyone made you do or did to you at some time in the past.

The problem is a problem to you in the here-and-now. It is a problem because it represents a constriction in your freedom of action. A stuck track. There are countless ways of attacking any problem. Some ways work *because* you believe they will work. And sometimes you can jar things loose by main force, get the needle to jump into another track. However, these "solutions" still leave the original problem intact and you'll probably run into it again.

Systems change consultants describe change in the specific performance as *first-order change.* As a solution to a problem, they feel that first-order change is Band-Aid stuff, a short-term fix at best. What is important, they say, is to create *second-order change*—a change in the way the whole thing hangs together. A change in the relationships framing and supporting the specific conduct that has become a problem to you is an example.

They take the perspective that an individual's problem behaviors are generally part of an interaction system. Ken complains about Barbie's withdrawal and coldness. Barbie withdraws and responds with coldness to Ken because he complains all the time. One consequence is that they both are dissatisfied with their sex life. Generally one or the other of them contacts the therapist and requests help, describing the problem in terms of discontent with their sex life and attributing it to the other person's problem (either Ken's constant complaining or Barbie's withdrawal and lack of affection, depending on the viewpoint).

How do you solve this problem? I don't know. But you aren't going to get very far by giving Barbie tranquilizers or antidepressants and telling her to practice being more responsive to Ken or by giving Ken psychotherapy and telling him to be more understanding of Barbie. Or teaching either him or her some new sexual techniques. *You have got to break the system.*

The Nobel laureate Ilya Prigogine's life work has been the study of chemical systems in a far-from-equilibrium state. What he has discovered is that if you push an open system far enough beyond its homeostatic state the system collapses into chaos.

As the poet, Yeats put it: Things fall apart; the centre cannot hold, / Mere anarchy is loosed upon the world.

That part wasn't much news, but Prigogine discovered that this phase of disorder is only temporary. *A new system spontaneously forms in the place of the old one.* Order out of chaos, as he describes it. Prigogine believes that his discoveries in the physical sciences have important implications for the social and behavioral sciences, and I am inclined to agree.

You force the old system to the point of breaking. A new system, also in a state of disequilibrium, will arise that is adapted to the new state of affairs. This disequilibrium is a necessary condition for growth as opposed to stagnation of any relationship, any social system, and also is the necessary resource for optimization of performance.

But—here's the really exciting part—if you do it right, you can have a say in what the new system is like. You can create the new system pretty much to your specifications, according to your preferred outcome. The creative part is always up to you. In this book I have provided some hints and pointers and tactics and strategies, but creativity always involves doing the unknown in an as-yet undiscovered way.

While the details are always unknown until you discover them in action, there is a basic method for facilitating change in any system. This is the tactical part of what I was talking about earlier.

Key Tactic Twenty-three: If what you have been doing hasn't done it for you, do something else. It is useful to consider a two-step strategy for creating *second-order change* to resolve problems and overcome constructions and blockages in action. The first step is to break the ongoing system by deliberately changing your performance in some way. Be prepared to encounter resistance, from others and from within yourself. Be prepared to have to grit your teeth and stick to your guns and assert this same change through every cycle of performance until the system breaks. This is one reason why systems consultants and therapists advise you to take it slow and to consider the dangers of improvement.

Use a lot of CSH, practicing and repracticing the necessary performances. Give yourself all the help you can get. For this first step, it doesn't really matter too much what change you make as long as it is do-able and it is something about which you can be persistent. Eventually, in its own time, the system will break, and then, for some period of time, there will be a state of chaos. Uncertainty. Ambiguity. Confusion. Just the sort of thing on which a true artist thrives as an opportunity for creative action.

It is during this interlude that your creative self-hypnosis and self-management comes into play. You will have been working on visualizing your preferred outcome all along, until it becomes something you can almost literally see, hear, feel, and touch. Something you feel that you can have. Something you know you want.

Step two in facilitating second-order change, then, is to become a bit compulsive about scanning your present and choosing your preferred future. If anything, increase the frequency and duration of your creative self-hypnosis sessions during periods of chaos. Put even more energy into visualizing and creating your preferred future. Use your performance tactics as appropriate, but remember that the only way to do it is to do it and there is no way to know what you will be in a position to do or have to do or need to do until you are actually there doing it. By your mindwork, you are focusing your creativity, building your creative energy, so to speak.

By all means use the methods from our Chapter Six to generate ideas about alternative courses of action and rehearse them in your mind or with other people. As long as you recognize that you will find out what you did to accomplish your preferred future only after you did it. And prepare yourself to accept change, to allow chaos, and to allow yourself to act when the time is right.

Exercise 7-B: Chaos, Change, and Opportunity

DIRECTIONS
1. Do CSH for Exercises through step 3.
2. Imagine as much chaos and change in your life as you can imagine tolerating. Build a sense of having as much as you can stand. Let images, situations, words, and whatever else float through your mind or deliberately use them to build this experience. Keep imagining it until you feel somewhat comfortable imagining it.
3. Imagine even more chaos and change. Keep building it up in your mind until you feel that you are just beyond your limit. Hold that level and meditate, contemplate, feel it for a while.
4. Go one step further in the same direction in your mind, but only one step. Get a sense of even more chaos and change.
5. Focus on how you are reacting to this perfectly safe fantasy—is your body tensing up? What are your mental "postures" as you confront it? What kinds of words and images are you noticing? Notice both words and images for what you are experiencing (how are you labeling and defining the situation itself) and for

how you are dealing with it (how are you labeling and defining your chaos-managing activities)?

6. Now relabel the situation for yourself; tell yourself that *what you were imagining to be chaos was really opportunity in disguise.* Build a brief fantasy along these lines.

7. Next, imagine literally embracing the chaos and change. Perhaps imagine welcoming it as a guest—imagine saying genuine words of welcome to it and embracing it as a friend and ally. I visualize myself bowing or giving it a big hug while saying, "Welcome, welcome, my dear friend." You do it your way! Maybe have tea with it or a glass of wine or something.

8. Imagine feeling comfortable with change. You can let the chaos part recede, but just imagine feeling physically, emotionally, mentally, and spiritually comfortable with change.

9. Visualize your preferred future. Feel it growing on you. Growing in you. Feel yourself growing toward it.

10. Do step 5 in CSH for Exercises. Take a break; you deserve it!

SUGGESTIONS FOR TEAMS

Why not role-play or sculpt Key Tactics Twenty-two and Twenty-three and then build a scenario of chaos and change in round robin fashion and keep making it worse. Imagine or sculpt or role-play welcoming that chaos, making it your friend and becoming comfortable with change.

FRIENDS CAN BE GOOD MEDICINE

I hope what I am going to say next is old news to most readers. Stale or not, the news is this: *Being connected to other people can literally save your life.* Our connections to other people seem to be a major source of resilience for us.

These connections have extraordinary impact on our mental health and also our physical health.

The resource guide for the Friends Can Be Good Medicine Campaign (California, 1982) summarizes the medical evidence:

- Compared with people who maintain supportive social relationships, socially isolated persons have *two to three times* the overall *risk of dying* prematurely.
- The existence of an available confidant confers significant protection against the development of depression.
- Pregnant women under stress and without supportive, confiding personal relationships have *three times* the *number of complications* experienced by women undergoing similar levels of stress but with supportive personal relationships.
- *Rates of mental hospitalization* are roughly *five to ten times* as great for separated, divorced, and widowed persons as for married people.

Skeptics might argue that these early studies didn't clearly prove that social isolation actually caused these ill effects. However, a new report by University of Michigan sociologist James House and his associates (summarizing studies of more than 37,000 people in the United States, Finland, and Sweden, conducted over a twenty-year period) has conclusively proven that social isolation is a more significant mortality risk than smoking, high blood pressure, high cholesterol, obesity, or lack of physical exercise. Furthermore, the study finds that social isolation not only affects physical health but makes people more prone to suffer an accident or commit suicide.

It appears that virtually all of us have drastically underestimated the depth to which we are social creatures. While some accused Herbert Blumer of overemphasizing the importance of social interaction, it now appears that he, if anything, underestimates it. The new evidence suggests that our social interactions affect us down to the level of our brain chemistry and immune system.

It is clear that we need somebody to interact with. Without other people in our lives, we wither and die. And that *positive* social relationships keep us mentally and physically well.

Key Principle Thirty-eight: Friends are good medicine, the best. As I write this book, I find myself reaching in my mind to the people whose opinion I most respect and who have taught me the most, whose ideas and opinions come to mind when I try to think of what I need to tell my readers. As I do this, I realize that these are not generally people I think of as mere acquaintances, or those with whom I have been involved in formal student–teacher relationships. Rather, these are people I think of as my friends.

You know, I hadn't realized until now how many friends I truly have! Now it's your turn to think about this—to literally count your blessings.

Exercise 7-C: Telling One's Friends

DIRECTIONS
1. Do CSH for Exercises through step 3.
2. Just think about the subject of friends for a few moments. Let the names, images, feelings, and memories of your past and present friends float through your mind.
3. Remember a time when you were down and your friends were there for you.
4. Remember a time when you were really up and you shared it with your friends.
5. Remember a time when your friend was really down and you were there for your friend.
6. Remember a time when your friend shared something happy and exciting with you.
7. Remember a bad time shared by you and your friends.
8. Remember a good time shared by you and your friends.

9. Imagine having all the friends you have ever had in your life gathered about you once again, including those who never knew how you felt about them, and imagine thanking them, each and every one, for being your friend and telling them how much you have cared about them.
10. Do step 5 in CSH for Exercises.

SUGGESTIONS FOR TEAMS

Why not share some of your experiences regarding friends and friendship and what they have meant for you in your life? Maybe try to formulate a joint definition of what it means to be a friend, and perhaps talk about ways of finding, making, and keeping friends that have worked for you.

SOCIAL SUPPORT

What exactly do we mean by social support? My very dear friend Susan Hillier Parks, and her mentor Marc Pilisuk, who have devoted many years to researching this issue explain it this way:

> Social support is the sum of the social, emotional and instrumental exchanges with which an individual is involved having the subjective consequence that the individual sees him or herself as an object of continuing value in the eyes of significant others. With social support, we are more secure in our interdependence. Without it, we are pushed toward greater independence and loneliness.

In summary, friends are not an option but a necessity. For optimum survival we need friends. We need caring, committed relationships. In the past (for example, in rural societies) our families and kin generally provided the social support we needed. In contemporary society we have to seek our own social support.

Key Tactic Twenty-four: Invest in creating a social support system; you're going to need it. Relationships are central to creative living. For you to succeed in your objectives, for you to have a life you can feel is worth living, you need to feel cared for and you need to care about others. At the most practical level, you need to have a network of socially supportive relationships to help you create and maintain desired changes in your life.

How do we find them? We don't. We have to create them ourselves. We construct our own support networks out of friends, we form self-help groups, we join community organizations, we act as support persons for our neighbors and co-workers. We invent our strategies and tactics as we proceed.

SUPPORT GROUPS

The concept of having and giving social support is, I have no doubt, enticing. However, the reality is that ours is a time of increasing loneliness and isolation from other people.

How many people with whom you are in daily or even weekly face-to-face contact can you say *really* care about you? And do you really care about them?

With how many people can you share your innermost feelings, desires, cares, and concerns? Who can you trust to offer support—physical and material assistance, information, guidance, or even a hug—if things go wrong?

James House's report confirms this impression that the trend toward social isolation is on the rise. We are increasingly less likely to live with other people, to be married, to belong to social clubs, or to visit with friends compared to twenty or thirty years ago.

We have come full circle, back to the sociological imagination, in that we are seeing the consequences of the social changes of the past half-century or so. Of a society in which interpersonal social bonds are subordinate to the individual's pursuit of material success.

Those in the middle classes may be immeasurably

wealthier than their forebears with respect to material things. But we are impoverished in relationships, in social support. Community and family were once our primary sources of social support. As these institutions fall into disrepair, nothing has replaced them. Corporations typically discourage close personal bonds among fellow workers. Our neighborhoods are places of temporary residence; there are those who seek homes where neighbors won't bother them. Our work lives are increasingly demanding of our time—blue-collar workers on overtime, white-collar workers on overload. We don't have much time or opportunity to develop supportive relationships.

So what do we do? As always, the first step is to evaluate our personal situation.

Exercise 7-D: Your Social Support Network

DIRECTIONS
1. Write the following at the top of a new journal page: "My Social Support Network."
2. Now, under this title list every person on whom you can currently count for social support and/or who can count on you for social support as defined by Parks and Pilisuk.
3. Review this list. Put a line through any names of people on whom you couldn't rely if you really got into bad trouble, who you would be embarrassed to ask for help, to whom you couldn't reveal things that might not be proper or respectable or morally upright or legal, who might demand something in return or hold what you said or did over you as a kind of emotional blackmail or to extract future favors.
4. Have there been times in the past when you felt you had more or better social support? What did you have that you do not currently have? Was there anything you were doing then that you are not doing now? Was the situation different, and, if so, in what way?

5. Now, close your eyes. Remember a time when you felt you had real social support, really good friends, caring relationships. Feel that way now.
6. Imagine yourself one year in the future. Imagine that you are again feeling securely supported by other people in your life. What kinds of relationships could be part of this story; what might you be doing to involve yourself in caring, supportive relationships? Do any specific individuals come to mind? Just let yourself focus on the feeling and let your creative imagination come up with some details. Don't try to organize it or make it make sense, just focus on having and giving social support.
7. When you are ready, tell yourself you are going to invest more of your energies in creating the social support networks that can help you feel this way, open your eyes, and, in your journal, jot down any ideas or observations that seem appropriate.

As Parks and Pilisuk point out, investing in friends is only one of the solutions people are finding to the problem of our increasing social isolation:

> Friendships develop on individual, one-to-one bases, and they also occur through associations with all kinds of groups. In the last fifteen years, we have witnessed a rapid rise in the number of groups specially designed to provide support, to help or to heal in some way.

This second solution is known as *support groups*. They range from highly organized groups for people sharing social or psychological problems (such as Alcoholics Anonymous) to virtually unstructured groups of peers helping one another through loneliness or divorce. According to recent estimates, about 15 million Americans are involved in more than 500,000 such groups, over half of which have formed in the past five years.

This is a pretty dramatic trend, as Parks and Pilisuk note:

> Support groups mark a turning point in social history. In whatever forms they take, they speak to the need to take friendships more seriously, to create intentionally the types of relationships that, in the course of busy lives, do not seem to be arriving on their own.

If a formally organized support or self-help group seems appropriate to your needs, you might contact your local mental health association, women's (or, where they exist, men's) centers, or religious groups for information, or simply ask other people about self-help and support groups in your area. On the other hand, if you don't want to get involved in anything organized or if you don't find a group that is right for you, you can create your own group. It can be something formal, with agendas and dues and membership, or as informal as just getting together regularly with a group of your friends and be there for one another.

In either case, the principle is the same:

Key Principle Thirty-nine: You don't have to do it on your own.

MOBILIZING SUPPORT

There is another, less recognized, part to the support system story that has particularly great relevance to creative self-management. This part is the fact that when you are trying to change you are bucking the forces of the world, as I have mentioned in the early chapters of this book.

Perhaps you want to lose weight. I'm sure you are aware that you have to change your eating patterns, to put less food in your mouth, and, ideally, to exercise more. And this means *you are going to have to change your interactions.*

Why? Because you can't afford to sit around with your friends and eat. Yet one of the most basic ways that we organize togetherness in our society (and, in fact, in most human societies) is to share food. There is a *symbolic* dimension to this eating together—our interactions of socializing over food constitute a sort of ritual that means sharing and friendship and caring for one another.

So you go ahead and say, "No thanks, I don't want anything." Probably you'd add some polite social noises to provide a neutral account for your conduct, like "I'm not feeling hungry right now."

This is likely to disturb your friends. Their radar will say, "Something's wrong here!" The ritual is disturbed, the reciprocity of shared eating is violated, the interaction isn't flowing in its accustomed tracks. This is a problem, an imbalance, a strain in the system. One that they will probably act to resolve—generally out of the best intentions. After all, you aren't behaving "in character." Something must be pushing you out of shape.

They'll ask, "Why, what's wrong? You aren't acting like yourself." And they'll say, "Come on, just have a little bite." While I am not sure that the road to hell is paved with good intentions, the road to failed change surely is! What is the solution to this kind of "sabotage"?

Key Tactic Twenty-five: To facilitate creative change, enlist the help of your social support system. If you don't have one, start one. For example, at my marketing research firm I know of at least two informal support groups that have developed among women who are trying to control their weight. I can see many positive effects of the support they have given participants. It is probably significant that one of these groups consists of younger women at the same level on our professional staff, while the other consists of slightly older women who are on our support staff. These groups seem to naturally form among people who share many personal characteristics (age, gender, educational background) and who also share social characteristics, in that they occupy positions of similar status in the organization that brings them together.

I am pretty sure that these groups do more than share

support and meals. By virtue of their similar organizational positions, these women are able to share problems, frustrations, strains, and *solutions,* which are relevant to their common work situation. Thus, groups of this sort provide not only *instrumental* help in accomplishing certain objectives (weight control) but also serve an important *stress management* role, illustrating the theme that our social support systems provide a buffer against and a means of dealing with the stresses and strains in our lives.

Now consider another situation. You have determined that you want to make a change in your performance or group affiliations. Maybe you want to change jobs or go through with a marriage or a divorce, or actively seek a promotion, or go out on your own. Perhaps you want to get somebody to stop behaving in a way that is really bugging you. Or maybe your entire group wants to make a change.

You can employ performance management strategies like the ones considered in Chapter Six. World-class consultants like Ron Lippitt are very clear about the folly of trying to create second-order changes on your own, however. And I very strongly concur. To optimize your life, invest in social support. To create second-order change in your life, take it one step further. *Enlist the help of your support group first.* If you persist in trying to do it on your own, you can enlist their help in picking up the pieces or helping you keep yourself together somewhat further downstream. But prevention is always easier and more pleasant than a salvage operation.

So talk it over. Brainstorm together. Perhaps do some practice exercises together. Lean on the wisdom and experiences of others. Set up an arrangement so that you can call on them if things get tough and ask for advice or merely go over to their house and know that they'll let you stay there for a while and cool off if you need to.

The hardest part is to ask for help, to ask for advice. To admit vulnerability and open yourself to being scorned, ridiculed, or rejected by others. To make this easier on yourself, establish your support in advance and do a lot of mindwork. However you choose to go about it, the bottom line remains the same: Facilitate creative change; enlist the help of your social support system.

Exercise 7-E: Mobilizing Social Support

DIRECTIONS

1. Think of (a) a dramatic change you have made in your life previously that went well for you and (b) a change in your life you are planning to make in the relatively near future. Perhaps identify and briefly describe each in your journal.
2. Do CSH for Exercises to step 3.
3. Remember that change you have made in your life previously. Recall what it was like for you at the time. How did you feel about it before it happened, as it was happening, immediately or long after it happened? How did these feelings change? How did it go for you?
4. Thinking back, assess to what extent you involved any or all of the social support systems in your life before you made the change, as you were making the change, and after the change. How did you involve them? What did you do? What happened—what were the interactions? What did they do for you? What did you feel you were getting out of them at the time? Looking back, how would you now evaluate your use and experience of social support at that time?
5. What lessons can you draw from this experience? How can you improve your mobilization, use of, and level of benefit from social support systems in the future? Perhaps open your eyes, make some notes about this in your journal, close your eyes again, and flash your centering place.
6. Think about and visualize the change you plan to make in your life in the near future. Consider how you can mobilize your social support systems to help you manage and stabilize this change and to prevent any well-meaning sabotage of your change attempt.

7. Now imagine realizing your preferred outcome, focusing on how you might conceivably mobilize and use your social support systems to facilitate your own personal efforts. Really build this image of your preferred outcome as a reality.
8. Do step 5 in CSH for Exercises.

SUGGESTIONS FOR TEAMS
Discuss social support and what you can do to support one another. (Hint. Hint. Nudge. Nudge.)

CREATIVE LIVING CAN BE GOOD MEDICINE

There are times and situations where people are not in a good position to create support groups, for example, if you are in the hospital for an extended stay, or even more aptly, if you were physically incapacitated or very old and in a nursing home. Think about it; imagine yourself in this position.

Most of us, I'm sure, do our best to care for aging relatives. But there often comes a time when illness and debilitation make it impossible for us to care for an aging parent by ourselves. Or for a person to live on his or her own any longer. That means a nursing home, if the elderly person is really sick or physically incapacitated, or perhaps a retirement home for those who primarily need help with their daily routine.

The research on social support has already begun to have an impact on the way we treat the institutionalized elderly. For example, based on the evidence that any caring relationship can help, even one with a cat or a dog, nursing homes are beginning to keep community pets. In fact, it appears that even a plant can help, as shown in an experiment related by Rina Alcalay and Meredith Minkler of the University of California's Berkeley School of Public Health:

Two groups of nursing home residents were selected. . . . Members of each group were then given a plant. Residents in the so-called "responsibility-enhanced" group were told that the plant was theirs to take care of—that how it fared would depend basically on whether they remembered to water it, etc. At the same time, *they were told that they were really competent men and women who should be making more decisions for themselves.*

Members of the control group were also given a plant, but they were told that the staff would take care of it, just as the staff would continue to take care of them and serve them since, after all, they were in the home to be cared for.

Within a very few weeks, the investigators found a noticeable difference between the two groups. The responsibility-enhanced group was showing greater improvement on a variety of measures of physical and mental well-being and exhibited a visible increase in activity level. Even more dramatic was the finding that eighteen months later, the responsibility-enhanced group showed a mortality rate only half that of the control group.

While these findings have been used to suggest that even plants can be good medicine, I think this interpretation misses a far more important implication of the study. As the researchers recognized, this was really an example of the power of our interpersonal definitions of the situation. The plants, I would argue, were really symbolic—the focal point of a systems-level intervention showing us the truth of Elliott Jaques' contention that the roles and role relationships into which we are thrust have a great deal to do with what kind of people we become.

The real story is that people were relegated to helplessness, placed by virtue of their age or physical disability into a total care facility in which they no longer had any control over their lives. They were cared for, placed back into the condition of little children without any power over their lives. This "infantilization" and stripping away of power and control was becoming a self-fulfilling prophecy.

But then the social science researchers redefined the situation for some of these folks. They communicated a new definition of these people's selves, telling them that they are competent and should be making more decisions for themselves. By getting the nursing home to go along with this idea and making it a social reality by actually granting more everyday life control to those in the "responsibility-enhanced" group, the researchers created a change in the system of social relationships in which this group was embedded.

And so *that* became a self-fulfilling prophecy. What's more, these people (who had been carefully matched with the control group with physical and psychological health status at the start of the experiment) not only improved but lived longer than the others.

This example is more than one of a sociological intervention; it is also a case study of the power of creative living. These old folks had been prevented from making everyday life choices and they had been deteriorating mentally, physically, and spiritually as a result. Now they were encouraged to take active responsibility for their plant and to take increasing responsibility for *doing* their own lives. The result was a measurable improvement in wellness.

WELLNESS AND CREATIVE LIVING

Wellness refers to enhanced well-being. To a positive condition, not merely to the absence of illness or disease symptoms. Wellness is a holistic phenomenon, meaning that it involves not only your body but your mind and everything else. Including, I might add, your social relationships.

While a lot of people have come to equate wellness with physical fitness or following a certain kind of diet or living a certain kind of life-style, even of believing certain kinds of things, that's not the original meaning of the term. One of the pioneers of wellness medicine, Dr. John Travis, explains it this way:

> Wellness is the right and privilege of everyone. There is no prerequisite for it other than your free choice. The "well" being is not necessarily the strong, the brave, the successful, the young, the whole, or even the illness-free being. A person can be living in a process of wellness and yet be physically handicapped, aged, scared in the face of change, in pain, imperfect. No matter what your current state of health is you can begin to appreciate yourself as a growing changing person and allow yourself to move toward a happier life and positive health.

Wellness, then, is a process, not a state. It is a by-product of creative living.

Key Principle Forty: You achieve wellness by creative living, not by following a physical or mental fitness routine. There is a lot of good information in print about the marvelous connection of mind and body. About holistic medicine and holistic health. I'll refer you to some classics in the Notes and References to this chapter. By all means educate yourself about wellness and what is now called *behavioral medicine*. Explore your options. And then use your creative self-management techniques to develop and work toward whatever goals you choose to set for yourself. But never forget that it's the process of living creatively that ultimately counts more than anything, and this means you need to pay at least as much attention to social support and friendships as to finding the best running shoes or health club.

Exercise 7-F: Wellness

DIRECTIONS
1. Do CSH for Exercises through step 3.
2. Imagine wellness. What would you need to be, feel, do, in order to feel positively well? Imagine yourself experiencing what wellness can mean to you. Really build. Let yourself really feel it.
3. Visualize your preferred future, making sure to build in a sense of positive wellness. Focus on that aspect of your preferred future. Tell yourself you can have it.
4. Do step 5 in CSH for Exercises.

THE MAGIC OF LAUGHTER

In our serious adult world we tend to forget the things we learned as children and thus we impoverish ourselves and diminish our capacity to grow and love and move and create. Particularly when you take a direct approach to overcoming life's problems and achieving your goals and desires, it's easy to get very serious about what you are doing and to lose at one and the same time your sense of balance and your sense of humor.

I'll tell it to you straight: If you can't laugh at yourself, you're in deep trouble. If you can't see the absurdity, silliness, and buffoonery in whatever it is in which you're involved, you've lost your sense of proportion. If you can't see the cosmic joke, you've not attained anything like wisdom. Humor is our species' basic means of spotting contradictions, inconsistencies, pomposity, self-serving sanctimoniousness, and general loss of balance.

Key Principle Forty-one: A sense of humor is the ultimate self-correction mechanism. This is not one of those cute, useless statements about how you shouldn't take things too seriously and just go with the flow. Laughter is a basic key to wellness, a means of unblocking yourself and of overcoming whatever is interfering with your internal and external optimization. Laughter can even be the key to restoring your body's homeostasis.

In his wonderful book, *Anatomy of an Illness*, Norman Cousins relates the story of how he literally laughed himself free of a crippling connective tissue disease in 1964. Systematically experimenting on himself, he found that the belly laughter he could obtain through a good dose of Marx Brothers films and readings from humorous books not only provided relief from pain that analgesics couldn't provide but proved to be a key ingredient in his recovery from a disease that had a one in five hundred cure rate. Since then, formal investigation of the medical and physiological effects of humor and laughter has confirmed that "laughter is good medicine." What we have learned about social support would suggest that laughter among friends may be even *better* medicine.

Laughter is not, in any case, really a private matter. Rather, as sociologist Rose Laub Coser remarks in a brilliant paper on the social functions of laughter, it plays an important, positive role in the development of relationships and in group life, generally. Just by laughing together, we become intimate in a way that can transcend physical intimacy. As every male teenager knows, laughter can break the ice and provide an opening for a seduction. But it goes deeper than that, as Coser tells us:

> To laugh in the company of others presupposes a minimum of common "definition of the situation." . . . In laughter, one must share and share alike.
> To laugh, or occasion laughter through humor and wit is to invite those present to come close. Laughter and humor are indeed like an invitation, be it an invitation for dinner or an invitation to start a conversation: It aims at decreasing social distance.

Coser studied how patients in a hospital ward used jokes, humorous stories, and jocular griping to relieve their common tensions and insecurities, to help one another deal with shared complaints they were powerless to resolve (such as the quality of hospital food), and to bring new patients into their collective life. She concludes that humor allows people

> . . . in a brief span of time and with a minimum of effort, mutually to reinforce their experiences, to entertain, reassure, and communicate; to convey their interest in one another, to pull the group together by transforming what is individual into collective experience, and to strengthen the social structure within which the group functions.

It is no wonder that tyrants of every stripe fear and discourage humor. Humor can be a powerful tool for individual and collective change, whether in the form of political cartoons or Monty Python satire or a bunch of friends cracking jokes about their common conditions. Humor not only cuts through the hypnotic qualities of postnatal suggestions but it brings people together around their commonalities, forges bonds, and strengthens relationships.

So do not neglect humor and laughter. While there are certainly times and places in which a serious demeanor is appropriate and an interjection of humor would be a fatal error, this is a matter of strategic performance and audience management and nothing more. Certainly, in your own leisure time, I cannot urge you too strongly to seek out comedy and share belly laughs and generally have fun. So much about our lives is serious that you can't afford not to balance it out with humor.

THE BALANCING ACT

Once again what we are aiming toward is optimizing your life, establishing a balance that is right for you. We are all juggling an infinite number of needs, demands, obligations, relationships, situations, goals, and groups. Pat yourself on the back, friend. You're doing an awful lot and almost getting away with it. I know that it is sometimes hard to accept how well we are actually doing (since each of us knows precisely where we are lacking and all the ways in which we have failed) so I have devised the following exercise to help you get a better perspective on this issue.

Exercise 7-G: Inner Journey

DIRECTIONS
1. Ask yourself the following question and brainstorm your answers, writing every answer that comes to mind in your journal: *Why am I so hard on myself?*
2. Repeat for this question: *What am I embarrassed about?*
3. And this one: *What am I afraid people might find out about me?*
4. Now do CSH for Exercises through step 3.
5. Imagine the following fantasy:
     You are wandering through your magical place or centering point and you come upon a path that leads further inward. For some reason, no matter how much you exert yourself, you seem to be moving very slowly

down that path. But you keep on trudging along and finally you come to an even more magical place. Standing before you is a glowing figure whose features, for some reason, you cannot quite make out and whose identity you know that you know but you can't remember. You feel a sense of absolute trust in that figure, however, knowing that this figure has immense wisdom and compassion and truly cares about you. So you tell this figure about the brainstorm exercise you just did and ask this figure for help in putting your feet on the path that is most right for you, the path that leads to creative living. And you listen to what this figure says, if there are any words, and you pay attention to whatever images and feelings this figure places in your mind. For however long or short a time it takes, you stay there and allow yourself to receive all the communications this figure shares with you. When this figure is done, you feel a gentle, reassuring touch at the center of your forehead, and you feel a sudden surge or rush of reassurance and positive energy flooding through every part and level of you. Knowing you are dismissed for now, you feel yourself instantly transported back to your usual centering point.

6. Do step 5 in CSH for Exercises. (If you were to ask me what this fantasy means, what the symbolism represents, I would tell you I don't know. It's just a metaphor. And I'd wink.)

   Special Note: Feel free to repeat step 5 above whenever you feel troubled or perplexed, need guidance or reassurance, or just feel that it is time to take a trip back there again. Always do this step within your longer CSH form or CSH for Exercises.

SUGGESTIONS FOR TEAMS

For the first and only time in this book, I urge you *not* to discuss or analyze the fantasy in step 5 above, although you may share your brainstorms.

CREATIVE LIVING

In Chapter Five, I brought up Bohr's concept of complementarity, the idea that there may be more than one accurate description of the same thing. Let's explore this somewhat further.

Exercise 7-H: Complementarity Revisited

DIRECTIONS
1. Look at this book you are reading. Fix in your mind *exactly* what you see.
2. Turn the book over. Now fix in your mind exactly what you see.
3. Turn the book back over and read the words.
4. Now describe this object we have called "the book" to yourself.
5. Consider these questions in addition to any questions step 4 raises for you directly:
   a. Is it the "same book" you are describing?
   b. How do you know?
   c. Can you entirely separate the book from your experience of it and, in particular, your self-interactive experience of reading it?

When Bohr described the concept of complementarity he was also suggesting that the reality of things exceeds our ability to capture the dynamic complexity in any single metaphor, image, or mathematical or verbal description. He was saying that you must sometimes look at things in several mutually exclusive ways (perhaps even an *infinite* number), each of which provides a partial description of what you are looking at.

It is up to us to exercise our creative intelligence and shift to a higher level of logic or an *expanded frame of reference* in which these apparently contradicting truths each have their place. Not always, but in many, many cases, the only reason why they appear to be contradictory is because of our limited perspective. We invent the problem by the way we think about it. If we change how we think, this kind of problem goes away.

This is not to suggest that you forget the realists' corollary to the Thomas theorem, which states that what you don't define as real might not pay any attention to what you think about it. Rather, I am asking you to consider the possibility that some things might appear to be problems for you because your viewpoint is too narrow. For example, by imagining that it is a matter of either this or that, that someone is either with you or against you, for the one side or for the other side, you miss an infinite range of other possibilities. This, I have found, is a general principle valid from the level of describing a book to understanding a problem to trying to make sense out of the whole shebang.

Somebody less serious-minded than myself might describe the way in which scholars and scientists bicker endlessly about which perspective is right and why the other is wrong as a kind of *sport*. Or even the quip that, if College Bowl is the varsity sport of the mind, this is the professional sport. It seems to me that a little clear communication among all of us and, especially, between disciplines could go a very long way.

For example, psychologists and sociologists rarely read one another's literature or study the history of their sibling discipline during their professional training. Consequently, cognitive psychologists believe that they have discovered something that Cooley, Mead, Thomas, and their symbolic interactionist inheritors have been researching, and, practicing as clinical sociologists for nearly an entire century. These psychologists have been showing that the language we use, the images we evoke in our minds, and the words we tell ourselves in our thoughts have a crucial impact on both our performance and the quality of our lives. And that we can do well to exchange negative, self-limiting or self-demeaning thoughts, feelings, and imaginings for more positive ones.

I have found a great deal to admire in the new school of cognitive behavioral therapy. However, I wish more cognitive psychologists would look into the symbolic interactionist tradition. And that popularizers of this school would not imply that it is all a matter of the words you tell yourself and would not ignore either social interaction or social structural reality.

INTEGRATED LEVELS OF FOCUS

As scholar–practitioner Jonathan Freedman has pointed out, clinical sociologists employ a perspective that he terms *integrated levels of focus*. We see that effective action for change must take into account the fact that one is *never* dealing with an individual alone or a relationship or problem alone. Rather, one is dealing with that person or relationship or problem in the context of all the groups: organizations, religious or ethnic affiliations, social worlds (such as the college students' world or the advertising world), and the entire society in which the human actor or actors involved participate, would like to participate, or do not want to participate.

As I've said before, everything is connected. You had best take your blinkers off and try to get a sense of the *big picture*. To be unconnected is to make nothing of yourself. Literally.

Creative living implies that you recognize the structural and situational facts of your life *and you treat them as resources*. We are all performance artists. Our lives are our ultimate work of art. Our lives are really all that we have to offer others, all that we have to share. How we live our lives, what we do with our lives, what we create in and with our lives—that is what we are, that is what we have and what will remain when our time on Earth is done.

In the end, as in the middle and in the beginning also, you are your act. You get what you create and you create what you get. So do your life well, as best as you can. Aim high, as high as you can. Be all that you can. Don't let anything get you down.

And that, my friends, is what I can tell you about creative living. The rest is up to you.

SUMMARY

This chapter concludes by bringing us full circle, back to our initial problem of how to create the life you want for yourself. It began with a discussion of the relationship between optimization and change, introducing the concept of *homeostasis,* the moving balance that is central to all organisms and living systems. It then suggested the notion of *creative optimization* as a way of creating forward motion in your life by allowing some variation in your performances. It contrasted this with *second-order* change, which involves straining an undesired system to the breaking point in order to allow a new system to form in its place. Our focus then shifted to the issue of social support and the buffering effects of friendship and supportive relationships on mental, physical, and social health. Some ideas about forming and mobilizing social support were discussed. We then considered how creative living can be, in itself, a source of wellness, which naturally raised the topic of *wellness.* The importance of humor to wellness and creative living was discussed and then we made our final swing into the issue of complementarity, the relativity of our categories and how these categories relate to doing our lives creatively. I leave the next step in your lap. Where it belongs.

Six Key Principles were introduced in this chapter:

THIRTY-SIX: Optimization depends on a moving equilibrium and, hence, on change.

THIRTY-SEVEN: Creative living means that you actively invite and use change to optimize performance.

THIRTY-EIGHT: Friends are good medicine, the best.

THIRTY-NINE: You don't have to do it on your own.

FORTY: You achieve wellness by creative living, not by following a physical or mental fitness routine.

FORTY-ONE: A sense of humor is the ultimate self-correction mechanism.

Four Key Tactics rounded out our list of pointers to help you in thinking about and designing your own creative self-management strategy:

TWENTY-TWO: To optimize your performance, play with it; try never to repeat yourself exactly.

TWENTY-THREE: If what you have been doing hasn't done it for you, do something else.

TWENTY-FOUR: Invest in creating a social support system; you're going to need it.

TWENTY-FIVE: To facilitate creative change, enlist the help of your social support system.

Technique Seven: Grand Finale

DIRECTIONS

Here is an initial "meditation" and then seven themes to use in working with CSH.

A. *Initial grand finale meditation*

Directed CSH

1. Tense/relax.
2. Imagine place.
3. Steer "up" or "down."
4. Visualize present.
5. Do tactical mindwork and/or visualize future.
6. Set mind.
7. Open eyes. Tell yourself, "That's it, end of session."

1. Do Directed CSH, using the "up" direction. Spend at least three minutes visualizing your magical place or centering point as you imagine yourself becoming more and more and more calm, centered, wide awake, and superconscious.
2. In step 3 of Directed CSH, first visualize your present self and life as clearly and as objectively as you can. Then imagine you have a split screen in your mind (as if there is a line or a division running down the middle) and hold this image

of your present on the left-hand side of this imaginary screen.

3. Next, recall what you were like the day before you began working with this book and visualize how you were then on the right-hand side of your mind. Congratulate yourself on what you have accomplished so far.

4. Now blank out that image of your past self, and on the right-hand side, in its place, visualize a preferred future, as far from now as feels appropriate. Keep that split screen going, so that you are visualizing your preferred future on the right-hand side and your present on the left.

5. Switch the screens back and forth a couple of times: Mock up your future on the *left* and your present on the *right*; then reverse them again.

6. Imagine your present in front of you and your preferred future behind you and then reverse them.

7. Imagine your centering point again and let go of these images of past, present, and future. Let go of all thoughts, all awareness of past, present, and future.

8. Instead, imagine the people to whom you feel most closely connected and imagine being connected to each one of them by shafts of light. Imagine receiving energy from them and, as you receive some energy, imagine sending back even more. Feel the lines of light that represent supportive relationships begin to glow brighter and brighter as energy moves back and forth between you and all the other people in your life. Feel the energy pulsing faster and faster.

9. Imagine now all the other people and groups and other living systems to which each of these people in your life is connected. Feel energy moving back and forth among these others, and between them and those to whom they are, in turn, connected. Feel the sphere of energy and connection

growing wider and wider, more and more radiant.

10. Feel this sphere of connectedness expanding even further, to embrace all people, all living things, all beings everywhere (including the spiritual realm if that is part of your world). Feel the energies flowing through you now, as if you are a channel of this wonderful sphere of connectedness. Feel them growing brighter and brighter still.

11. Now, imagine that pure love somehow enters this system and begins to flow through it and through you. And with that cosmic, unselfish love, feel joy. Feel these pulsing through you and through all, between you and all.

12. If at any point you begin to feel as if you are unable to continue focusing like this or as if you just don't want to, let it go and just follow wherever your mind and spirit choose to go; if everything wants to vanish for a while, let it. There are no rules here and nothing you have to do.

13. Whenever you are ready, complete steps 6 and 7 of Directed CSH.

Hint: Consider taping this session, just as you did for Technique One. I made a tape so that I can lie back and imagine along with it. On the tape, I just give myself the above directions, only I describe things more fully, and, pretty much extemporaneously, add additional suggestions as they come to mind. I even added a musical background, again as in Technique One. You might find that this approach works well for you, too. If you choose to make a session tape, feel free to play it as often as you like.

B. *Themes for use in step 5 of your daily CSH this week.* Work with one of these themes each day for a week, in addition to whatever else you are doing with your self-hypnosis. Follow the sequence given here.

When you do step 5 of Directed CSH, just read the theme aloud or in your mind (from the book or from a note card) and allow yourself to follow the suggestions in whatever way comes to mind.

1. Remember being asleep.
2. Remember dreaming.
3. Remember forgetting.
4. Remember discovering something truly amazing.
5. Remember feeling glad to be alive.
6. Remember feeling as if you were in a dream.
7. Remember feeling as if you were finally waking up and it was wonderful.

SUGGESTIONS FOR TEAMS

You may have completed this book, but you have only begun to explore the possibilities of creative living and creative self-hypnosis. Perhaps do the Grand Finale exercise together and see what happens.

I strongly urge you to continue meeting as a group, for social support, mutual exploration, and just as an excuse to get together and have fun.

NOTES AND REFERENCES

For those interested in a fuller introduction to the clinical sociology perspective and the work of the early authors cited in the first three chapters, see my textbook, *Using Sociology: An Introduction to the Clinical Perspective* (Dix Hills, NY: General-Hall Publishers, 1985). Specific references to the works cited in the present chapter can be found there. Two other excellent sources are Barry Glassner and Jonathan Freedman, *Clinical Sociology* (New York: Longman, 1979) and Harry Cohen, *Connections: Understanding Social Relationships* (Ames, IA: Iowa State University Press, 1986).

For more general information about sociology, I suggest two eminently readable works: Peter L. Berger's classic *Invitation to Sociology: A Humanistic Perspective* (Garden City, NY: Doubleday-Anchor, 1963) and a splendid book of readings, Lewis A. Coser (ed.), *The Pleasures of Sociology* (New York: Mentor, 1980).

CHAPTER ONE

Page 10. Quotation from C. H. Cooley, *Human Nature and the Social Order*. New York: Scribners, 1902.

Page 14. Quoted in Lewis Wirth, "Clinical Sociology," *American Journal of Sociology*, 1931.

Page 18. See John Lofland, *Doing Social Life: the Qualitative Study of Human Interaction in Natural Settings.* New York: Wiley-Interscience, 1976.

Page 25. The quotation and material on the internal community are taken from the late Ronald Lippitt's Clinical Sociology Intervention Skillshop, October 1984, under the auspices of the Sociological Practice Association. His enormous influence on my own thinking and practice is reflected in many of the exercises to be found in this and subsequent chapters.

Page 32. The "superconscious" technique employed here is technically known as *hyperemperia*. The method was introduced by my friend, Don Gibbons, Ph.D., who demonstrated its equivalence to traditional hypnosis with respect to enhancement of performance on the standardized scales of hypnotic performance employed by researchers. Like Don, I have found this approach to be extremely well received by younger, active people—many of whom reject or prove resistant to conventional hypnotic induction. See Don Gibbons, *Applied Hypnosis and Hyperemperia.* New York: Plenum Publishers, 1979.

CHAPTER TWO

Much of this material was initially presented as a Bergren Forum, Alfred University, March 12, 1986.

Page 42. One of the better books available on contemporary brain research is Robert Ornstein, Richard Thompson, and David Macaulay, *The Amazing Brain.* Boston: Houghton Mifflin, 1984.

Page 46. Robert Sheckley, *Mindswap.* New York: Delacorte, 1966. As his newer books are becoming popular again, it is likely that this book will be reprinted in paperback in the near future. One of my favorite books.

Page 47. Aldous Huxley, *The Doors of Perception.* New York: Harper and Row, 1954. See also *Writings of William James,* John T. McDermott (ed.). Chicago: University of Chicago Press, 1977.

Page 50. The story and later references are adapted from Gregory Bateson, *Mind and Nature: A Necessary Unity.* New York: Dutton, 1979. A difficult book to grasp, but, I believe, destined to be a classic of late twentieth-century thought.

Page 52. For clear thinking, in addition to what is covered here, you might want to check some of the literature on rational decision making and to learn enough about probability and statistics to become proficient in evaluating the likelihood of various outcomes and selecting the best way to hedge the odds in favor of realizing your objectives. One of the best introductions to this "science" is Robyn M. Dawes' *Rational Choice in an Uncertain World*. New York: Harcourt Brace Jovanovich, 1988. Check it out.

Page 54. Cooley is quoted in Wirth, 1931.

Page 55. I am indebted to Theodore R. Sarbin for sensitizing me to the concept of metaphors, metaphor to myth transformation, and the like. For an early statement of this approach, see Theodore R. Sarbin and William C. Coe, *Hypnosis: a Social Psychological Analysis of Influence Communication*. New York: Van Nostrand, 1972. I would also recommend Sarbin's own source, Stephen Pepper, *World Hypotheses*. Berkeley: University of California Press, 1942. This is a serious philosophical treatise.

Page 55. General Semantics quotes are from Alfred Korzybski, *Science and Sanity*. New York: Science Press, 1941.

Page 57. The best statement of the Theory of Logical Types is to be found in Bateson, from which my approach has largely been drawn.

Page 60. See Robert Sommer, *The Mind's Eye*. New York: Delacorte, 1976. A full treatment of sensory imagery. Another important source is Arnold Lazarus, *In the Mind's Eye: The Power of Imagery for Personal Enrichment*. New York: Guilford Press, 1984.

Page 61. W. I. Thomas and Dorothy Swaine Thomas, *The Child in America: Behavior Problems and Programs*. New York: Knopf, 1928.

Page 66. See *The Collected Writings of Milton H. Erickson*, Ernest L. Rossi (ed.), Volumes I–IV. New York: Irvington, 1981. Or see any of the numerous references to Erickson's work in other books. For more on Sarbin's approach, see Sarbin and Coe, 1972 (cited above) and for Barber, see T. X. Barber, N. P. Spanos, and J. Chaves, *Hypnosis, Imagination and Human Potentialities*. New York: Pergamon, 1974. A more recent volume in the same general tradition as Sarbin and Barber is Daniel Araoz, *The New Hypnosis*. New York: Brunner Mazel, 1984.

CHAPTER THREE

Page 74. For a good, highly provocative discussion of the New Physics for laypersons, I suggest Gary Zukav, *The Dancing Wu Li Masters: An Overview of the New Physics*. New York: Bantam, 1979. Don't be misled by the title; this is a superb introduction to the subject.

Page 76.   Quotation is from Wirth, 1931.

Page 82.   Quote from Suzanne Powers, "The Role of the Clinical Sociologist in a Multispecialty Health Facility," *American Behavioral Scientist*, March/April 1979.

Page 91.   Quote (and inspiration) from Harry Cohen, "Sociology and You: Good Living," Chapter 3 in my textbook *Using Sociology*.

Page 99.   See Robert Fritz, *The Path of Least Resistance*. New York: Ballantine, 1989. Fritz has developed several programs around his concepts and approach, which he calls DMA. I have found this material highly useful and have incorporated some of its elements in the present book.

Page 99.   Nathan Hurvitz, "The Sociologist as Marital and Family Therapist," *American Behavioral Scientist*, March/April 1979. I am currently preparing for posthumous publication a manuscript providing full details about Hurvitz's concepts, methods, and approaches.

Page 102. Herbert Benson, *The Relaxation Response*. New York: Morrow, 1975.

CHAPTER FOUR

Page 105. C. H. Cooley, *Human Nature and the Social Orders*. New York: Scribners, 1909.

Page 106. Herbert N. Blumer, *Symbolic Interaction: Perspective and Method*. Englewood Cliffs, NJ: Prentice-Hall, 1969.

Page 107. Harry Cohen, "Sociology and You: Good Living," Chapter 3 in *Using Sociology*. I owe Harry for Key Principle Nineteen.

Page 110. Blumer, 1969, cited above.

Page 113. Erving Goffman, *Strategic Interaction*. Philadelphia, Penna.: University of Pennsylvania Press, 1969. The best introduction to Goffman's work, however, is his *The Presentation of Self in Everyday Life*. Garden City, NY: Doubleday-Anchor, 1959.

Page 114. Quote is from John Lofland, *Doing Social Life*, cited above.

Page 116. Robert K. Merton. "The Self-Fulfilling Prophecy," reprinted in Lewis A. Coser (ed.), *The Pleasures of Sociology*.

Page 120. Robert Fisch, John H. Weakland, and Lynn Segal, *The Tactics of Change*. San Francisco: Jossey-Bass, 1976. This is probably the most accessible statement of the MRI school's ideas and approach.

Page 121. The acknowledged dean of humanist sociology is Alfred McClung Lee. See his books: *Sociology for Whom?* New York: Oxford University Press, 1978. *Toward a Humanist*

Sociology. Englewood Cliffs, NJ: Prentice-Hall, 1973. *Sociology for People: Toward a Caring Profession.* Syracuse, N.Y.: Syracuse University Press, 1989. I would like to acknowledge my gratitude to Al and Betty Lee for their example and their unstinting support.

Page 122. See, for example, Bateson's *Mind and Nature,* cited above.

Page 127. See Sarbin and Coe, cited earlier.

Page 128. As always, my thinking and approach in this volume is deeply influenced by that of Ted Barber, another person whose support has been invaluable to me.

Page 136. Quotation from Arthur J. Lange and Patricia Jakubowski, *Responsible Assertive Behavior.* Champaign, IL: Research Press, 1976.

Page 137. From Thomas Gordon, *Parent Effectiveness Training.* New York: Peter H. Wyden, 1970.

CHAPTER FIVE

Page 144. The concept of sculpture is borrowed from Bunny S. Duhl, *From the Inside Out and Other Metaphors.* New York: Brunner Mazel, 1983. She presents an approach to understanding human systems highly compatible with my own (so I like it) along with excellent exercises for training therapists in systems that have influenced some of the exercises you will find here.

Page 145. C. Wright Mills, *The Sociological Imagination.* New York: Oxford University Press, 1959.

Page 145. Also from Mills, 1959.

Page 146. See discussion of complementarity in Gary Zukav, *The Dancing Wu Li Masters,* cited above.

Page 149. This exercise was inspired by the exercises Harry Cohen developed for his chapter in *Using Sociology.*

Page 152. See Jay Haley, *Reflections on Therapy.* Washington, DC: Family Therapy Institute of Washington, DC, 1981.

Page 156. The quotation is from Harry Cohen, *Connections,* cited above.

Page 161. The ideas developed in this section are based on Lilian B. Rubin, *Intimate Strangers: Men and Women Together.* New York: Harper, 1984.

Page 164. Quote from Rubin, 1984.

Page 165. Quote from Rubin, 1984.

CHAPTER SIX

Page 195. Quote from *The Complete Works of Chuang Tzu,* translated by Burton Watson. New York: Columbia University

Press, 1968. As far as I am concerned, there is no other translation worth mentioning.

Page 196. Quote from the Burton Watson translation, cited above.

Page 200. Ludwig von Bertalanffy, *General Systems Theory*. New York: George Braziller, 1968.

Page 205. Elliott Jaques, *A General Theory of Bureaucracy*. New York: Halstead Press, 1976. See also the chapter by John Glass on "Understanding Organizations and the Workplace" in *Using Sociology*, cited above.

Page 208. Grace Baruch, Lois Biener, and Rosalind C. Barnett, "Women and Gender in Research on Work and Family Stress," *American Psychologist*, February 1987.

Page 209. Arthur Shostak, *Blue Collar Life*. New York: Random House, 1969.

Page 212. S. C. Kobasa, "The Hardy Personality: Toward a Social Psychology of Stress and Health." In J. Suls and G. Sanders (eds.), *Social Psychology of Health and Illness*. New York: Lawrence Erlbaum Associates, 1981.

CHAPTER SEVEN

Page 223. Walter B. Cannon. *The Wisdom of the Body*. New York: W. W. Norton and Company, 1963 (reprint).

Page 223. Gregory Bateson and Mary Catherine Bateson. *Angels Fear: Towards an Epistemology of the Sacred*. New York: Bantam, 1988. Completed by his daughter, this posthumous work discusses the nature of such biological mechanisms and goes on to discuss other issues referred to in this chapter. Fascinating.

Page 226. Dennis Wrong's article, "The Oversocialized Conception of Man in Modern Sociology," is reprinted in Lewis A. Coser (ed.), *The Pleasures of Sociology*, cited above.

Page 228. See Ilya Prigogine and Isabelle Stengers, *Order Out of Chaos: Man's New Dialogue with Nature*. New York: Bantam, 1984. (Rather heavy for the nontechnically inclined, but well worth the effort); the excerpt is from W. B. Yeats' poem, "The Second Coming."

Page 232. From Lisa Hunter, *Resource Guide: Friends Can Be Good Medicine*. California Department of Mental Health, Mental Health Promotion Branch, 1981.

Page 232. James S. House, Karl R. Landis, and Debra Umberson, "Social Relationships and Health," *Science*, vol. 241, July 29, 1988. See also *Science* for August 4, 1988. For a detailed yet popular presentation of the research evidence regarding the relationship between social interaction, brain physiology, health, and immunity, see Robert

Ornstein and David Sobel, *The Healing Brain*. New York:
Simon and Schuster, 1987.

Page 234. The quote is from Marc Pilisuk and Susan Hillier Parks,
The Healing Web: Social Networks and Human Survival.
Hanover, NH: University Press of New England, 1986.
This book presents an unrivaled summary of what is
known about social networks and a provocative discussion of the implications of this new area of study for
both laypersons and professionals.

Pages 237–38. These quotes are also from Pilisuk and Parks. For
information about self-help and social support groups,
see *The Self-Help Sourcebook*, which you can obtain by
sending $9 to St. Clares–Riverside Foundation, One Indian Road, Denville, OH 07834 or contact National Self-
Help Clearinghouse, 33 West 42nd Street, Room 1227,
New York, NY 10036.

Page 242. This discription of an experiment by E. Langer and J.
Rodin is taken from *Friends Can Be Good Medicine*.
State of California Department of Mental Health, 1981.
(Italics added for emphasis.)

Page 244. Quotation from John Travis, M.D. is from the same
source.

Page 245. See, for example, Kenneth R. Pelletier, *Holistic Medicine:
From Stress to Optimum Health*. New York: Delta, 1979.
Dennis T. Jaffe, *Healing from Within*. New York: Alfred
A. Knopf, 1980.

Page 246. Norman Cousins, *Anatomy of an Illness*. New York:
Bantam, 1979.

Page 247. Quotations from Rose Laub Coser, "Some Social Functions of Laughter," reprinted in Lewis Coser (ed.), *Pleasures of Sociology*, cited above.

Page 251. Good examples of the cognitive behavioral approach
include David D. Burns, M.D., *Feeling Good: The New
Mood Therapy*. New York: Signet 1980. J. Mark G. Williams, *The Psychological Treatment of Depression: A
Guide to the Practice of Cognitive-Behaviour Therapy*.
New York: Free Press, 1984.

INDEX